Can Democracy Be Saved?

Can Democracy Be Saved?

Participation, Deliberation and Social Movements

Donatella della Porta

polity

First published in 2013 by Polity Press

Polity Press
65 Bridge Street
Cambridge CB2 1UR, UK

Polity Press
350 Main Street
Malden, MA 02148, USA

ISBN-13: 978-0-7456-6459-0
ISBN-13: 978-0-7456-6460-6 (pb)

A catalogue record for this book is available from the British Library.

Typeset in 10 on 12 pt Sabon
by Toppan Best-set Premedia Limited
Printed and bound in Great Britain by the MPG Printgroup

For further information on Polity, visit our website: www.politybooks.com

To Alessandro, Colin and Philippe,
with whom – without their knowing – this project started

Contents

Acknowledgments

I began to reflect on this volume in 2003 when – together with Colin Crouch, Alessandro Pizzorno and Philippe Schmitter – I organized my first seminar at the European University Institute. The subject was 'Transformations in Democracies', and the debate was not only engaged, but deliberative as well.

Subsequently I went on to study changes in the conceptions and practices of democracy in the framework of the comparative research project 'Democracy in Europe and the Mobilization of Society' – 'Demos' (financed by the European Commission under the 6th framework). I am grateful for their many reflections to Massimiliano Andretta, Marco Giugni, Raffaele Marchetti, Lorenzo Mosca, Mario Pianta, Herbert Reiter, Dieter Rucht, Simon Teune and all my other colleagues, both junior and senior.

While the results of that research were published in various volumes, dedicated in particular to the global justice movement, this book was helped along by other additional stimuli. First and foremost was the preparation of a comparative research project on experiments in deliberative democracy (developed with the help of Bernard Gbikpi, Joan Fonts and Yves Sintomer), as well as that project's first study, a piece of research carried out with Herbert Reiter, and supported by the Region of Tuscany.

The second (I believe), chronologically speaking, came to me from Alessandro Pizzorno who asked me to write a chapter on social movements and democracy for a project he was coordinating on the democratic state – specifying, however, that I was to concern myself not, as I usually do, with the post-1968 era, but with the last three centuries (or more). For suggestions and inspiration for that chapter, discussed at the conference organized by the Feltrinelli Foundation in Cortona in 2010, I am grateful – in addition to Alessandro Pizzorno – to Roberto Biorcio, Pietro Costa, Colin Crouch, Klaus Eder, Leonardo Morlino, Bernardo Sordi and the other participants.

The third stimulus came from Mauro Calise who, as the then president of the Italian Society for Political Science, asked me to give the inaugural speech at the association's annual conference in 2009. It was in preparing that speech that I entered the normative debate on democracy, albeit seeking to link it with the results of many pieces of empirical research – both mine and others' – on transformations in democracies. It was on that occasion, finally, that Massimo Baldini asked me to write the Italian version of this book. My thanks also go to Mauro and Massimo for their trust and advice.

This book is, in any case, more than the final part of a journey, it is that journey's continuation. Some of the reflections contained in this work have helped me prepare the project 'Mobilizing for Democracy', now financed by an Advanced Grant from the European Research Council (ERC), and its preliminary results are reported in various chapters. While the responsibility for what I have written remains mine, I'm grateful to the ERC and the European Commission for their support to my research.

Throughout these years, I have had the immense luck of enjoying the most stimulating environment, in the Department of Political and Social Sciences at the European University Institute. I have also carried out part of my research while I was a visiting scholar at the Wissenschaftszentrum für soziale Forschung in Berlin and at the Humboldt University. I thank my colleagues Dieter Rucht, Michael Zuern and Klaus Eder for their support there.

In this volume, I have developed ideas presented in 'State Power and the Control of Transnational Protests' (with Herbert Reiter), in Thomas Olesen (ed.), *Power and Transnational Activism*, London: Routledge, 2011; 'Movimenti sociali e stato democratico', in A. Pizzorno (ed.), *La democrazia di fronte allo stato*, Milan: Feltrinelli, 2010; 'Communications in Movements: Social Movements as Agents of Participatory Democracy, in *Information, Communication and Society*, 14 (6), 2010; 'Democrazia: Sfide e opportunità', in *Rivista Italiana di Scienza Politica*, 40 (2), 2010; *Democracy in Social Movements*, London: Palgrave, 2009; *Another Europe*, London: Routledge, 2009; 'La partecipazione nelle istituzioni: concettualizzare gli esperimenti di democrazia deliberative e partecipativa', in *Partecipazione e conflitto*, 0, 2008 (with Bernard Gbikpi); *The Policing of Transnational Protest: In the Aftermath of the*

'*Battle of Seattle*', Aldershot, Ashgate, 2006 (with Abby Peterson and Herbert Reiter); 'E-democracy: Internet e democrazia', special issue of the *Rassegna italiana di sociologia*, 47 (4), 2006; 'Deliberation in Movement: Why and How to Study Deliberative Democracy and Social Movements', in *Acta Politica,* 40, 2005; and 'Globalization and Democracy', in *Democratization*, 12, 2005.

1

Models of Democracy: An Introduction

There is a striking paradox to note about the contemporary era: from Africa to Eastern Europe, Asia to Latin America, more and more nations and groups are championing the idea of democracy; but they are doing so at just that moment when the very efficacy of democracy as a national form of political organization appears open to question. As substantial areas of human activity are progressively organized on a regional or global level, the fate of democracy, and of the independent democratic nation-state in particular, is fraught with difficulties. (Held 1998, 11)

Many recent contributions on democracy start – like David Held's above – by mentioning a paradox. On the one hand, the number of democratic countries in the world is growing – according to Freedom House, from thirty-nine democracies in 1974 to eighty-seven countries free and democratic, and sixty partially free, in 2011 (Freedom House 2012). On the other, there is a reduction in the satisfaction of citizens with the performances of 'really existing democracies' (Dahl 2000). Some scholars even suggested that the third wave of democratization risks developing into economic wars and armed conflicts (see, in particular, Tilly 2004). Certainly, research on quality of democracy by Larry Diamond and Leonardo Morlino (2005) pointed at the low quality of many democratic regimes. The question 'Can democracy be saved?' became central in the recent political debate faced with a most serious financial crisis, as well as apparent institutional incapacity to address it. Not only have these developments triggered harsh societal reactions and calls for politics to come back in, but also the austerity measures to address them have accelerated the shift from a social model of democracy, with its development of the welfare state, to a neoliberal one, that trusts free-market solutions.

As we will see in this volume, to understand this paradox it is necessary to distinguish between different conceptions of democracy, both as they have been theorized and as they have been applied in real-world, existing democratic institutions. As Robert Dahl observes about the idea of democracy, 'Ironically, the very fact that democracy has such a lengthy history has actually contributed to confusion and disagreement, for "democracy" has meant different things to different people at different times and places' (2000, 3).

In this volume, I shall in fact contrast four models of democracy, assessing the challenges and opportunities that recent social, cultural and political changes represent for them. If we want to save democracy, we have in fact to acknowledge its contested meaning, as well as the different qualities that are stressed in different conceptions and practices of democracy. Saving democracy would mean going beyond its liberal model, broadening reflection on participation and deliberation inside and outside institutions. This would imply looking at the same time at normative theories as well as at empirical evidence on different models from the liberal one. Referring to research I carried out on social movements, but also to other scholars' work, I aim to discuss general challenges and opportunities for democracy. In this chapter, I will start this journey first of all by introducing different conceptualizations of democracy, which will then be discussed in depth in the rest of the volume.

Conceptions and practices of democracy: an introduction

The search for a shared conceptualization of democracy in political science was for a long time oriented towards procedural criteria which mainly considered free, competitive and periodic elections as a sufficient indicator for the presence of democracy. The choice of a minimalist definition of democracy was justified at the time with reference to the ease of its empirical operationalization. Normative definitions – which look at the ability of democracies to produce a government 'for the people', realizing its wishes and preferences – are instead considered difficult to apply in empirical research:

> How may we see to what extent certain real problems are close to, or far away from, the ideal 'correspondence' or responsiveness postulated as necessary?...How is it possible to pinpoint the 'wishes' or

'preferences' of citizens? Who is entitled to express them without betraying or modifying them? Is it only the 'preferences' of the majority that count? But should a democratic regime not also protect minorities? How, then, do we measure the 'correspondence' or responsiveness, that is the 'congruence'? (Morlino 1996, 84)

More recently, however, it has been observed that a minimalist, procedural definition is not, in reality, the only empirically verifiable one. As Leonardo Morlino (2011) has argued, all the different ideals of democracy can be operationalized in the sense that adequate empirical indicators can be found to determine whether, according to a specific definition, a country at a particular moment in time is democratic or not. It should be added that definitions of democracy are always changing, linked as they are to specific problems (theoretical and empirical, scientific and real) that emerge and change in different historical periods.

In addition, every definition of democracy necessarily has a normative dimension. As rightly observed by David Held, empirical theories of democracy, focusing on the meaning normally attributed to the term, have thus tended to normatively legitimate that specific conception:

> Their 'realism' entailed conceiving of democracy in terms of the actual features of Western polities. In thinking of democracy in this way, they recast its meaning and, in so doing, surrendered the rich history of the idea of democracy to the existent. Questions about the nature and appropriate extent of citizen participation, the proper scope of political rule and the most suitable spheres of democratic regulation – questions that have been part of democratic theory from Athens to nineteenth-century England – are put aside, or, rather, answered merely by reference to current practice. The ideals and methods of democracy become, by default, the ideals and methods of the existing democratic systems. Since the critical criterion for adjudicating between theories of democracy is their degree of 'realism', models which depart from, or are in tension with, current democratic practice can be dismissed as empirically inaccurate, 'unreal' and undesirable. (2006, 166)

It could be added that, over time, the research focus on representative institutions has produced a partial vision of the real functioning of existing democracies.

If a large part of political scientists' attention has been concentrated on democracy, this does not mean that a unanimously accepted definition of the concept exists. There is no doubt that the concept of democracy is not only 'stretched' but also contested. In a recent *APSA-CP Newsletter* symposium dedicated to conceptualization, Thomas Koelbe (2009) rightly lamented the use and abuse of the concept of democracy to describe a plethora of different political systems, and indeed a basic disagreement on its conceptualization.

Different types of definitions of democracy do in fact exist. The classical normative definitions underline the legitimizing role of citizens. Democracy is power *from* the people, *of* the people and *for* the people: it derives from the people, belongs to the people, and must be used for the people. Those general principles are, however, combined in very different ways. Charles Tilly (2007, 7) has distinguished four approaches to democracy in the social sciences:

- A *constitutional approach* concentrates on laws a regime enacts concerning political activity...
- *Substantive approaches* focus on the conditions of life and politics a given regime promotes...
- Advocates of a *procedural* approach single out a narrow range of government practices to determine whether a regime qualifies as democratic...
- *Process-oriented* approaches...identify some minimal sets of processes that must necessarily be continuously in motion for a situation to be considered as democratic.

If we look at actually existing democracies, we can generally observe that they in fact combine different conceptions. Representative institutions are flanked by others. As Pierre Rosanvallon has recently noted, 'the history of real democracies cannot be dissociated from a permanent tension and contestation' (2006, 11).[1] Indeed, the democratic state needs not only legal legitimacy through respect for procedures, but also the trust of its citizens. In the evolution of 'really existing democracies' this has meant that, alongside the institutions that guarantee electoral accountability (or responsibility), there is a circuit of surveillance (or vigilance) anchored outside state institutions (2006, 11). A public sphere developed from the encounter between the state's search for efficiency and the intervention of civil society seeking to express requests and rectify mistakes (Eder 2010). Placing emphasis on elections often ends up obscuring the need for critical citizens who make governors accountable. Thus, 'When the electoral institution is chosen as the institution characterising democratic regimes the much more important presence of a sphere that is both public and distinct from the regimes is obscured. Deprived of this, deprived that is of open public discourse, and despite being governed by persons regularly elected, such a regime could only misleadingly be called democratic' (Pizzorno 2010, xiii).

Rosanvallon suggested that democracy needs not only legal legitimation, but also what he calls 'counter-democracy', that is 'a specific, political modality of action, a particular form of political intervention, different from decision making, but still a fundamental aspect of the democratic process' (2006, 40). In the historical evolution of democratic regimes, a circuit of surveillance, anchored outside state institutions, has developed side by side with the institutions of electoral accountability. Necessary to democratic legitimacy, confidence requires defiance, in the sense of instruments of external control and actors ready to perform this control; in fact, democracy develops with the permanent contestation of power. Actors such as independent authorities and judges, but also mass media, experts and social movements, have traditionally exercised this function of surveillance. The latter, in particular, are considered as most relevant for the development of an 'expressive democracy' that corresponds to 'the *prise de parole* of the society, the manifestation of a collective sentiment, the formulation of a judgment about the governors and their action, or again the production of claims' (2006, 26).

The definition of democracy also changes over time. Through self-reflexive practices, democracy is in a permanent process of definition and redefinition (Eder 2010, 246). Although extremely young as an institution (just a few decades old in the majority of states, if we take universal suffrage as a fundamental condition), democracy does have a long history as a subject for reflection (Costa 2010). If electoral responsibility was privileged in the historical evolution of the discourse on really existing democracy, today the challenges to procedural democracy bring our attention back to other democratic qualities (Rosanvallon 2006).

Democracies are also varied. Different democratic qualities have been intertwined in the construction of diverse typologies. Political scientists have often looked at different arrangements in terms of functional and geographical distribution of power, involving more or less centralization in public decision making. Other scholars have pointed at the varying capacity of democratic states to implement their decisions. Tilly has, for instance, classified political regimes on the basis of some of their capacities: 'How wide a range of citizens' expressed demands come into play; how equally different groups of citizens experience a translation of their demands into state behaviour; to what extent the expression of demands itself receives the state's political protection; and how much the process of translation commits both sides, citizens and the states' (2007, 13).

Not one, but four models

Noting the diversity between different conceptions and practices of democracy, my aim in this volume is not to reconstruct various ideas of democracy, but rather to analyse the way in which they have been prefigured by different actors, as well as translated into requests and proposals, thus penetrating and transforming real democracies, and so the democratic state. From this point of view, in addressing the question 'Can democracy be saved?', the original contribution I wish to develop in this volume lies in the combination of normative theory with empirical analyses of how some conceptions have developed and have inspired concrete institutional changes.

Throughout the analysis, some general considerations will emerge on the status and content of the liberal model of democracy. If this is dominant today, it is, however, challenged by other conceptions, variously discussed as participatory democracy (Pateman 1970; Polletta 2002), strong democracy (Barber 2003), discursive democracy (Dryzek 2000a), communicative democracy (Young 1996), welfare democracy (Fitzpatrick 2002) or associative democracy (among others, Perczynski 2000).

In the intense debate in normative theory, we can single out two dimensions of democratic conceptions that are relevant for our reflections. The first dimension refers to the recognition of participation as an integral part of democracy; a second one looks at the construction of political identities as exogenous versus endogenous to the democratic process. In political theory from Dewey to Habermas, it is often observed that the principle of representation is balanced by the presence of participatory spaces, and the majoritarian principle, central to liberal definitions of democracy, is in various ways, balanced by the presence of deliberative spaces.

First of all, a general mantra of discussion on democracies in so-called 'empirical theories of democracy' is that democratic institutions are representative. While the ideal of democracy as government of, by and for the people stresses the source of all power in the citizenry at large, democratic institutions are called to restrict the number of decision makers and select them on the basis of some specific qualities. A distinction is in fact usually made between the (utopistic) conception of a *democracy of the ancients*, in which all citizens participate directly in the decisions about the public goods, and a (realistic) *democracy of the moderns*, where an elected few govern. The volume and complexity of decision making in the modern state is often quoted as imposing severe constraints on the participation in public decisions of the many and, especially, of the normal citizens, often considered as too inexperienced, if not too emotional, to have a say in the choices which will affect them. Electoral accountability should then give legitimacy to the process, by allocating to the citizens-electors the power to prize or punish those in government, every once in a while (see chapter 2).

If the liberal theories have underlined delegation, or electoral accountability, this has, however, been considered to be insufficient in other theorizations (see chapter 3). In particular, so-called participatory theories have affirmed the importance of creating multiple occasions for participation (Arnstein 1969; Pateman 1970). Elections are in fact, at best, too rare to grant citizens sufficient power to control the elected. Additionally, elections offer only limited choices, leaving several themes out of the electoral debates and citizens' assessment. More and more, elections have been seen as manipulated, given the greater capacity of some candidates to attract financial support, licit or illicit, as well as to command privileged access to mass media. In parallel, the quality of decisions could be expected to decline with the decline in participation, as the habit of delegating tends to make citizens not only more apathetic, but also more cynical and selfish. Participation is instead praised as a school of democracy: capable of constructing good citizens through interaction and empowerment.

Not only delegation, but also majoritarian decision making has been criticized. A 'minimalist' view of democracy as the power of the majority has been considered not only as risky in terms of thwarting the rights of the minorities, but also as reducing the quality of decision making. As there is no logical assumption that grants more wisdom to the preferences which are (simply) more numerous, other decision-making principles should at least temper the majoritarian one (see chapter 4). In normative debates, deliberative theories have in fact promoted spaces of communication, the exchange of reasons, the construction of shared definitions of the public good, as fundamental for the legitimation of public decisions (among others, see Miller 1993, 75; Dryzek 2000a, 79; Cohen 1989, 18–19; Elster 1998; Habermas 1981, 1996). Not the number of pre-existing preferences, but the quality of the decision-making process would here grant legitimacy as well as efficacy to the decision. By relating with each other – recognizing the others and being recognized by them – citizens would have the chance to understand the reasons of the others, assessing them against emerging standards of fairness. Communication not only allows for the development of better solutions, by permitting holders of different knowledge and expertise to interact, but would also change the perception of one's own preferences, making participants less concerned with individual, material interests and more with collective goods.

Participation and deliberation are in fact democratic qualities in tension with those of representation and majority decisions, and are alongside these in a precarious equilibrium in the different conceptions and specific institutional practices of democracy.

Crossing the dimensions of delegation versus participation and majority vote versus deliberation, I single out four different models of democracy (see table 1.1) that I will refer to in the following chapters.

Table 1.1 Conceptions of democracy

	Majority vote	Deliberation
Delegation	Liberal democracy	Liberal deliberative democracy
Participation	Radical, participatory democracy	Participatory deliberative democracy

Liberal democracy privileges – as mentioned – delegation and the majority vote. The assumption is that deciding on public issues is too complex a task to be left to the mass of citizens. Their task is rather to legitimize the power of an elected elite. As power originates, indeed, from the people, they are expected to exercise it, as electors, at specific moments. Electoral campaigns should be able to inform the citizens about past performances and political programmes, as well as personal skills, of candidates; elections should allow the citizens to choose those who will then govern for an allocated time-span. The fear of losing power at the coming elections should make the elites in government sensitive to the people's judgement. The distinctive institutions of Dahl's polyarchal democracy are in fact based upon the presence of officials elected in free, fair and frequent elections, as well as freedom of expression and association and alternative sources of information (Dahl 1998).

Moreover, in liberal democracy, even if with some caveats, the majority wins. This means, decisions are made by measuring the degree of support for opposing views and allocating the victory to those who are more numerous. In principle, ideas, interests, preferences and/or identities are assumed to develop outside the democratic process, which channels them inside the political system. Decisions are then made on the basis of measurement of the support for each of them among the citizens. The legitimizing principle is 'one head, one vote'. In Anthony Downs' (1957) influential version, democracy works as a market where politicians aim at collecting votes, and citizens have (exogenously generated) preferences. While, of course, interests differ, a broad consensus is assumed among compatible interests, and conflicts tend to be considered as negative, as they risk overloading the system (Crozier, Huntington and Watakuni 1975). The actors carrying conflictual interests are seen as anti-systemic (Sartori 1976).

This liberal conception of democracy, however, does not sufficiently reflect the real functioning of democracy in any periods of its existence. As we are going to see, in the rest of this volume, really existing democracy incorporates institutions based upon different principles of legitimation. Referendums, considered as a residual vestige of direct democratic procedures, are spreading, and so are institutions based on principles of restricted delegation or including representatives chosen by lot (see, e.g., chapter 9). Moreover, that conception is partial as it implicitly looks at the public institutions as the only democratic arena. Research on social movements, but also on political parties, called instead for attention to be paid to the many arenas in which democratic forms are based upon different principles from the liberal ones. Mechanisms of institutional accountability, through control by the people as the source of democratic legitimacy, require (many and varied) societal institutions that work as channels of political communication and socialization to the public good. Not only (negative) controls but also (positive) stimuli have to come from the citizens continuously if good decisions are to be made. Along the same lines, research on the long processes of first democratization stressed the importance of non-electoral circuits for the functioning of the demo-cratic state. The influence of protest in regimes with restricted electoral participation did not operate through elections, even though the parlia-ments were targets of claims-making. In fact, in their concrete evolution, the existing democratic states and societies have amended the ideal-typical principles of liberal democracy, mixing them with others, linked to other conceptions of democracy.

The liberal conception of democracy has been, first of all, challenged by a *participatory* one. Recognizing the existence of deep conflicts in society, the theorists of participatory democracy have stressed the impor-tance of involving citizens beyond elections (Arnstein 1969; Pateman 1970; Barber 2003). Participation in different forms and in different moments of the democratic process is in fact considered as positive both for individuals, who are socialized to visions of the public good, and for the very political institutions, as it might lead to increased trust and support for them. Challengers to the elites, in particular – from the labour movement to the most recent *indignados* – have nurtured a participatory vision, extending the forms of legitimate political involve-ment well beyond the vote. Conceptions of democracy as open partici-pation tend, in fact, to limit the functions of delegates and instead expand (assembleary) arenas for decisions open to all. Moreover, the space for politics broadens in participatory visions, as democracy is considered as fundamental not only in parliaments, but also in civil society organizations: from parties to social movements, from working places to neighbourhoods. While collective identities are still, as in the liberal model, formed outside of the democratic process, and might lead to conflictual interests, agreement on the basic principles of decision making is a precondition for managing those conflicts peacefully.

Beyond the set of criticisms addressed to delegation, there is also one addressed to the principle of the majority vote. A second alternative to liberal conceptions of democracy has, in fact, stressed the importance of the communicative dimension. Decisions are, in this sense, not made by counting votes, but rather through the more complex process in which opinions are formed. While liberal democracy assumes a political market in which candidates try to sell their products to electors, who already have their preferences, the *liberal-deliberative* conception of democracy is most attentive to the way in which those preferences are formed. The assumption is, in fact, that decisions are more legitimate and, additionally, better, the more interests and collective identities emerge – at least in part – throughout a high-quality deliberative process. In Habermas' (1981) theorization, deliberation should be based on communicative rationality, through an exchange of opinion based on reasons. While the extent to which deliberation implies the actual building of consensus is debatable (Dryzek 2010), good communication certainly implies a recognition of the others', and an open-minded assessment of one's own, reasons. With this in mind, the theorists of deliberation have looked at the ways in which preferences are formed within democratic institutions (Dryzek 2000a, 79). Even though the decision process often ends up with a vote, democracy should not, however, be identified with the principle that the majority wins over the minority. What counts as democratic is rather the possibility, during the democratic process, for holders of different points of view to interact and reciprocally transform each other's views. Empirical research on deliberative democracy has looked at deliberation within political parties (Teorell 1999), parliaments (Steiner et al. 2004), public journalism (Dzur 2002), cyberspace (Dahlberg 2001; Gimmler 2001), the European public sphere (Schutter 2002; Chalmers 2003), citizens' juries (Smith and Wales 2000), deliberative pollings (Fishkin 2003), referendums (Uhr 2000) and social movement organizations (della Porta 2009a and 2009b).

Combining both criticisms of the liberal conceptions of democracy, a fourth model of democracy stresses *participative-deliberative* qualities. In political theory, the feminist critique of Habermas has, in fact, stressed the importance of looking not only outside public institutions, but also beyond a mass-mediatic public sphere, creating places in which the weakest groups in particular can be empowered. Free spaces, with high-quality communication, are here considered as fundamental for the formation of collective identities. Not the bourgeoisie, but rather the subaltern classes are seen as the carriers of this democratic vision. The most recent waves of social movements, in particular, from the global justice movement to Occupy Wall Street, tried to put these norms into practice, by creating public forums, open to the participation of all citizens, in which a plurality of opinions is represented. The public sphere is here considered as a conflictual space, but there is also a reflection on the conditions for the formation of collective identities during the democratic process.

This volume

In what follows, I aim to bridge theory and empirical evidence, debates on democracy and debates on social movements, in order to look at the normative characteristics of these four different models, but also at their historical evolution. In this sense, I will seek to move beyond the gap that exists between normative theory and empirical studies, responsible for a lack of comparative studies, informed by theory, on democratic innovations (Smith 2009, 8; also Shapiro 2003). That gap is linked to the separation between the institutional analysis of democracy and the analysis of democratic principles, as if they belonged to two different worlds (Beetham 1999, 29). I will try, therefore, to contribute to the dialogue between normative theories and empirical explanations, whose absence, or at least weakness, has been seen as a considerable obstacle to progress in the analysis of democracy (Smith 2009, 9).

As will be seen, not only the conceptions but also the institutions of democracy themselves have been transformed to include, with differing levels of tension and in different balances, diverse understandings of democracy. After presenting the challenges to the liberal model (chapter 2), I will introduce conceptions and practices of participatory and deliberative democracy (chapters 3 and 4, respectively), with particular attention to the role of social movements as promoters of another democracy. Later on, I will address the use of new media in the search for new forms of participation and deliberation (chapter 5), the challenge of building a global democracy (chapter 6), and the contribution of social movements to the democratization process (chapter 7). Chapters 8 and 9 look at two, very different, state responses to social movement challenges, in the forms of protest policing and institutional experiments aimed at innovating democracy.

2

Liberal Democracy: Evolution and Challenges

The idea of popular sovereignty found historical expression in two different ways. The first was the right to vote, the right of citizens to choose their own leaders. This was the most direct expression of the democratic principle. But the power to vote periodically and thus bestow legitimacy to an elected government is almost always accompanied by a wish to exercise a more permanent form of control over the government thus elected. (Rosanvallon 2006, 12)

This is how French sociologist Pierre Rosanvallon reminds us of the different legitimating pillars of democracy. In political discourse, as well as in the mainstream social sciences, the attention is focused in a more and more narrow (and myopic) way on a liberal conception of democracy. As we are going to see in this chapter, it is mainly this conception that has been challenged by recent transformations. Saving democracy implies therefore the recognition and implementation of different democratic models. In this chapter, I shall present some tenets of the liberal conception of democracy and its evolution. I shall then discuss the challenges that developments such as the weakening of the identifying capacity of the political parties, the shifting of power to international organizations, and the retrenchment of the welfare state bring about for liberal democracy. Finally, I'll mention, however, some opportunities for different models of democracy, to be discussed in the following chapters.

The conception of liberal democracy: an introduction

Robert Dahl, one of the most influential political scientists in the field, has defined the fundamental characteristic of democracy as 'the continuing responsiveness of the government to the preferences of its citizens, considered as political equals' (1971, 1). This definition underlines a normative element: it is affirmed, that is, that democracy should involve a necessary correspondence between politicians' decisions and the wishes of the population. Moving to empirical research, Dahl has also suggested, however, that a series of procedures guarantees the response capacity of democracy.

A government capable of responding to the preferences of its citizens should guarantee that each is able:

1. to formulate their own preferences;
2. to present them to their fellow citizens and to the government via recourse to individual and collective action;
3. to ensure that their preferences are 'weighed equally in the conduct of the government, that is, weighted with no discrimination because of the content or source of the preference' (Dahl 1971, 2).

For these three conditions to be achieved, according to Dahl (1971), eight constitutional guarantees must be in place:

1. the freedom to form and join organizations
2. the freedom of expression
3. the right to vote
4. the right to compete for support and votes
5. eligibility for political roles
6. alternative sources of information
7. free and fair elections
8. institutions that make the government dependent on the vote and other forms of expression of political preferences.

Elections play indeed a very central role in the definition of liberal democracy – in particular in the passage from normative to procedural definitions of democracy. In this conception, those regimes that guarantee the right to vote to all citizens are thus democratic. Elections and institutions constituted by elected members are considered as indispensable guarantees for democracy: 'a representative system cannot exist without periodic elections used to render those who govern responsible before those who are governed...a political system is qualified as representative when honest electoral practices assure a reasonable level of responsiveness among governors before the governed' (Sartori 1990, 230).

In order for there to be democracy, elections must be competitive, fair and recurrent. It is not, in fact, sufficient for there to be elections – elections must involve real competition among the candidates, the competition must be fair, and the elections must be repeated regularly (in order that those elected know they must give account to electors for their actions within a certain amount of time). Elections must therefore function as elements of accountability, obligating the principal actors in the government – given that democracy involves an institutionalized system of representation, 'realised through the free electoral designation of certain fundamental organs (mostly parliaments)' (Cotta 1990, 933).

Liberal democracy is certainly representative, locating in representative institutions the possibility of limiting the risks linked to the power elections confer on the masses, considered as ignorant and potentially dangerous. Democracy here is conceived as the right of the citizenship to participate in the determination of the collective will through the mediation of elected representatives (Held, 1997, 168). It is not accident that John Stuart Mill underlined the difference between controlling the government and exercising the functions of government, leaving the latter to specialists. Although citizens participate in the selection of representatives, the principle of an unbinding mandate defends the capacity of the latter to make their decisions autonomously. Many theorists of a liberal model of democracy have explicitly defined direct democracy as unrealistic, especially when the territory to govern exceeds a certain size or when there is a high qualitative differentiation of administrative functions (Weber 1974, 256).

In this vision, electoral competition is central to the functioning of the cycle of electoral control. According to Sartori, democracy is an ethical-political system in which the influence of the majority is based on the power conferred on minorities, in competition among themselves, through elections (Sartori 1969, 105). Democracy, then, requires competition in the electoral market as the mechanism to attribute power to the people and to enact the responsiveness of the leader (Sartori 1987, 156). Political parties fulfil a fundamental function in implementing the principle of electoral responsibility, structuring the competition. Since they are present in the long term, they give the elector the possibility to judge, and eventually punish, those responsible for bad government.

Simplifying greatly, competition and electoral accountability are central to the realization of individual autonomy aspired to in the conception of liberal democracy. An effect of this should be the realization of a certain level of responsiveness to the preferences of citizens (Dahl

1970), normally operationalized as the preferences of the majority, but including the protection of the basic rights of minorities.

Liberal democracy does not, however, rely on electoral legitimation alone – so the observation that 'in democracy the majority wins' is inaccurate. A widespread *constitutional* conception underlines the necessity of limiting every type of power, including that of representative organs, by submitting it to the law. Liberal democracies in fact subordinate the power of the majority to judicial control regarding respect for the law and the constitution (Kelsen 1995, 123).

In democracy, obtaining the majority in parliament confers the right to decide on many things, but not on everything. Principally, liberal democracies exclude decisions that can contribute to corrupting the democratic rules of the game (Bobbio 1983, 316). Minorities are protected through the constitutionalization of some rights – that is, the protection of some fundamental elements of the social pact that democracies are based upon from the whims of majorities. As Morlino notes, even though allowing for a large indeterminancy in decisions to be taken, 'this uncertainty is always *relative* and cannot exceed certain boundaries' that are defined in the 'compromise agreement which recognizes the collectively accepted rules for the peaceful resolution of conflicts between social, politically represented and significant parties' (Morlino 2011, 30–1).

Similarly, in what has been called the genetic definition of democracy, democracy is considered as that bundle of norms and procedures that derive from a compromise oriented to the peaceful solution of the tensions that emerge among relevant actors in a specific political system (for example, Przeworski 1991, 26–34).

Even if we speak of competition (above all between parties) and of majority and opposition, the liberal conception of democracy is founded on the recognition of individual rights, while conflicts between collective actors tend to be considered as pathological. Citizens with a base of similar values, interested principally in their own material wellbeing, have the power to decide between political leaders in constant competition amongst each other. Indeed, the need for generally shared values is often affirmed, even if there are ever-increasing doubts as to the real extent to which these are shared in contemporary democracies (Held 1997). As David Held observes, in this competitive elitism, 'the sole role of the elector is to accept or reject one boss over another. The boss guarantees order and the capacity to manage the complexity of the political world; the vote of the electorate supplies legitimacy to subsequent political action' (1997, 265). Competition must however be limited on some themes. As summed up by David Held, 'the competition between rival leaders and parties must regard a relatively limited range of political questions: these must be reciprocally bound by consensus on the overall orientation of national politics, on a reasonable parliamentary programme and on general constitutional business' (1997, 266).

In this vision, participation must be limited and channelled in order to avoid an overload in demands, particularly from infantile citizens. Indeed, J. A. Schumpeter underlined that 'the electors must respect the division of labour between themselves and the politicians they elect. They must not withdraw their trust too easily in the interval between one election and another and they must understand that from the moment they have elected someone, political action is his competence and not theirs' (1967, 280–1). Even letters and petitions would, in this view, reduce the necessary freedom of action of the representative (1967, 280–1).

According to a much discussed study, in the 1970s it was the growth in participation that threatened the 'disintegration of the civil order, the breakdown of social discipline, the debility of leaders, and the alienation of citizens' (Crozier, Huntington and Watakuni 1975, 2). The governments of the United States and European democracies were described here as being subjected to excessive stress as a result of the growth in participation, seen as a challenge to institutions. According to Huntington (1975, 37–8), the problem of Western governments derived from an 'excess of democracy': 'The effective operation of a democratic political system normally requires some measure of apathy and disengagement in the population. The vulnerability of the democratic government in the United States derives from the internal dynamics of democracy in a highly educated, mobilized and participatory society.' The paradox was that it was precisely those most educated groups that seemed to present the greatest danger for democracy – as they were the ones that placed most demands on the system.

The emergence of democracy in the liberal state

The history of democratic regimes, defined by the right to vote for all citizens, is brief. As observed by Dahl (1998, 5–6), 'if we accept universal adult suffrages as a requirement of democracy, there would be some persons in practically every democratic country who would be older than their democratic system of government'. The concept of democracy has, however, a history thousands of years long.

Democracy, as developed in the last century, has some distant predecessors where the first rumblings of democracy developed. Some of the independent cities in Greece and the Roman republic in 500 BC are in fact often referred to as examples of forms of government that foresaw the participation of a consistent number of citizens. Specifically, in Athens between 500 and 300 BC, an assembly open to all those who enjoyed the status of citizens assigned some administrative posts, while others were decided by drawing lots. Limited forms of popular government were also seen in ancient Rome up to 100 BC. After 1,200 years, forms of popular participation in government then re-emerged, in particular in the city-states of northern Italy, and survived for around two centuries (Dahl 1998).

These first experiences did not, however, include some of those accountable institutions which are fundamental to the definition of a regime as democratic (in particular a parliament elected by universal suffrage), which were, instead, (slowly) developing beginning in Great Britain, Scandinavia, Switzerland and the Netherlands.

The study of 'first democratization' has focused in fact on the extension of political rights and the institutions linked to them. In an important piece of comparative work on different countries, the Norwegian political scientist Stein Rokkan spoke of *institutional thresholds* that each political movement had to pass in order to be fully integrated into democratic institutions. Similar to locks on a canal, these institutional thresholds allow for the growth of new actors that will then flow into institutions, but also allow the tide to be stemmed and the waves to be contained. Each rising political movement must pass through a series of locks, moving along the road that leads to the heart of the political system and the central arena of the decision-making process (1982, 142). There are four 'locks' or institutional thresholds: the *legitimation* threshold, linked to the right to express one's own ideas and to organize; the *incorporation* threshold, linked to the capacity to influence the choices of representatives; the *representation* threshold, linked to entrance into parliament; the *executive power* threshold, linked to the capacity to control the government.

During this process, the very quality of liberal democracy changes: extremely important for the quality and stability of democracy is the *timing* – that is temporal evolution – of the passing of the various thresholds. Rokkan presents the objectives of his research as follows:

- Regarding the *legitimation* threshold: at what moment in the history of the formation of the state and the construction of the nation did the effective recognition of the rights of petition, criticism and demonstrations against the regime take place?
- Regarding the *incorporation* threshold: how much time passed before formal rights to participate in choosing representatives were granted to the supporters of the opposition movements?
- Regarding the *representation* threshold: what barriers prevented the representation in parliament of the new movements and when

and in what ways were they lowered, facilitating the conquest of seats in the legislative assembly?

- Regarding the *executive power* threshold: how much were the executive organs influenced by the legislature, and how much time was needed before the parliamentary force could be transformed into direct influence on the decision-making process of the executive, through proportional rule and cabinet responsibility towards parliamentary majorities? (1982, 142)

The temporal evolution of passing the first two thresholds is linked, according to Rokkan, to elements such as the level of territorial consolidation in the Middle Ages and the continuity of medieval organs of representation. Electoral systems and executive accountability also vary subsequently, influenced by the dimensions of the country as well as specific historical circumstances.

The affirmation of liberal democracy followed diverse paths. In Robert Dahl's analyses, these can be distinguished based on the two principal theoretical dimensions of his concept of democracy:

1. the *right to opposition*, which refers to the level at which a series of constitutional guarantees 'are openly available, publicly employed and fully guaranteed to at least some members of the political system who wish to contest the conduct of the government' (Dahl 1971, 4);
2. the *level of inclusion*, that is the proportion of citizens to whom rights of opposition are guaranteed – as 'regimes also vary in the proportion of the population entitled to participate on a more or less equal plane in controlling and contesting the conduct of the government' (1971, 4).

Crossing the two dimensions, Dahl constructs a typology of political regimes, distinguishing:

- *closed hegemonies*, where no citizen has any right to opposition;
- *competitive oligarchies*, where strictly defined groups have a right to opposition;
- *inclusive hegemonies*, where low level participation is granted to all citizens;
- *polyarchies*, with wide-ranging opposition rights granted to all.

Dahl has defined the concession of opposition rights as *liberalization*, and the extension of those rights to the majority of the population as *inclusion*, or participation. Historically, the evolution of the two dimensions has not been in parallel. Paths of democratization – that is evolution towards polyarchies – have been varied.

In a first path, *liberalization precedes inclusion*: 'a) a closed hegemony increases opportunities for public contestation and thus is transformed into a competitive oligarchy; b) the competitive oligarchy is then transformed into a polyarchy by increasing the inclusiveness of the regime'. The English case is an example of liberalization, with the widening of opposition rights preceding the extension of participation: the opposition system was in fact well developed before the concession of universal suffrage. There was therefore an intermediate passage from a closed hegemony to a competitive oligarchy.

In the second path *inclusion precedes liberalization*: 'a) a closed hegemony becomes inclusive; b) the inclusive hegemony is then transformed into a polyarchy by increasing opportunities for public contestation'. The evolution towards polyarchy took place via a path that privileged inclusion in diverse countries, with an intermediate passage from closed hegemony to inclusive hegemony, principally through the extension of a single right of opposition: the vote.

In the third path there is a 'short cut', with a direct passage from closed hegemony to polyarchy. In these cases, 'a closed hegemony is abruptly transformed into a polyarchy by a sudden grant of universal suffrage and rights of public contestation' (1971, 34).

According to Dahl, the first type of path has been the healthiest for democracy, allowing the gradual socialization of new groups to the rules of the game. Indeed, this applies for the oldest and most stable polyarchies, where 'the rules, the practices, and the culture of competitive politics developed first among a small elite' (1971, 36). In these cases, the sometimes bitter conflict surrounding democratization was 'restrained by ties of friendship, family, interest, class and ideology that pervaded the restricted group of notables that dominated the political life of the country. Later, as additional social strata were admitted into politics they were more easily socialized into the norms and practices of competitive politics already developed among the elites' (1971, 36). The second path was generally more risky: 'When the suffrage is extended *before* the arts of competitive politics have been mastered and accepted as legitimate among the élites, the search for a system of mutual guarantees is likely to be complex and time consuming' (1971, 38). The short cuts have only rarely led to stable polyarchies. Unfortunately, while the liberalization path is the best for allowing the elaboration of a system of reciprocal guarantees that stabilize the regime, this is no longer a realistic option for contemporary non-democratic regimes (1971, 39).

Different paths towards democracies of different qualities are also described in other accounts of first democratization. Again in Dahl, democratization is a long process, during which degrees of inclusion and participation vary, together with the very quality of liberal democracy. Historical sociologists have also noted that the different and more or less easy paths of democratization have been influenced by some socioeconomic structures. In a wide-ranging historical study covering many countries, Barrington Moore demonstrates how some socio-economic configurations have been more favourable to the development of liberal democracy. In his work, three roads to modern society are identified: 'The earliest one combined capitalism and parliamentary democracy after a series of revolutions: the Puritan revolution, the French revolution, and the American civil war...The second path was also a capitalist one, but, in the absence of a strong revolutionary surge, it passed through reactionary political forms to culminate in fascism...The third route is of course the communist one' (1973, 413).

Only in the first path does modernization pass via the development of democracy, defined as

> a long and certainly incomplete struggle to do three closely related things: 1) to check arbitrary rulers; 2) to replace arbitrary rules with just and rational ones; 3) to obtain a share for the underlying population in the making of rules. The beheading of kings has been the most dramatic and by no means the least important aspect of the first feature. Efforts to establish the rule of law, the power of the legislature, and later to use the state as an engine for social welfare are familiar and famous aspects of the other two. (1969, 414)

The factors that favoured the affirmation of democracy in Western Europe were multiple. In the first place, absolute monarchy filled an important function in 'checking the turbulence of the nobility. Democracy could not grow and flourish under the shadow of prospective plunder and pillage by marauding barons' (1969, 417). On the other hand, however, the presence of a nobility strong enough to counterbalance the power of the monarchy was also an important element for the development of democracy. From the feudal relationship of vassalage, typical of the medieval Europe, both the idea of the right to resistance to unjust authority and the conception of a contract as a reciprocal commitment, freely entered into by free persons, were maintained. This permitted 'that delicate balance [...] between too much and too little royal power which gave an important impetus to parliamentary democracy' (1969, 415–6) to exist in Western Europe. Indeed, 'In early modern times too, a decisive precondition for modern democracy has been the emergence of a rough *balance between the crown and the nobility*, in which the royal power predominated but left a substantial degree of independence to the nobility' (1969, 417, emphasis added).

A final element that favoured democracy was the existence of a numerous and vigorous *urban bourgeoisie* – 'No bourgeoisie, no democracy' (1969). As various scholars agree, the bourgeoisie in fact had an interest in the development of a series of individual rights – first and foremost rights to private property and concluding contracts – that indirectly favoured the development of political rights.

And, again, democracy was facilitated by the *mercantile evolution of the landed aristocracy* – a typically English phenomenon. The need to find money to pay rising taxes and the development of trade with cities pushed the English aristocracy towards a form of mercantile agriculture that in fact liberated peasants from many of the constraints of subjugation to lords and created solidarity with the interests of the emerging bourgeoisie in the cities.

If the alliance between city and countryside helped democratic evolution, a necessary condition to the development of democracy was in any case *the absence of a coalition between the aristocracy and the bourgeoisie against peasants and workers*.

In the historical experience of Great Britain, France and the United States, finally, *violent revolutions* formed part of the process of industrialization and democratization which took place via the weakening of the power of the agrarian elite and the destruction of peasant society. The revolutionary break with the past is thus seen as another necessary characteristic for the development of democracy.

Various studies have also emphasized how the development of democracy was closely linked to some paths of construction of the nation state. If 'the state makes war, but wars make states', some of the main stages of development of democracy and mass politics have also been reached through the recognition of ever greater rights for citizens. Indeed, 'it was in the interests of a State that confronted other States to have well fed soldiers and healthy workers with none of the problems of old age' (Pizzorno 2010, xxiii). This served not only to keep soldiers quiet and tamed through material advantages, but also to construct collective identities that legitimated the state's demand for loyalty.

The recognition of these rights, as we will see in the next chapter, contributed to a profound transformation of the democratic institutions that were initially founded upon elitist and individualist conceptions. The elitist conception of representation, present in the first French and American republics, is explicit in the often cited affirmation by James Madison, 'To the people of the state of New York' published in the *Federalist*, which defines elections as an instrument 'to refine and enlarge the public views, by passing them through the medium of a chosen body of citizens, whose wisdom may best discern the true interest of their country, and whose patriotism and love of justice will be least likely to sacrifice it to temporary or partial considerations' (in Sintomer 2007, 37). In contrast, drawing lots, as was already done in some local contexts, was rapidly abandoned insofar as it risked giving power not to the best, but to common citizens. It was not by chance that, in the nineteenth century, it was the Left that defended the institution of the popular jury, including their use in judicial proceedings, which conservatives considered instead as technically incapable and prone to emotional influence (2007).

Democratic states were also born with an idea of democracy as linked to individual rights and/or negative freedom. As David Held observed (1997, 138), the theorists of liberal democracy (from Jeremy Bentham to J.S. Mill, to utilitarians in general) have justified the liberal state on the basis of its capacity to secure 'for individuals those conditions that are necessary to follow their own interests without the risk of arbitrary political interference, to participate freely in economic transactions, exchange labour and goods on the market and appropriate resources in a private manner'. In the nineteenth-century conception of liberalism, 'the state was to play the role of arbitrator and guarantor while individuals pursued their interests in civil society according to the rules of competition and free exchange' (1997, 238).

All concerted action in the pursuit of specific interests (wages, working conditions) remained illegal for a long time. Indeed, the conception of the state as guarantor was accompanied by intolerance towards those who contested some of its rules: 'Those that threatened the security of property, or the market society, threatened the realization of the public good' (Held 1997, 138–9).

The dominant Enlightenment discourse of the French revolution supported individual freedom and competition, opposing trade corporations and proclaiming individual liberty (Sewell 1980, 73). Private property was defended as deriving from men's work, in nature, preceding the intervention of the state; society was presented as a voluntary act of association between independent individuals. Suppressed by the Turgot edict of 1776, corporations were in that discourse considered as responsible, by blocking trade and industry, not only for causing prices to rise, but also for depriving many of the right to work. After the French revolution, there were in fact several attempts to destroy the traditional corporatist order in favour of a society based instead on individuals, contracts and private property (1980, 167). Consequently, the Le Chapelier law affirmed the right to meet as private citizens, but not as members of corporations, for the promotion of common interests. In the constituent assembly, in fact, the right to work outranked the right to association, the masters won over the workers (1980, 167).

In England too civil and religious freedoms were linked to free trade (Thompson 1991, 57), and individual freedoms did not at first include a full right of association. Tom Paine, while promoting social measures that could reduce disorder and thus legitimize the government, did not think any state intervention on private property wise (1991, 105). Here, as well, individual freedoms did not initially include a full right of association. The Combination Acts of 1799–1800 banned the trade unions, and the Seditious Societies Act of 1799 confirmed opposition to national associations, making, e.g., the Corresponding societies, that were pushing for a constitution, illegal.

This conception of liberalism accompanies a specific vision of society as composed of individuals possessing prevalently material interests. As David Held writes, 'democracy is a logical necessary requirement for the direction of a society now free from tradition and absolute power, in which individuals with enlightened desires constitute a mass of consumers whose aim is to obtain the maximum of private satisfaction' (1997, 140).

Transformations in democracy: the challenges

In the next chapters we are going to see how the liberal model of democracy was, de facto, bridged with other democratic conceptions – such as participatory and deliberative ones – in the institutional evolution of really existing democracies. As liberal democracy remained dominant, an understanding of contemporary challenges requires an assessment of the mechanisms which needed to function in order for liberal democracy to be legitimate. I suggest below that three such mechanisms were necessary. First, liberal democracies needed functioning political parties as actors that could implement the principles of electoral accountability. Second, the majoritarian assumption needed a nation state as defining the border of the demos in whose name (and interest) decisions were made. Third, and more subtly, even though liberal democracy did not call for social justice, it still relied upon the assumption that political equality was to reduce social inequality that otherwise risked undermining the very principle of free access to political rights. The liberal form of democracy developed, that is, in contexts characterized by well-established welfare states, party democracies and the full sovereignty of the nation state.

At the turn of the millennium, these conditions have, however, been challenged as neoliberal globalization, as well as other general evolutions in contemporary democracies, have produced:

- A shift of power from parties (and representative institutions) to the executive;
- A shift of power from the nation state to international governmental organizations (IGOs);
- A shift of power from the state to the market, which also implies a shift from welfare state to warfare state.

Even though these are neither complete nor natural or irreversible trends, they are, however, certainly challenges to the liberal model of democracy. In fact, they contributed to the shifts towards a neoliberal conception of democracy, based upon an elitist vision of electoral participation for the mass of the citizens and free lobbying for stronger interests, along with low levels of state intervention (Crouch 2003, 5).

From the parties to the executive?

Competition between well-structured parties is an essential mechanism for electoral accountability as a legitimating device for liberal democracy. The assumption that elections give citizens the power to punish bad governors and confirm good ones requires collective actors that are able to give transparency and, especially, continuity to the accountability process. Citizens need, that is, information from trusted sources, as well as a certain degree of continuity in the actors that are to be prized or punished. Additionally, as many aims cannot be achieved in the short term, citizens must trust some actors to interpret and promote their claims in a long-term perspective. Political parties have been pivotal in playing these functions, in what have been – not by chance – called party democracies.

Recent research has, however, repeatedly confirmed a rapid decline in the capacity of political parties to function as mediators between the civil society and the political institutions (della Porta 2008). In particular, parties seem to have lost much of their 'power of identification', that is, their capacity to function as powerful identifiers, helping to define long-term collective identities (Pizzorno 1981). Analyses of political parties describe (with particular intensity after the Second World War) a progressive rapprochement of parties to institutions, and their moving away from civil society. As Pizzorno has observed, parties maintain their function of selecting political personnel, but 'political participation as a contribution to proposals for the (re)organization of society no longer pass through parties, which see their associative and political socialization activities greatly reduced' (1996, 1028). In fact, in the last quarter of the twentieth century and the first decade of the new one, there has been a substantial and growing disaffection with respect to numerous specific democratic institutions, and no institution is considered worse than parties (Diamond and Gunther 2001, ix; della Porta and Reiter 2012).

First of all, the *trust* of citizens in parties is dramatically falling. In seventeen of the nineteen democracies for which there were data, at the turn of the millennium the proportion of the population identifying with parties, along with attachment to parties, had declined (Diamond and Gunther 2001, ix). According to Eurobarometer data, the percentage of respondents declaring attachment to parties also dropped in almost all European countries between 1975 and 1992. The decline appeared particularly acute in countries such as Italy (where the percentage of interviewees who declared themselves close to a party fell from 46 per cent in 1978 to 31 per cent in 1992), France (from 28 per cent to 16) and the Netherlands (from 40 per cent to 28 per cent). On average the percentage of European citizens close to parties fell from 37 to 29 per cent in the same period. In advanced democracies, the percentage of those who strongly identify with parties is in decline in all twenty-one countries analysed (Dalton 2004; see also della Porta 2001; Dalton and Wattemberg 2000). It has been noted that, in particular, the trust of electors in the competences and ability of their own parties decreased (as did the conviction that politicians listen to citizens) (Dalton 2004, 28 and 149). The weakening of parties' capacity to root themselves in civil society was particularly marked in Italy, where the proportion of members of the main political parties to voters collapsed from about 12 in the 1940s, 1950s and 1960s, to around 9 in the 1970s and 1980s, then to 4 in the 1990s and 2000s (Raniolo 2007, 125). Apathy has also been singled out as an important characteristic of political culture in democratic countries such as the United States (Eliasoph 1998). In general, comparative research has indicated that, at the beginning of the new millennium, citizens have become more distant from political parties, more critical of elites and political institutions, and less positively oriented with respect to governments (Dalton 2004, 46).

Decline in trust had *electoral* effects. Research carried out on Austria, Germany, Denmark, Finland, the Netherlands, Norway, Switzerland and the United Kingdom indicates that the percentage of electors that has changed parties between one election and another (among those that voted at both elections) has increased constantly, passing from 11 per cent in 1950–4 to 26 per cent in 1990–4 (Lane and Ersson 1999, 195). In addition, another effect of the changes is the growth of electoral abstention. If we look at the trend of participation in elections in European countries between the period immediately after the Second World War and the end of the 1990s, despite noteworthy differences among countries, we note a downward trend, particularly strong in countries as different as Norway

(–9.8 per cent), Italy (–9.9 per cent), Ireland (–11 per cent), Finland (–16.9 per cent) and the Netherlands (with –22.2 per cent).

With the parties reeling from declining trust and loyalty, party organization also changed. The centralization of decisions in the hands of a few visible leaders is intertwined with the merely formal involvement of members (considered mainly as card-payers). In particular, there is a much reduced number of and influence from the activists, normally considered more intransigent than both the leaders and the rank and file, and therefore as obstacles to moderate political choices (Crouch 2003). The personalization of leadership has led to talk of an Americanization of European parties, oriented more and more to an individualistic management of gains, and less and less to the creation of collective identities, progressively assimilated into the state (depending on the state for finances and profits) and less and less autonomous from public institutions (Calise 2010). Party activists as channels of communication to potential voters are thus replaced by the mass media, in particular television, which facilitate direct identification of electors with leaders able to transmit a self-assured, confident and warm image, as well as to appropriate some relevant themes (Barisione 2007), thus side-stepping the mediation of the party. In this frame, the use of an 'anti-political' language by leaders also becomes an instrument for reinforcing personalized leadership by politicians who underline, paradoxically, their estrangement from politics (Campus 2006). Similarly, populist appeals (to the people against the elites) by parties (prevalently, but not only from the Centre-Right) seek to utilize low party identification and mistrust in institutional politics to create an electoral following. In a vicious circle, the decrease in trust and identification in parties could lead to further personalization as a strategy to win back consent (Diamanti 2007), especially (but not only) from the most socially marginalized and least politically interested electors.

While parties appear less and less able to mediate between the state and the society in the most advanced democracies, cynicism towards them is very widespread in new democracies as well. As Philippe Schmitter observes, however – unfortunately for the prestige of their discipline – political scientists are not sure about what to do to 'fix the parties' (Schmitter 2001, 67), and, with them, the basis of the legitimacy and efficiency of liberal democracy.

From the national to the international

Liberal democracy developed within national borders that defined the community whose (majoritarian) will had to be represented. Political rights were part and parcel of national citizenship, and often jealously protected: not by chance, they have often been the last type of citizens' rights to be granted to non-national residents. Liberal democracy applied only within national borders, and states were the only recognized actors of international politics. In the realist approach, long dominant in the discipline of international relations, states are considered to compete amongst themselves in different forms in the name of their national interests inside a wholly anarchic system. This vision has, however, been challenged from various points of view.

First of all, an increasing relevance of international politics is shown by the growth in the *number* of international organizations (from 37 in 1909 to 350 in 1995 – see Princen and Finger 1994, 1), international agreements (from 15,000 in 1960 to 55,000 in 1997), of international conferences (from a couple per year in the nineteenth century to about 4,000 per year at the end of the twentieth century). The number of international agreements at the United Nations increased from the 8,776 registered at the end of 1960 to the 63,419 registered in March 2010 (http://treaties.un.org/pages/Home.aspx?lang=en).[1]

What is more, there are indicators of an increasing *power* for some of these international organizations. In particular, international financial institutions have made economic help conditional upon national governments accepting some specific policies. The World Bank (WB) and the International Monetary Fund (IMF) – during the Cold War accused of distributing help according to political loyalty (Thacker 1998) – increased their power of injunction through the negotiation of structural adjustment programmes with debtor countries. At the end of the 1990s, half of the world's population and two-thirds of its countries were subject to the influence of those two institutions (Pieper and Taylor 1998). With its growing involvement in liberalization policies (in Eastern Europe but also, e.g., in Greece), the IMF linked provision of long-term loans to the approval of its plans for liberalization, deregulation, privatization and fiscal reform (O'Brian et al. 2000, 162). As for the WB, since the late 1970s the move from financing development projects to supporting structural adjustment has brought about an attempt at reorganizing domestic economies, with 'considerable influence on the daily lives of the world's population' (2000, 11). Also macro-regional organizations (e.g. the European Union) increased their sanction capacity, as is seen very clearly in the conditionalities imposed on member states who want access to some form of financial support.

Furthermore, there has been a change in the internal decision making of some of these international organizations. While the majority of them still function mainly as meeting places and discussion forums where decisions are taken unanimously and then ratified by national organs, there is a growing number of supranational organizations within which decisions binding for all member states are made on a majority basis. Vis-à-vis its predecessor, the GATT, the World Trade Organization (WTO) dispute settlement procedures moved from a system of negotiation to one of adjudication (O'Brian et al. 2000, 71).

International organizations have thus contributed to the spread of *international regulations and norms* that in some cases supersede national sovereignty. As has often been pointed out, 'no official authority controls states in the contemporary world system, but many are subject to powerful unofficial forces, pressures and influences that penetrate the supposed hard shell of the state' (Russett and Starr 1996, 62). Increasing acknowledgement of global interdependences has contributed to the creation of supranational norms that, as in the case of the human rights regime, help to defend some citizens' rights, especially against authoritarian regimes. At the same time, some international organizations became norm entrepreneurs for neoliberal visions, privileging deregulation and reducing social services. A neoliberal model in fact implies an elitarian conception of citizens' participation, and yet a large sphere of influence for the lobbies which represent strong interests (Crouch 2003, 5). Market deregulation and the privatization of public services are not 'natural' effects of technological development, but a strategy adopted and defended by international financial institutions and by the governments of the most powerful nations (in particular through the G7 and the G8) to the advantage of multinational corporations. As Colin Crouch (2003, 95) has observed, the establishment of the ideology of a free market has clearly been facilitated by the WTO, whose 'postdemocratic' aim is the liberalization of international exchanges of goods and services. Neoliberal globalization, therefore, is a matter not only of new technologies and modes of production, but also of the *political* tools set in place to regulate and reproduce this social structure through, among other things, the proliferation of international organizations (Beck 1999; Boli and Thomas 1999). Labels such as 'judicial globalization' reflect the expansion of international courts (Zolo 2004, 96).

Finally, while the types of recognized actors in international arenas go well beyond states (see below), there is a growing *politicization* of international relations, in the sense of its increased contestation, but also the emergence of a world order based on the diffusion of shared norms. As observed by Zürn, Binder and Ecker-Ehrhardt, politicization means entrance into the political sub-system, which is characterized by the presence of 'public communication and by contestation about the common good and collectively binding decisions necessary to advance it....In brief then, politicization means making a matter an object of public discussion about collectively binding decision making' (2010, 7). In fact, a shift from hegemony to contestation has been observed in the configuration of discourses that address international issues – among them, nowadays, international political economy, in particular (Dryzek 2010, 183). The scope of the debates, in terms of issues addressed, increased in fact together with the number of actors participating in them (2010, 185).

This does not mean, of course, that states (especially some of them) have no power left. First of all, the growing political globalization is not particularly related to technological challenges and opportunities or market dynamics. It is rather the product of political decisions that the states (especially some of them) participated in. The liberalization of trade and particularly of financial markets is driven by political actors within single states (and in particular within the most powerful one, the United States) – as well as by the mentioned international actors. Moreover, as in the past, sovereignty is formally equal, but substantively unequally distributed, as some states have more power over their own territory, others much less. Also, as research on the European Union clearly indicates, states retain a (differential) capacity to influence the international organizations (suffice to compare Germany with Greece in the EU) they belong to, and especially play an important role in the implementation of international treaties.

It is uncontestable, however, that the growing number, power and visibility of international organizations challenge the very principles of legitimation of liberal democracies as representing the will of their citizens.

From the state to the market?

While not directly claiming that they aimed at reducing social inequalities, liberal democracies tended to legitimize themselves as efficient in granting wellness to their citizens: freedom was assumed to produce healthy competition and, therefore, economic growth and political equality to grant power to the (more numerous) less privileged citizens and, therefore, policies were oriented to reducing inequalities. This assumption seemed to be confirmed when democracy became synonymous with welfare states that, even if following different models, were all oriented to granting a modicum of social protection to the citizen, so reducing the inequalities produced by the market. Many agreed (and some still agree) that a high-quality democracy should not only respect individual freedom, but also pursue the second aim of democracy: equality. As Leonardo Morlino (2011, 43) observed:

If these aspects, which are essential for the achievement of freedom and equality, are to be effectively pursued, contemporary democracies will also have to attend to issues such as environmental conservation, the right to health care, assistance for the elderly and invalid, the right to a job, provisions for the unemployed, the need to ensure everyone has a reasonable standard of living, the right to greater educational opportunities, and also the promotion of equity in private disputes or between public and private interests. Not to include in an analysis of the ideal democracy the safeguarding of the substantive elements outlined above would paradoxically mean ignoring the steps already taken by many real democracies to promote equality.

What is more, failing to recognize the protection and promotion of social rights as indispensable for democracy and the implementation of its main principles, such as participation and political equality, 'In short...would result in a definition of the ideal democracy that in some ways falls short of what real ones have already achieved' (2011).

The so-called mid-century compromise between capital and labour, which had allowed for the development of the welfare state, was, however, not going to last. Since the 1990s, and more and more in the new millennium, research on the welfare state has pointed at its retrenchment, and the consequent rapid increase in social inequalities. Deregulation of financial markets, reduction of taxes, and privatization of public services have indeed been common trends in advanced democracies, although with some differences between European countries and the United States (Crouch 2003). Administrative reforms, often presented as applications of the theory of 'public management', were, until a few years ago, almost unanimously appreciated as capable of limiting parasitic behaviour among public actors, of simplifying baroque administrative procedures and of re-launching economic initiative. Deregulation and the privatization of public services were seen as functional for the rejuvenation of local economies thanks to the space liberated for private initiatives. Especially since the beginning of the new millennium, the weaknesses and criticality of the new model – in terms of both the reduction in quality of a series of public utilities (Crouch 2003) and the delegitimation of local government organs – have become increasingly clear.

In the last few decades, politics and governments have lost ground, being conquered by privileged elites and their anti-egalitarian conception (Crouch 2003, 9), which tends to substitute social right with charity (Dore 2010, 177). In his *Post-Democracy*, Colin Crouch (2003, 9) points at the reduced capacity for intervention by elected politicians, as well as citizens' growing dissatisfaction with their performance. Neoliberal conceptions are said to have undermined the moral basis of capitalism and with it the capacity to define a general interest (Dore 1998, 244), or at least to allow the development of those social rights that have been posited as the bases for some conceptions of democracy (Marshall 1992; Tilly 2004). In some sectors more than in others, economic globalization has produced not competition but high barriers to entry, favouring a small number of huge multinationals (Crouch 2010, 182). The effects of deregulation and privatization are not seen in a competitive market, but in the growth of multinationals and oligopolies. At the same time, there is an involution of the state – that is, the regression to a penal state, which concentrates on repression, and progressively abandons its social functions of education, health and welfare (Bourdieu 1998, 34). Indeed, public funds for social services have been cut, but not the public spending related to the pre-democratic roles of the state, such as the extension of official honours and symbolic privileges for the rich and powerful, the development of a complex apparatus of laws, prisons and police forces to protect private property, and the distribution of lucrative public contracts (Crouch 2010, 185).

These changes have been linked to those mentioned at international level as 'national governments, terrified of the implicit threat of capital flight, have let themselves be dragged into a cost-cutting deregulatory frenzy, generating obscene profits and drastic income disparities, rising unemployment, and the social marginalization of a growing population of the poor' (Habermas 2001, 79). Additionally, thanks to the opening of borders to goods, services and finance, multinational corporations have grown in size and influence upon (weaker) states while labour has not been given such freedom. In a vicious circle, removing borders for goods, services and finance has reinforced multinational corporations. Not only are they growing in number (there were 60,000 at the beginning of the 2000s), they have also grown in terms of size and the capacity to influence states, progressively increased in their ability to intervene. Suffice to remember that in 2000, the large multinationals accounted for 42 per cent of world exports and 10 per cent of production, employing 40 million people (Pianta 2001).

The effects of this dominance are seen in the 2010s, with the recent dramatic crisis in the Eurozone. Neoliberal economic policies have renounced policy intervention oriented to promoting economic growth, so leaving territorial inequalities unchallenged while the financialization of the economy grew exponentially. The financial crisis that started in the United States in 2007 and spread at global level the following year thus hit those economies that had always been weaker: Ireland and Southern Europe. As Italian economist Mario Pianta noticed, 'The causes of the financial crisis are in the lack of sustainability of a system that let speculation prevail over rules, finance over real economy, the market over politics' (2012, 9). When banks became insolvent, governments rushed to save them, with transfers of money. But without any structural intervention that could increase control over financial speculation (through, e.g., a tax on financial transactions or limits on bank and stock-market transactions), this brought about a growth in public deficits and increasing dependence from financial markets, with consequent economic recession. Austerity policies (with cuts of salary and pension, as well as flexibilization of the labour market through reduced protection for workers) have been unable to improve the economies, instead reducing productivity and increasing unemployment and poverty, with an improvement in the conditions of the richest 10 per cent of the population and a decline in those of the remaining 90 per cent (2012, 72). In all this, public authority has been accused of being not powerless, but, rather, 'actively committed to increasing the power of actors in the global markets and finance and reducing that of everyone else' (2012, 61).

Economic globalization, in this neoliberal version, therefore challenges a conception of democracy as development of social rights that is deep-rooted in public understanding, as well as in sociological theory (Marshall 1992; Tilly 2004). The effects on the legitimacy of democracy are immediate:

> With the chance (or even the possibility) of a welfare policy being revoked, the image of a democracy looking to the future, given to the progressive actuation of equality is weakened...As soon as the ground that forms the complementary (or at least credible) relationship between the various rights and their connection with democracy dries out, another of the characteristic elements of constitutional democracy disappears. (Costa 2010, 39)

While the satisfaction of users of public services is decreasing, the state appears no longer to be able to fulfil the functions of regulation, service provision and balancing of social inequalities once considered its fundamental duties.

In sum, although to differing degrees in different states, and certainly not in any irreversible way, we can note the diffusion of a neoliberal doctrine that has reduced the capacity of the state to intervene in the economy. If the recent financial crises have shaken these convictions, they have not yet led to any paradigm change.

Challenges and/or opportunities?

In sum, the weakening of the parties' states, nation states and welfare states present serious threats to a notion of democracy based upon a liberal conception. We have pointed out several indicators of a general malaise in democratic countries that challenges democracy both inside and outside national borders.

At the national level, procedural legitimation of democracy as a regime based upon electoral accountability is limited by widespread phenomena such as the decline of electoral participation (visible on all territorial levels), but also the profound transformation in the political parties as the main actors that, giving continuity in time from pre-electoral promises to judgement on post-electoral performances, allowed electoral accountability to function. As the recent mobilizations for democracy show, the retrenchment of public expenditures has, moreover, reduced the potential for states to get a sort of 'legitimacy by the output' – linked, that is, to their capacity to meet citizens' claims.

At the transnational level, challenges to democratic legitimacy on the input side arise from the necessity to adapt conceptions and practices developed at the national level to a reality in which transnational actors and global events have an increasingly larger influence. As John Markoff (1999, 283) observed, globalization changes the ways in which democratization is addressed in a world of transnational connections: democratization of the states is no longer the central issue. The normative conceptions and empirical implementations of democracy developed in and about the nation state are not easily applied at the supranational level where political institutions and civil society are concerned. Indeed, 'democracy as we know it within countries does not exist in a Globalized Space. More accurately, to the extent that Globalized Space is marked by conventional democratic procedures, these are ad-hoc, non systematic, irregular and fragile' (Rosenau 1998, 39). Not only do international organizations usually have no electoral accountability, but also a transnational conception of citizenship and citizenship rights is hard to develop. The fundamental principles of nation-state democracy – such as territoriality, majority principles, and use of coercive power – 'have to be reformulated, if they are to be applied globally' (Archibugi 2003, 7). At the same time, however, democratic accountability, transparency and participation are more and more needed faced with processes of politicization of international relations (Zürn and Ecker-Ehrhardt 2011).

From the output side, an additional challenge comes (at both national and transnational levels) from the transformations in economic politics, and their effects on the capacity of democracies to produce public goods. Economic globalization as 'return to the market' has certainly reduced the potential for state intervention on economic inequalities, challenging the assumption (previously dominant in Europe, but also in Keynesian political economy) about its role in ensuring economic development, and also social justice. In turn, the reduced effectiveness of public administration affects the legitimacy of state institutions as well. In fact, 'As markets drive out politics, the nation-state increasingly loses its capacities to raise taxes and stimulate growth, and with them the ability to secure the essential foundations of its own legitimacy' (Habermas 2001, 79).

If a narrative in terms of a crisis of democracy, or at least of a reduction of democratic qualities even in advanced democracies, has been long widespread, a sort of counter-narrative, however, started to develop, stressing the opportunities that some recent transformations bring about for democracy. Some empirical research has in fact also singled out potential chances for improvement in (some) democratic qualities triggered by recent changes (see table 2.1).

There has been an increase not only in the number of democratic countries after the third wave of democratization, but also in citizens' participation. While some more conventional forms of participation (such as voting or party-linked activities) are declining, protest forms are instead increasingly used (Dalton 2004). Citizens vote less, but are no less interested or knowledgable about politics. And if some traditional types of associations are less and less popular, others (social movement organizations and/or civil society organizations) are instead growing in resources, legitimacy and members. Media studies have discussed the increasing participatory opportunities linked to the new technologies, which also to a certain extent allow the shortcoming of increasing commercialization of traditional media to be bypassed. Both trends increase the capacity to watch over elected representatives, even if their electoral accountability is declining. In the analysis of public policies, the term 'governance' assumed a vaguely positive meaning to identify flexible and participatory forms of decision making. Experiments with deliberative democracy developed as means to increase citizens' participation, creating high-quality discursive arenas and empowering the people. Even though this process continues to be an exception, it is becoming more

Table 2.1   *Challenges and Opportunities for Democracy*

Challenges	Opportunities
– democracy in democratic countries	+ countries with at least a minimal level of democracy
– conventional forms of participation	+ innovative forms of participation
– media commercialization	+ partial public spheres
– electoral accountability	+ capacity for scrutiny of institutions
– state intervention against social inequalities	+ recognition of other-than-social rights (gender, environmental, human rights...)

and more tried and tested (della Porta and Gbikpi 2008). Moreover, if the capacity of state intervention on market inequalities is reduced, civil right issues have entered the political debate more and more. In international politics, research on transnational relations singled out the – admittedly difficult – development of norms in defence of environmental protection, gender rights and human rights. In different ways in different international organizations, civil society organizations carved out channels of access to international decision making.

More generally, the very reflection on democratic qualities testified to the perceived need to balance the acknowledged crisis of the representative (electoral) conception of democracy with a sort of revival of other ones that – even though far from hegemonic – belong to deep-rooted traditions in democratic thinking, and with development of democratic institutions that go beyond electoral accountability.

Conclusion

In summary, while the weakening of political parties, nation states and welfare states challenges the liberal conception of democracy, it might have produced some opportunities (at least discursive ones) for other conceptions of democracy. As Pierre Rosanvallon has suggested, the understanding of democratic experiences requires the consideration, at the same time, of the 'functions and dysfunctions' of electoral representative institutions, but also of the organization of distrust (Rosanvallon 2006, 8).

Thinking in terms of other conceptions of democracy paves the way to addressing contemporary changes as not only challenges to, but also opportunities for, democracy. The weakening of liberal democracy (variously defined as crisis or decline) has led the state to pay more attention to the variety of arenas in which different models of democracy developed – something I will deal with in what follows. These diverse models are often combined and balanced in the practices and discourses of different actors.

3

Participatory Democracy

We seek the establishment of a democracy of individual participation, governed by two central aims; that the individual share in those social decisions determining the quality and direction of his life; that society be organized to encourage independence of man and provide the media for their common participation. (Port Huron Statement, 1964)

Although the meetings were frequently long and tedious, many occupiers point to these open, participatory assemblies as embodying an alternative to the current representative democratic order disproportionately influenced by the 1%. (Juris 2012, 263, on #Occupying Boston)

The often-quoted Port Huron Statement by the US student movement in 1964 is considered to be a manifesto for democracy as participatory, claiming free speech and the right to participate in collective decisions. About fifty years later, as Juris observed on the Occupying movement, participatory democracy is still central for the movements that have mobilized against financial crises and austerity measures. Some of the transformations-as-opportunities identified at the end of the last chapter tend to favor the development of some specific democratic qualities, which are central for conceptions of democracy other than the liberal one discussed in the last chapter. In particular, the growth of diverse and multiple forms of unconventional political participation reflects the development of participatory conceptions of democracy. To this conception and related practices, and the long path of their development, this chapter is devoted. After defining participatory democracy and reviewing normative theories devoted to it, I'll turn to history to show how social movements (in particular, the labour movement) have put forward different conceptions of democracy from the liberal one, emphasizing collective and social rights over individual (negative) freedom as well as participation by citizens over delegation to politicians. In their complex evolution, the labour movement, and other left-wing movements, have not only succeeded, often in alliances with other actors, in changing political institutions, but also experimented with different democratic qualities within their structures and struggles.

Participatory democracy: an introduction

The theme of participation is central to politics and to democracy. The very concept of politics, with reference to its etymological root in the Greek *polis*, recalls an image of participation: in the agora one intervenes in the making of decisions. If so-called 'ancient democracy' included this element of direct intervention, however, it is often said that 'modern democracy' has little in common with the Greek *polis*, being prevalently representative.

Yet another conception of democracy has survived in contemporary democracies, alongside the liberal one – one which underlines the necessity for citizens, naturally interested in politics, directly to assume the task of intervening in decisions that regard public issues. Where liberal democracy foresees the constitution of bodies of specialized representatives, participatory democracy instead posits strong constraints on the principle of delegation, seen as an instrument of oligarchic power. If liberal democracy is based on formal equality – one head, one vote – participatory democracy underlines the need to create the conditions for real equality. While liberal democracy is often bureaucratized, with decision making concentrated at the apex, direct democracy insists on the necessity of bringing decisions as close to the people as possible.

If the tension between representation and participation is always present in debates on democracy, with the first clearly prevalent in the actual evolution of democratic institutions, a certain level of participation is nevertheless necessary to legitimate representatives. The very idea of popular sovereignty presupposes the participation that developed in Europe halfway through the eighteenth century together with the public sphere, and which allowed interaction between citizens and institutional representatives (Mayer and Perrineau 1992, 10). This was then extended through the different stages of the widening of electoral suffrage, removing – albeit very slowly – census and gender barriers. As Pietro Costa (2010, 9) has observed:

The driving force of democratization (its principal rhetorical device) is equality, employed as an instrument capable of shedding light on differences and denouncing the illegitimacy of the barriers that fragment the national society creating mutually estranged classes of citizens. And it is the participation–equality–rights nexus that continues to hold up democratic claims throughout the nineteenth century...It is in this perspective that attacks on the census constraints of suffrage are conducted, in which the political and social elite who form a considerable share of public opinion oppose tenacious resistance.

Theories of participatory democracy have also criticized liberal conceptions of democracy, which spoke of free and equal citizens, as unrealistic, underlining instead the power asymmetries that a purely political equality failed to neutralize. Influenced by the most powerful interests, the state is in fact seen as not fully able to guarantee real freedom and equality. To fight inequalities (and their delegitimizing effects), greater transparency in the functioning of public – both representative and otherwise – institutions is thus called for, along with the democratization of societal institutions. The involvement of citizens must be continuous and direct, widening towards a capacity to intervene in all the different areas of a person's everyday existence. The democratization of parties and associations is considered particularly important, as these mediate between society and state. According to Held:

> if we want democracy today to bloom it is necessary to rethink it as a double-faced phenomenon, with one side regarding the reform of state power and the other the restructuring of civil society. The principle of autonomy can only be realized if we recognize that a process of 'double democratization' is indispensible, that is the independent transformation of both the state and civil society. (1997, 435)

In this conception, participation at all levels, institutional or not, is oriented to rebalancing power inequalities that the liberal conception does not question. In fact, in this vision, while democracy is challenged by powerful organizations, in order for democracy to survive the challenge, 'economic groups and associations must undergo rearticulation by political institutions, in order to become part of the democratic process itself. This is possible with the adoption, within the modus operandi of such actors, of principles, rules and democratic practices' (1997, 451).

We can add that a delegated conception of democracy does not take into account the problem – acknowledged by Dahl (2000), among others – of the different intensity of preferences. At elections, each vote counts equally, but in reality the strength of citizens' opinions and emotional attachments, as well as competences, on different issues varies enormously. While this unequal distribution of preference makes representative democracy inefficient in its very claim to reflect preference distribution (Pizzorno 2012), participatory democracy takes this into account, by granting more decisional capacity to those who are more committed, and therefore participate more.

To a certain extent, participation has indeed survived even in representative regimes. Even if they are representative, participation (not only electoral) is considered essential for contemporary democracies, which gain legitimacy not only through votes but also through their capacity to submit decisions to the 'test of the discussion' (Manin 1995). As Pierre Rosanvallon noted, in the historical evolution of democracy, along with the growth of institutions of electoral accountability, a circuit of oversight anchored outside of state institutions took shape. In fact, the understanding of democratic experiences requires the consideration, at the same time, of the 'functions and dysfunctions' of electoral representative institutions, but also of the organization of distrust. The different elements of what Rosanvallon defined as counter-democracy do not represent, in fact, 'the opposite of democracy, but rather a form of democracy that reinforces the usual electoral democracy, a democracy of indirect powers disseminated through society – in other words, a durable democracy of distrust which complements the episodic democracy of the usual electoral representative system' (2006, 8). If mistrust is the disease, it might be part of the cure as 'a complex assortment of practical measures, checks and balances, and informal as well as institutional social counter-powers has evolved in order to *compensate for the erosion of confidence, and to do so by organizing distrust*' (2006, 4).

In the same vein as Rosanvallon, other scholars have stressed at the same time the crisis of the traditional, liberal (representative) conceptions of democracy and the revival of democratic qualities often considered under the label of a 'democracy of the ancients' that stresses the importance of a (free and committed) public. In particular, Bernard Manin described the evolution from a 'democracy of the parties', in which the public sphere was mainly occupied by the political parties, to a 'democracy of the public', in which the channels of formation of public opinion are freed from their ideological control (1995, 295). This also means that the cleavages within public opinion no longer reflect electoral preferences, developing instead from individual preferences formed outside of the political parties:

Individuals may have different opinions on a certain theme (for example, some are in favour, others against). A fracture then forms in public opinion on the theme in question...but this fracture does not necessarily reproduce partisan divisions between those that habitually

vote for one party and those that vote for another. The fracture forms
on the basis of the preferences of individuals on a specific subject, not
on the basis of the partisan political preferences. The fracture of public
opinion on different themes may not coincide with the line of division
established at the vote. (1995, 295)

Normative theorists of participatory democracy have, as mentioned,
stressed the importance of involving citizens beyond elections (Arnstein
1969; Pateman 1970; Barber 2003). In sum, participatory theory – which
David Held defines as the conception of the 'New Left' – promotes a
'direct participation of citizens in the regulation of the key institutions
of society, including the spheres of work and the local community' (Held
1997, 379), or 'the participation of citizens in the determination of the
conditions of their associational lives, which presumes the authentic and
rational nature of the judgements of each individual' (1997, 416).

In Carole Pateman's theorization, citizens should be provided with as
many opportunities to truly participate as there are spheres of decision.
While in *partial* participation, 'the final power of decision rests with the
management, the workers if they are able to participate, being able only
to influence that decision' (Pateman 1970, 70), *full* participation is a
'process where each individual member of a decision-making body has
equal power to determine the outcome of decisions' (1970, 70–1). In a
similar vein, 'strong democracy' has been defined as a government under
which citizens participate, at least some of the time, in the decisions that
affect their lives (Barber 2003).

Participatory theorists have in fact criticized ritualistic forms of participation, calling instead for real empowerment. As Arnstein (1969,
216) noted, 'citizen participation is a categorical term for citizen power'.
This means that 'there is a critical difference between going through the
empty ritual of participation and having the real power needed to affect
the outcome of the process' (1969). Any process which does not transfer
power is a manipulation of public opinion; no meaningful participation
is achieved until direct democracy comes into play. This is why, for
instance, Arnstein's ladder counts eight rungs corresponding to eight
degrees of power. From the bottom to the top, these eight rungs are:
manipulation, therapy, informing, consultation, placation, partnership,
delegated power and citizen control. The first two bottom rungs are
equivalent to non-participation; the three successive ones are degrees of
tokenism; but the three upper rungs are degrees of citizen power.[1]

Participation is called for as not only just, but also useful. Among the
instrumentally positive contributions of participation, we find defence
from arbitrary power, the production of more informed decisions and
the growth of the legitimacy of those decisions (Smith 2009, 5). Yet the

advantages of participation are praised in terms not only of immediate legitimation, but also of a growing socialization to interest and action for the collective good. Participation is seen to have a positive effect on citizens. Spaces of participation become 'schools of democracy': the more citizens participate in the decision-making process, the more they are informed and enlightened, and the more they will vote in national elections (Pateman 1970). Active, knowledgeable and informed citizenship will increase the systemic efficiency and individual and collective wellbeing.

Participation creates, then, a virtuous circle: opportunities to participate stimulate trust and activism, thus reproducing the stimulus to participate and improving the effects of participation itself. Indeed, participation in civic activity educates individuals with respect to how to think in public, given that citizenship permeates civic activity with the necessary sense of public-spiritedness and justice; in this sense, to paraphrase Barber, politics becomes its own university, citizenship its gym, participation its teacher (2003, 152).

Free spaces (horizontal and participatory) offer a school of citizenship, socializing in those competences and values that are essential to support effective participation (Evans and Boyte 1986, 17). Participation in social movements and other associations often broaden the personal identities of participants and offers satisfaction and self-realization (Gamson 1992, 56; Blee 2011). Indeed, identities and motivations are transformed, during collective action: while participation often starts for limited, immediate, even selfish reasons, many activists develop in time a political and social conscience and a more public and trusting sense of the self (Szas 1995, 154).

Similar effects were detected in the case of decentralized institutions. As Tocqueville (1986, vol. I, 112–13) wrote long ago, 'Town-meetings are to liberty what primary schools are to science; they bring it within the people's reach, they teach men how to use and how to enjoy it.' It is from encounters that solidarity is born: 'Feelings and opinions are recruited, the heart is enlarged, and the human mind is developed by no other means than the reciprocal influence of men upon each other' (Tocqueville 1986, vol. II, 158). Similarly, according to J.S. Mill, it is local institutions that carry out

> the practical part of the political education of a free people, taking them out of the narrow circle of personal and family selfishness, and accustoming them to the comprehension of joint interests, the management of joint concerns – habituating them to act from public or semi-public motives, and guide their conduct by aims which unite instead of isolating them from one another (Mill 1947, 112)

In this sense, it is by participating that people learn to participate. As Carole Pateman writes (1970, 42–3), 'the principal function of participation is...the educational, educational in the widest sense of the term, that includes both psychological aspects and the acquisition of the practice of capabilities and democratic procedures...Participation develops and forges those same qualities that are necessary to it: the more an individual participates, the more he is able to participate.' Personal involvement in the participatory process may significantly change one's attitude, perspective and value priorities (Bachrach 1975, 50).

The need to create multiple and varied channels of participation is justified by the recognition of the presence of conflicts between actors possessing different resources and powers. Bachrach and Baratz (1986), in particular, have theorized a dichotomy between those who have power and those who do not. The former can realize the mobilization of prejudice, excluding some ideas and requests from the public debate through the activation of a bundle of norms, values and rules that prevent some matters from becoming subject to public decision. Part of the activity of exercising power is thus oriented towards imposing and reinforcing this selectivity, preventing controversies from emerging on questions of fundamental importance to the group in power. Decisions are thus often taken on issues of little relevance, while non-decisions are taken with regard to the most important conflicts.

Increasing participation by the excluded therefore becomes necessary in order to introduce new, important issues into the political debate. Participatory democracy thus has elements in common with *associational* democracy (Hirst 1994), which focuses upon the need for citizens to self-organize. Associational experiences in civil society are here considered not only to be capable of replacing the state in some of its functions, but also to produce social solidarity, contributing to the democratic socialization of the citizens as well as to the production of social goods.

Participation should thus be an instrument for redistributing resources to the advantage of the weakest. While interest groups favour the most resourceful through less visible lobbying, these arenas of participation should give more power to the powerless. For Peter Bachrach, democratic participation is 'a process in which persons formulate, discuss, and decide public issues that are important to them and directly affect their lives. It is a process that is more or less continuous, conducted on a face-to-face basis in which participants have roughly an equal say in all stages, from formulation of issues to the determination of policies' (1975, 41). The participation of those who are excluded is an instrument for reducing inequalities as a democratic public sphere should provide the mechanisms for recognition and representation of the voices and perspectives of those who are oppressed (Young 1990, 184). From this point of view, the participatory approach tends to stress also the substantive, social dimension of democracy (Schmidt 2010, 225–35).

Conflicts are central in the conceptions of radical democracy (Laclau and Mouffe 2001), which presents agonist democratic *politics* as a peaceful way to manage conflictual interests that emerge in the (antagonist) *political*. So, for Chantal Mouffe, the political is 'the dimension of antagonisms that I take to be constitutive of human society', while politics is the 'set of practices and institutions through which an order is created, organizing human coexistence in the context of conflictuality provided by the political' (Mouffe 2005, 360). In this sense, agonism recognizes the conflicting relations with, but also the legitimacy of, the Others:

> while antagonism is a we/they relation in which the two sides are enemies who do not share any common ground, agonism is a we/they relation where the conflicting parties, although acknowledging that there is no rational solution to their conflict, nevertheless recognize the legitimacy of their opponents... This means that, while in conflict, they see themselves as belonging to the same political association, as sharing a common symbolic space within which the conflict takes place. (Mouffe 2005, 20)

What is shared in this vision is 'adhesion to the ethical–political principles of liberal democracy: liberty and equality. But we disagree concerning the meaning and implementation of those principles, and such a disagreement is not one that could be solved through deliberation and rational discussion' (Mouffe 2000, 245).

Visions of participatory democracy thus tend to consider the formation of collective identities as exogenous to the democratic process: that is, they emerge in the society, and then participate in politics. This is the case also for the radical democratic approach which leaves the formation of interests and identities outside of the (conflictual) political sphere. The interest in 'articulation' – as practices that establish a relation among elements, so that identities are modified (Laclau and Mouffe 2001, 105) – does not bring about a definition of the (democratic) conditions under which this 'articulation' might happen. Additionally, there is a separation between political institutions and society. Identities are not constructed through democratic processes; rather, the function of democracy is 'to provide institutions that will allow them to take an agonistic form, in which opponents will treat each other not as an enemy to be destroyed, but as adversaries who will fight for the victory of their position while recognizing the right of their opponents to fight for theirs' (Mouffe 2009, 53).

The historical development of participatory democracy

In European history, a participatory vision of democracy developed with the mobilization of the labour movement, also bringing about relevant institutional changes. The initial phases of the democratic state have been defined as characterized by widespread activism in the public sphere (cf. Eder 2010), which remained autonomous from political parties. During the first phase of representative democracy, which Bernard Manin (1995, 260) defined as *parliamentarism*, candidates were elected on the basis of personal trust, linked to their networks of local relations and reputation. In society, opinion movements were organized around varied themes, and applied pressure, often through public demonstrations in parliaments, conceived as the place where representatives formed their opinions through open discussions. It is in this phase – which in the history of England and France stretches from the late eighteenth century to the early nineteenth – that the public sphere asserted itself, and not only for the bourgeoisie. Studies on the formation of the labour movement describe this period as characterized by identities still oriented to trades, fragmented organizational structures and local, sporadic protests, but also by a certain participatory ferment.

In this phase, electoral accountability was limited, as electoral suffrage was still very restricted. Notwithstanding the low levels of electoral participation, participation in the public sphere was intense, with the multiplication of autonomous and influential opinion movements. Summarizing numerous historical studies, Alessandro Pizzorno observes that, halfway through the eighteenth century, in England public opinion 'manifested itself in ever more numerous petitions, in discussions in public places, or in semi-private places (taverns, cafés, clubs), where the new middle class of tradesmen and professionals, readers of periodicals gathered...Numerous societies and associations were formed...the political press spread in a manner previously unimaginable' (Pizzorno 1996, 972).[2] In the period, which, according to E.P. Thompson (1991), saw 'the making of the English working class', street marches for reform mobilized hundreds of thousands of citizens, while some of the radical magazines achieved circulations of tens of thousands of copies. In France, as in England, extra-parliamentary political associations gathered hundreds of thousands of signatures for petitions on themes such as the freedom of the press, the emancipation of slaves, freedom of religion, electoral reform, and public education (Pizzorno 1996, 488–9). Here too, processions and barricades mobilized hundreds of thousands of people (Sewell 1980).

In Habermas' analysis of the formation of public opinion, social conflicts that emerged outside of parties were expressed in the bourgeois *public sphere*, a sphere that 'develops in the field of tension between State and society, in such a way as to itself remain a part of the private arena' (Habermas 1988, 171).[3] The birth of the public sphere coincides with the rise of demands by social movement organizations for an active role in decisions that regarded their constituencies. In this sense, the notion of public opinion, connected to that of publicity, was affirmed during the eighteenth century. Peculiar to the public sphere is, according to Habermas, the instrument used for political confrontation: public and rational argumentation. Cafés, drawing rooms, linguistic societies and Masonic lodges were the social spaces where this public sphere took form and the taste for debate was satisfied. It is in these spaces, then, that the institutions that led to the physical enlargement of the public space developed – first the press, but also public meetings, reading societies and various associations. After the French and American revolutions, journalism, freed from the censorship of absolutist regimes, became an instrument of wide discussion, albeit limited to an elite.

In Habermas' historical reconstruction, the commercial bourgeoisie progressively assumed a hegemonic position in civil society. Financial and commercial capitalism required the international circulation of both goods and news, thereby creating a social class interested in influencing government action (1988, 37). According to research on social movements, however, the public sphere was not (only) bourgeois, in the sense of being limited to the elites of literary cafés. Even though it is debated whether emerging conflicts should be read as motivated by the beginnings of class consciousness, or the survival of community or trade identities (Calhoun 1982), social movement organizations, with their scarce links with political parties, occupied an important space in the public sphere

At the origins of democracy lies, in fact, what Bendix called 'the entrance of the masses into history': indeed, 'the 18th century represents a rupture on a grand scale in the history of western Europe. Before that moment, the masses were barred from exercising their public rights. From that moment, they became citizens and in this sense members of the political community' (Bendix 1964, 72). In contrast to the Marxist school, Bendix underlines the primarily political character of those social movements:

> the growing awareness of the working class expresses above all an experience of political alienation, that is, the sense of not having a recognized position in the political community or of not having a civic community in which to participate.... the recently politicized masses protest against their second class citizenship, demanding the right to

participate on equal terms in the political community of the nation state. (1964, 73)

The struggle for universal suffrage was thus also and principally a struggle for recognition: 'it is to oppose a conception of foreignness and social invisibility that impacted the majority of society. Overcoming existing discrimination in the name of equality meant being recognized as full members of society' (Costa 2010, 13).

Popular participation through unconventional forms went along with its politicization. Between the late eighteenth century and the early nineteenth, the importance of demonstrations and strikes grew, with workers forming associations focusing on the defence of wages and working conditions, but also allied to political movements calling for democratic reforms. In France, newspapers written by workers for workers appeared, denouncing the partiality of the bourgeois press (and journalists) (Sewell 1980, 197). In England too, political reading societies (including working-class ones) met in public cafés where up to ninety-six newspapers were bought and read, including those printed illegally (Thompson 1991, 789). Not only, recalls E. P. Thompson, were there around a million literate people among English workers, but in addition 'Illiteracy... by no means excluded men from political discourse' (1991, 782). We can speak, then, of numerous and diverse *reading publics* (ibid., 790), not only bourgeois ones, that addressed political (public) issues.

A central element in the conception of democracy that developed in this way is the *collective* dimension of rights as opposed to a liberal conception of freedom (of contracts, property, etc.) as merely individual. If the public sphere emerged in these years, the actors who participated in it were only partly new. In both France and England the continuity between the trade corporations and the labour movement is underlined. In France, the societies of *compagnonnages* and mutual aid societies remained active, reproducing post-revolutionary versions of the old confraternities that later transformed into free associations. The leaders of the *compagnonnerie* maintained their influence in negotiations with masters, and in deciding eventual strikes (Sewell 1980, 180). The English workers' movement combined the traditions of the secret societies with that of trade unionism (Thompson 1991, 570). Here as well, the representatives of the old trades had a say in the emerging public sphere (Calhoun 1982).

The social and political demands of the budding workers' movement intertwined with claims that may be defined as meta-democratic, addressing the very conceptions and practices of democracy. The battle for the freedom of the press was a founding experience of the English working class (Thompson 1991, 805). There, the Luddites formed a transitional movement with their mix of defending the past yet anticipating the future through, among other things, the elaboration of specific proposals against the exploitation of women and children, for a minimum wage, and indeed for the right to form unions (1991, 603). The Chartists' claims for political reforms (such as universal suffrage and the secret ballot, the abolition of limits on eligibility to stand for election, and paid parliamentarians) were in fact supported by workers' organizations (Tilly 2004, 46). In France, in 1848, trade corporations and political clubs marched together to demand civil and political rights.

The emerging social movements in the public sphere not only discussed specific political reforms, but also constituted arenas for the meeting of different conceptions of democracy, with an explicit challenge to the minimalist, individualistic and liberal vision of the developing democratic state. From this point of view, liberal democracy unintentionally offered the relational and cognitive resources for its own transformation. Even if the discourse of individual rights that dominated the collective order hindered the organization of the workers at first, it nevertheless triggered the development of alternative conceptions of democracy.

In England, it was precisely the resistance to repression and limits to the freedom of association that led to an alliance between radical clubs and trade unionism (Thompson 1991, 675), with the accompanying emergence of popular radicalism and militant trade unions. If the Combination Acts reflected the alliance of aristocrats and manufacturers, they also produced, as a reaction, the alliance between radicals and workers' organizations (1991, 217). Similarly, the repression of 1817–19 contributed to the bridging of calls for political reform and calls for social reform, in a reaction that E. P. Thompson sees as principally determined, in terms of initiative and character, by worker associationism. The Peterloo Massacre (eleven demonstrators killed) in 1819, by bringing hundreds of thousands onto the streets to protest, caused a polarization of public opinion ('nobody could remain neutral': 1991, 757) and the consequent alliances between moderates and radicals in the struggle for civil and political rights. Indeed, if the liberal language of rights defined these as the natural rights of the free man, 'it was primarily through the prism of their rights as citizens that workers came to discover and articulate their interests in the first place' (Somers 2008, 13, and 152).

In France, too, although a series of laws benefiting property-owners on a basis of competitive individualism emerged from the revolution (see also chapter 2), some of its ideological elements were nevertheless taken up by workers and their associations to justify demands for not only the widening, but also the transformation of the meaning, of those rights (Tilly 1995, 142). In the 1830s, the tension between the Enlightenment conception of freedom (according to authorities, if workers had requests they had to present them individually to the competent authorities) and the workers' demands for the recognition of trade unions was obvious. Presenting the middle class as a new aristocracy, some of the labour organizations claimed their right to free themselves from oppression.

A central claim for the worker movement was in fact the right 'to combine', which began with the right to associate, but differentiated itself from this (Bendix 1964). While the freedom to associate with others formed a part of the freedom of conscience, of speech, of industry, of religious belief and of the press, it had not, like these others, been promoted by the revolution, which had rather, as mentioned, aimed to abolish the bodies between the state and the society. It emerged instead as an invention of the workers' organizations that, exploiting the ambiguities of the revolutionary discourse, defined the demands for collective negotiations in terms of brotherhood. In the burgeoning workers' movement, associations were thought of as workers' corporations, cooperatives, but also as confraternities of proletarians, initially with a mutual aid function, but then elaborated as instruments for opposing a vision of freedom as isolation, promoting instead reciprocal links and common intelligence (Sewell 1980, 216). Work was presented as the foundation of sovereignty, and the organization of workers in associations as a principle of social order, of a unique and indivisible republic. The language of association in fact allowed a redefinition of the workers' corporations as free and voluntary societies, combining cooperative language with a revolutionary one.

In the protest campaigns for the expansion of citizens' rights, other models of democracy were also conceptualized and practised: direct, horizontal and self-managed conceptions developed. In the public sphere, old and new intertwined: traditional forms of associationism (corporations, etc.) combined with emerging ones. In France, the conception of democracy emerging in working-class mobilizations included the federation of self-governing trade unions. With a mix of continuity and discontinuity, horizontal terminology began to spread in the trade associations – such as 'associate' rather than 'member', 'president' or 'secretary' rather than 'head' or 'captain'. The sans-culottes had already imagined the direct exercise of popular sovereignty in the name of a single popular will, calling for the public spiritedness of action, unanimity and equality (Sewell 1980, 103). Notwithstanding the defeat of the workers' motions in June 1848, the Luxembourg Commission (which functioned as an arena for interest mediation) remained an example of an attempt at self-management against the disorder of the market.

In a similar manner, the associations of the radical movement in England tended to organize in 'divisions', which were to divide as soon as they reached forty-five members (Thompson 1991, 167). A delegate from each division participated (along with a vice-delegate with no voting rights) in weekly meetings of the general committee. The principle of payment for services was affirmed with the aim of preventing 'the taking over of its affairs by men of means or leisure' (1991, 169). In many Corresponding Societies, which met at private houses or taverns, the presidency of the session rotated, changing each time. Influenced by the events in France, the English Jacobins took up the 'zealous egalitarian underpinning' of the *sans-culottes* (1991, 171). Predominantly artisans (but also journeymen), the participants at the meetings brought the spirit of mutuality of that culture along with them (1991).

Returning to the model of liberal democracy presented in the previous chapter, we may observe that this was contested and, at least in part, disregarded in the construction of the democratic state – not only in the continuation of the visions and institutions of the 'old order', but also in the emergence of different visions and practices of democracy.

If requests that had formed in the public (not only bourgeois) sphere were granted and identities recognized, this does not seem to have occurred (only or principally) through mechanisms of electoral account-ability. In his research on France and England, Tilly describes a transfor-mation in the form of collective action between the late eighteenth century and the early nineteenth, in which a local and parochial reper-toire became a national and autonomous one, based on public assemblies and ad hoc free associations among its interest groups. According to Tilly, in the eighteenth century the assumption was that citizens, grouped into known bodies (guilds, communities, religious sects), exercised col-lective rights, protected by the law, through the actions of their repre-sentatives who had the ear of the authorities (1995, 142). The modern repertoire that developed in the following century was made up of forms of action independent of the authorities, carried out in public places with the participation of associations that deployed their symbols of belonging (1995, 362). In England, the concentration of capital and proletarianiza-tion transformed the structure of interests, while urbanization changed the fabric of relations and the growth of the state (linked to military efforts) politicized the conflict, in what Tilly defines a 'para-parliamen-tarization' (1995, 49). Alongside parliamentarization, in fact, a public sphere grew, including even those citizens who, despite not having the right to vote, followed elections and participated in electoral campaigns (1995, 143). The parliamentarization of politics thus made elections important not only for the candidates, but also for their clientele (1995, 147). The French evolutionary path is similar, with growing demands by the state corresponding with a process of centralization of decisions and nationalization of political power (Tilly 1986).

Tilly linked the influence of social movements to the electoral moment, insofar as elections marked the presence of mass support for a few proposals (and thus a potential electoral pool of support). Nevertheless, the parties of the time were initially rather indifferent to these movements. Despite the odd exception (for example, candidates who supported the ideas of the English radicals), the parties were parties of notables, based on *individual representation* (Neumann 1956). *Patron* parties in the Weberian definition, they sought to:

> install their leader in a position of control in order that he would assign state offices to his followers, that is to the apparatus of functionaries and party propagandists. Lacking any principled content, the latter would from time to time include in their programs, in competition among themselves, those requests to which they attributed the greatest propagandist strength among the electors. (Weber 1974, vol. II, 709)

According to Neumann, this party 'is typical of a society with a limited political field and a low level of participation. This is manifested, in party terms, only by voting, and the party organization (if it even exists) remains inactive in the period between one election and another. Its principal function is to choose representatives who, once chosen, are invested with a complete mandate' (1956, 153).

Nevertheless, under pressure from social movements of various types, the system of representation that had been constituted with continuity and discontinuity with respect to the old order soon began to build institutions and practices for recognizing collective identities. Notwithstanding the individualizing rhetoric, the democratic state-in-formation developed traits of organized or associative democracy, constructing channels of access for interests organized in parties or associations. Both pluralist and, even more, neo-corporative models (Schmitter 1981) then recognized those bodies intermediate between the individual and the state that had previously been stigmatized. In addition, diverse conceptions and practices of democracy were present within these intermediate bodies, in some cases involving claims for direct participation, in some versions invoking self-management.

The labour movement has been a most important actor in the transformation of the individualistic liberal conception of right through a recognition of organized forms of participation. If, according to common wisdom, the Left privileged equality and the Right freedom, in reality the history of the workers' movement is one of claims for civil and political rights as inextricable from social rights. The relation between workers' struggles and demands for freedoms emerges continually in the historiographical reconstructions of the evolution of the workers' movement over the course of the nineteenth century.

In Great Britain, the tangling of claims for justice and for freedom appears evident in historical reconstructions. Chartism is presented as a development of radicalism in the eighteenth century, but also as the last spark of working-class revolutionary politics (Biagini and Reid 1991, 3). Halfway through the nineteenth century, the Reform League (65,000 members and 600 sections, 100 of which were in London) had an 'overwhelmingly working class' membership (Hinton 1974, 11). In tacit alliance with the more moderate Reform Union, the League organized huge demonstrations against the limits on the right to political assembly (in 1866, 150,000 protestors converged on Hyde Park, challenging a government ban), pushing the Disraeli government to concede an enlargement of suffrage. The 1850s also witnessed hard-fought battles for the recognition of trade union rights, among which the right to register was recognized only in 1855 with the Friendly Societies Act. In addition, it was only in the 1870s that the question of trade unions' legal status was finally settled, despite the earlier explosion in the numbers of those signing up. And even then, disputes over work on the law on conspiracy, the abolition of incarceration for breaking a contract (used until then against strikers) and the introduction of the right to peaceful picketing were excluded (Hinton 1974, 22). In the 1880s, the Democratic Federation continued its mobilization against repression in Ireland, for the nationalization of land, for democratic reform (along Chartist lines) and for a further extension of suffrage. Demands for social, civil and political rights thus became more and more intertwined, in complex ways:

> Unfortunately, it is all too often assumed that the world of the working-class politics can be understood simply by deploying categories such as 'socialist', 'Lib.-Lab.' or 'Labourist' to divide the labour movement into its ideological parts. In reality, working-class politics was far more complex. Individuals frequently shifted between these supposedly discrete ideological positions, or, more revealingly, behaved as though they were completely ignorant of their existence. (Lawrence 1991, 83)

Historians have in fact noted reciprocal influence between the organizations active on political rights and those active on social rights. Distinct from socialism, Chartism nevertheless had an impact on the workers' movement: while the Liberal party is normally seen as the heir to the traditions of radicalism, its effects are also strong in the Labour party (and in the organized working classes) (1991, 18). In fact, the Liberal party was viewed sympathetically by many trade unionists in the late Victorian period (for example, on the labour-law reform of 1875, Spain 1991, 110). The Tichborn movement of the 1870s has been described as the link in the chain between the end of Chartism and the development of socialism (and thus of the Labour party in the 1890s) (McWilliam 1991, 44). Over the course of the century, popular constitutionalism was indeed invoked in support of working-class mobilizations:

> It was the repertoire of constitutionalist action – the mass petition, the remonstrance to the Crown, the mass demonstration and platform agitation, the convening of conventions – that could be relied on to rally the force of popular radicalism. It was not merely what could be said but what could be done that gave the constitutional force, allowing certain things to happen, certain political dramas to unfold. (Epstein 1994, 11)

In the beginning of the eighteenth century, this mostly came about in a defensive manner, in particular against the restrictions placed on trade union rights by the government Whigs, repression in Ireland and the new Poor Law, as well the Rural Police Act. Protests developed against restrictions of the right to meet in public and the suspension of *habeas corpus* in 1817.

In France, too, social movements intervened in the public sphere, raising demands for justice and liberty, but also presenting diverse conceptions of democracy. Sewell (1986, 63) writes that 'the fall of 1833 saw not only the creation of a new and powerful sense of class-consciousness among artisans working in different trades, but also the first steps towards a political alliance between radical republicanism and socialism'. In particular, the role played in the 1833 strikes by the Société des Droits de l'Homme has been underlined: initially a republican and bourgeois society, it soon became dominated by the working class. Together with the diffusion of socialist ideology, the demand for freedom was considered to be the central characteristic of the French working-class conscience. At the beginning of the twentieth century, the working-class identity, linked to a widespread popular culture, was characterized by:

> the sense of being manual workers; of being exploited by employers who, in the popular imagination, had replaced feudalism; a lively attachment to freedom, which formed the basis of the *sans-culotte* spirit as well as direct-action trade unionism; extreme suspicion towards all forms of authority, towards those referred to as 'them', ranging from the state to the workshop and even including other unions, whenever the 'little leaders' took advantage of their functions to act as big shots. (Perrot 1986, 105)

Although they were a minority, critics of the vote (and of 'votards') as an individual instrument in contrast with the collective will expressed in assemblies, testified to the survival of conceptions of direct democracy (1986, 109).

Similarly in Germany, where end-of-century repression had favoured the centralization of struggles and working-class representation in the party (Nolan 1986), the workers' movement was born and grew from the bottom up: 'even apart from the strikes, to many workers self-organization and collective self-help appeared to be a quasi-natural way to protect against the insecurities of the market economy and the superiority of employers' (Kocka 1986, 338). The Verband Deutscher Arbeitervereine grew as the umbrella organization of workers' associations that had developed close links with left-wing and democratic liberals (Kocka 1986, 345). It was the defeat of the mobilizations of 1848–9 that rendered these alliances more difficult, contributing towards the creation of a strong yet isolated social democratic party.

From an organizational point of view, the interweaving and tensions between working-class struggles and conceptions of democracy were reflected in frequent waves of criticism of parties and trade unions 'from below'. As early as the end of the nineteenth century, in Germany, the political police had registered in the workers' *Kneipen* (bars) complaints about the coldness of the party and the loss of working-class spirit (Evans 1989, 246). In France, in 1936, the occupation of factories demonstrated how these had substituted trades as the focus of identity. As Perrot recalled:

> The occupations of factories in 1936 implied an entirely different relationship not merely to the instrument of work, but also to space. Dispersed with respect to residence, the workers were reunited daily in the factory, which became the locus of their collective existence; dislocated with respect to their crafts, they were reunited in the firm, which became the locus of their convergence, and thereby all at once the epicentre of the labour movement. (1986, 91)

In Great Britain, if the explosion in the numbers of those joining trade unions in the 1890s, and the mobilizations linked to this, led to the Labour party's running in the general elections of 1892, dissatisfaction over the lack of direct representation for the poor nevertheless accompanied the development of ideas of direct revolutionary action.[4]

Conceptions and practices of different models of democracy (and different democratic qualities) with respect to those foreseen in the definition of the liberal state were indeed developed and prefigured during waves of protest. In Great Britain, from 1910 to 1914, a new surge in membership of trade unions accompanied 'bottom-up' actions organized during the depression of 1908–9. Spontaneous transport strikes led to alliances negotiated from below among up to eighteen trade unions at a time, all pledging not to leave the negotiating table until the requests of each had been satisfied. Community mobilizations included the strikers' wives, who marched under the banner 'Our poverty is your danger. Stand by us'. Currents of trade unionism in defence of working-class autonomy developed, criticizing existing trade unions as too sectarian in structure, oriented to compromise in their politics and internally oligarchic in their conception of representation (Hinton 1974, 91). These examples of working-class autonomy are described as 'loosely-coordinated, fragmented and lacking a coherent body of theory'; in this sense, 'trade unionism failed to organize the grassroots leaders of industrial militancy into a disciplined force capable of leading a fight for revolutionary politics within labour politics' (1974, 94). Nevertheless, 'in a period when the Labour Party achieved little and was wracked by internal dissension, the trade union explosion provided a base for a renewal of socialist politics' (1974, 89). Even during the Great War of 1914–18, spontaneous protests saw alliances between skilled and unskilled workers, who pushed the Labour party to adopt some socialist goals. After the war, resistance to the moderate turn of the Labour government was expressed in the 1920–1 protests by the unemployed people's movement (organized in the National Unemployed Workers Movement), taking the form of hunger marches, which saw the participation of, among others, the party's local councillors, often at odds with the national government (1974, 134–5). The trade unions also expressed their disappointment about the second (minority) Labour government in 1929. In the 1930s, Labour re-emerged under the control of the trade unionists, with calls for promises to enact socialist legislation when in government, and a bottom-up opposition to the alliance with Churchill emerged in 1944.

Moments of tension and innovation also developed in the course of waves of strikes, accompanied by processions, assemblies and occupations. According to E. P. Thompson's formula, 'class formation occurs at the intersection of determination and self-activity: the working class made itself as much as it was made' (1978, 299). It was especially during strikes that a working-class consciousness was formed. In Michelle Perrot's reconstruction (1974), the strikes that spread through France at the end of the nineteenth century [5] were in fact organized not just by trade unions, but also by various local committees, with strong involvement from grassroots activists, who were often very young. In this sense, action produced and reproduced the workers' community – as Perrot noted:

> Revolt is not instinctive. It is born of action, and community in action. The strike, in this view, offers a remarkable occasion for basic training, an antidote to isolation, to the mortal cold that the division of labour

reduces workers to. With its leaders, its assemblies, its demonstrations, its language, sometimes even its financial organization, it forms a community with Rousseauian aspirations, anxious for direct democracy, avid for transparency and communion. (1974, 725)

In its everyday dimension, the long strike of this period (ten times longer than the average contemporary strike), 'even if rational in its reasoning and objectives, is not purely functional, but experience, history, event. Experienced as a liberating force, able to break the monotony of the days and force the retreat of the bosses' power, it crystallized an ephemeral and often-regretted counter-society. Strike nostalgia carries the seed of its recommencing' (1974, 725).

Pushed by the workers' movement, the debate on democracy also spread to include not only an emphasis on participation, but also themes of social equality. In the first period of the development of capitalism, equality in civil and political rights sanctioned by the concept of citizenship was not normally considered to be in conflict with the social inequalities produced by the market, notwithstanding the fact that these weakened the enjoyment of civil and political rights (Marshall 1992, 27). In the twentieth century, the growth of economic wellbeing, the diffusion of education, and the use of those same civil and political rights affected this balance:

Social integration spread from the sphere of sentiments and patriotism to that of material satisfaction. The components of a civilized and cultivated life, at first the monopoly of the few, were progressively placed within reach of the many, who were encouraged to reach out their hand to those who still eluded their claims. The diminution of inequality reinforced the pressures for its abolition, at least with regard to the essential elements of social wellbeing. These aspirations were in part heeded for incorporating social rights in the *status* of citizenship and thus creating a universal right to a real income that is not proportional to the market value of the claimer. (1992, 28)

Social rights began then to be discussed as essential conditions for a true enjoyment of political rights.

In the nineteenth and twentieth centuries it was therefore Bendix's 'masses' that conquered the rights of citizenship, organizing in political parties which then contributed to their integration. In particular, the socialist parties included the working class in the system, allowing the nationalization of society: 'above all integrating the working class into the procedures of the representative regime, "giving it a voice" and thus leading it to enter into dialogue with the other components of the political system, then contributing with success to enlarge the attributes of the

State' (Pizzorno 1996, 1023). With respect to the democratic state, the 'masses' exercised constant pressure for the enlargement of rights to dissent, as well as 'civility control'.[6] Further, they kept alive a focus on participatory democracy – open, direct and horizontal.

A participatory revolution?

Going back to the definition of liberal democracy, we can observe that it does not reflect some of the main elements which are present in the conceptions and practices of democracy which have developed in the last two centuries. While the electoral moment certainly played an important role, it was, however, neither the only nor the most important one in a democratic participation which instead flourished in associational forms, often independent of the representative circuit. Like the labour movement in the past, more recent movements also became arenas for debating and experimenting with different conceptions of democracy.

The protest movements of the late 1960s were already interpreted as an indication of the widening gap between parties and citizens – and indeed of the parties' inability to represent new lines of conflict (Offe 1985). This could be seen in the growing separation between movements and parties, that had together contributed to the development of some main conflict lines. Despite the obvious tensions between movements and parties, especially on the European continent, relations with parties long continued to play a central role for movements (Tarrow 1998; della Porta 1995). In fact, social movements have tended to form alliances more or less tightly with parties – and parties have sought to co-opt social movements, to absorb their identities, and to represent them in institutions. Social movements have indeed been extremely sensitive to the characteristics of their political parties of reference: they have privileged action in society, leaving parties the job of bringing their claims to institutions. They have placed themselves on the political Left–Right axis, and have constructed discourses compatible with the ideologies of their allies. For their part, parties have not been impermeable to the pressures of movements: from the Labour party in Great Britain to the Social Democrats in Germany, from the French socialists to the Italian communists, the programmes and members of the institutional left have changed following interactions with social movements and increasing awareness on themes such as gender discrimination or environmental protection. Comparative research has indicated that, in general, the old Left has been more disposed to supporting movements in locations where exclusive regimes had for a long time hindered the moderation of conflicts on the Left–Right axis (Kriesi et al. 1995, 68; della Porta and Rucht 1995).[7]

Between parties and movements, tensions continued to develop, however, over the appropriate organizational format. Faced with more and more bureaucratized parties (see chapter 2), the democratic quality of participation has remained central in the visions and practices of left-wing social movements. The 1968 movements (or the 'sixty-eight years', as they have recently been defined) called for an extension of civil rights and forms of political participation. The Berkeley Free Speech Movement influenced European student movements, which also organized debates on freedom of opinion as well as the 'state of emergence of democracy' (in Germany, for example) (for recent analyses, see Tolomelli 2008; Klimke and Scharlot 2008). The anti-authoritarian frame, central to these movements, was in fact articulated in claims for 'democracy from below'. Democracies in the form of councils and self-management were also discussed in the workers' movements of those years. Beyond the expansion of forms of political participation, the student movement and those that followed it (the first being the women's movement) experimented internally with new democratic practices, considered to be early signs of the realization of non-authoritarian relations (a libertarian dimension).

The so-called new social movements of the 1970s and the 1980s also insisted on the legitimacy – if not the prevalence – of alternative forms of democracy, criticizing liberal visions. In fact, 'the struggle of the left libertarian movements thus recalls an ancient element of democratic theory, which promotes the organization of the collective decision-making process variously defined as classical, populist, communitarian, strong, grassroots or direct democracy, against a democratic practice defined in contemporary democracies as realist, liberal, elitist, republican or representative democracy' (Kitschelt 1993, 15). According to this interpretation, against a liberal democracy based on delegation to representatives who may be controlled only at elections, movements affirm that citizens, naturally interested in politics, must directly assume the task of intervening in political decisions. As carriers of a participatory conception of democracy, the new social movements of the 1970s also criticized the monopoly of mediation through mass parties and by a 'strong' structuration of interests, aiming to shift policy making towards more visible and controllable places. Democracy as self-management was much discussed among social movements in this period.

In part, these conceptions did penetrate the democratic state through reforms that widened participation in schools, in factories and in local areas but also through the political recognition of movement organizations and the 'right to dissent'. Beginning from the 1960s, there has also been an increase in institutional and other forms of participation. In an important piece of comparative research carried out in the 1970s in different western democracies, Samuel Barnes and Max Kaase noted that, with respect to laws and decisions considered unjust or illegitimate, ever larger groups of citizens were ready to resort to forms of action characterized by their unconventionality, as in advanced industrial societies techniques of direct political action were no longer carrying the stigma of deviance, nor were seen as anti-systemic in their orientation (Barnes and Kaase 1979, 157). For example, between 1960 and 1974, the percentage of those who responded 'Non-conventional political actions, such as demonstrations' to the question 'What can a citizen do with respect to a local regulation judged unjust or damaging?' increased in Great Britain, the United States and the Federal Republic of Germany from less than 1 per cent to over 7 per cent.

The conclusion here is that increasing participation, including unconventional forms, is not an indicator of political alienation but, on the contrary, of the growth in political competences, in particular among the young. It was an expression of an enduring increase in potential citizen interventions, a broadening of the repertoire of political action that they rightly predicted was going to be reproduced over and over again (1979, 534).

In line with those predictions, a large-scale comparative research project – which used data from different surveys carried out at various points in numerous western democracies – underlined that, at least until 1990, political participation in western Europe grew considerably, with a reduction in the percentage of entirely inactive people (from 85 per cent in 1959 to 44 per cent in 1990) and a parallel growth in people partaking in some political activity (from 15 per cent in 1959 to 66 per cent in 1990) (Topf 1995, 68). While traditional political participation has remained stable, non-institutional participation has increased enormously in the years that followed. This growth has affected not only all the countries analysed, but, within the individual countries, it has reduced the differences in participation levels linked to gender, age and educational attainment – so as to lead scholars to speak of a 'participatory revolution' (1995, 78).

The most recent research also confirms that unconventional forms of participation are complementary, not alternatives, to conventional forms. In the 2000s, survey-based research has repeatedly underlined the decline of conventional forms of political participation (Putnam 2000; see also chapter 2), but the corresponding rise in unconventional forms (Torcal and Montero 2006). In Italy, for instance, unconventional forms of participation, such as signing petitions or participating in boycotts and marches, have spread – in 2005 the percentage of citizens that participated in unconventional forms stood at 37 per cent, equal to that of citizens participating in conventional ways (Lello 2007, 433; also Diamanti,

2007). In addition, while parties are losing members and trust, voluntary associations have gained. The number of people declaring that they never discuss politics has also tended to decrease: in Italy from 47 per cent in 1981 to 32 per cent in 2000 (Lello 2007, 416).

Conclusion

In conclusion, at the normative level, the concept of participatory democracy has suggested, with growing success, the need to increase the number and power of arenas open to citizens' participation. Concretely, real existing democracies developed by multiplying channels of participation, and extending the civil, political and social rights that made that participation possible. In fact, at least partially, participatory conceptions have penetrated the democratic state, through reforms that increased participation in public institutions, but also through the political recognition of the 'right to dissent'. This evolution has been neither linear nor peaceful: rights to participation were affirmed through various waves of protest, with strong resistance and frequent U-turns. Different democratic qualities – based on participatory principles – were nurtured in social movement organizations, re-emerging with more strength in times of struggle. The broadening of participation rights was reflected in a growth in unconventional forms of participation. Most importantly, the criticism of liberal democracy was expressed in the theorization of and experimentation with other models of democracy in a growing number of social movements.

4

Deliberative Democracy: Between Representation and Participation

After a march on 15 May 2011, about forty protestors decided to camp in Madrid's main square, Puerta del Sol, calling for supporters on the Internet. By 20 May, 30,000 people were in that square, and many more followed the protest online, while the movement spread to many other localities, both large and small. As sociologist John Postill (2012), present during the events, recalled, 'The encampments rapidly evolved into "cities within cities" governed through popular assemblies and committees. The committees were created around practical needs such as cooking, cleaning, communicating and carrying out actions. Decisions were made through both majority rules vote and consensus. The structure was horizontal, with rotating spokespersons in lieu of leaders. Tens of thousands of citizens were thus experimenting with participatory, direct and inclusive forms of democracy at odds with the dominant logic of political representation. Displaying a thorough mixture of utopianism and pragmatism, the new movement drew up a list of concrete demands, including the removal of corrupt politicians from electoral lists, while pursuing revolutionary goals such as giving "All power to the People".' By mid-June 2011, consensus-oriented assemblies decided it was time to move from the central squares to the neighborhoods (barrios).

From Spain, the emphasis on the creation of open spaces moved to Greece and the US, following mobile activists. Describing Occupy Boston, and citing an activist who talked about the 'small slice of utopia we are creating', Juris (2012, 268) singled out some of the tactical, incubating and infrastructural roles of the occupied free spaces: among the first are attracting media attention and inspiring participation; among the second, 'providing a space for grassroots participatory democracy; ritual and community building, strategizing and action planning, public education and prefiguring alternative worlds that embody the movement's visions'; among the third, networking and coordination. Beyond the prefiguration of a different society, the activists already imagine that these spaces, as Ratza and Kurnik (2012) noted, are also important in the invention of alternative, but not yet imagined, futures, through what has been called a politics of becoming. In the Occupy movement they studied in Slovenia, the encounters between diverse minorities transform them and their visions.

Protestors in the Puerta del Sol, or those in Zuccotti Park in New York, certainly went back to conceptions of participation from below, cherished by the progressive social movements I mentioned in the previous chapter. As this short account indicates, however, they combined this with special attention to the creation of egalitarian and inclusive public spheres. In this sense, their actions resonate with the conceptions and practices of deliberative democracy, which we are going to discuss in this chapter. Here as well, I shall first introduce the debate on normative theory and then refer to empirical research on democratic conceptions and practices in social movements, looking in particular at two waves of protest at the turn of the millennium.

Deliberative democracy: an introduction

A different type of criticism of the liberal democratic model from the one discussed under the 'participatory' label came from the theorists of a deliberative democracy, initially defined as 'liberal-deliberative democracy'.

What emerges as most innovative in the definition of deliberative democracy is the importance given to preference (trans)formation during the discursive process oriented to the definition of the public good. In fact, deliberative democracy requires a transformation of preferences during the interaction (Dryzek 2000a, 79). It is 'a process through which initial preferences are transformed in order to take into account the points of view of the others' (Miller 1993, 75). In this sense, it differs from conceptions of democracy as aggregation of (exogenously generated) preferences (or opinions) as it aims instead at their (democratic) formation.

With varying emphases, theorists of deliberative democracy stressed the importance of communication, as in deliberative democracy people are convinced by the force of the better argument. In particular, (good) deliberation is conceived as being based on horizontal flows of communication, multiple producers of content, ample opportunities for interaction, confrontation on the basis of rational argumentation, and a positive attitude to reciprocal listening (Habermas 1981, 1996). To use Barber's (2003, 173) words, 'at the heart of strong democracy is talk', and democratic talk requires listening as well as uttering.

Some deliberative conceptions stress consensus, as decisions are reached by convincing the others of one's own good argument. Decisions must therefore be approvable by all participants, in contrast with majoritarian democracy, in which decisions are legitimated by votes. According to Joshua Cohen (1989), an ideal deliberation aims to reach a rationally motivated consensus thanks to reasons that are persuasive to all.

Changes of preferences regarding the public good should occur through the process of argumentation wherein reasons are exchanged in support of respective and different positions. The central tenet of deliberative democratic theory is, in fact, that it is through argumentation that participants in deliberation convince one another and come to decisions. In deliberative democracy, the debate is oriented to finding endorsable reasons (Ferejohn 2000).

Finally, deliberation enables individuals to abstract themselves from the mere appeal of self-interest, in such a way that the solution should reveal the general interest (Cohen 1989, 23–4; Elster 1998). In this model, 'the political debate is organized around alternative conceptions of the public good', and, above all, it 'draws identities and citizens' interests in ways that contribute to public building of public good' (Cohen 1989, 18–19). A deliberative setting thus facilitates the search for a common good (Elster 1998). Indeed, while I can consider my preferences as sufficient reason to make a proposal, deliberation in conditions of pluralism requires that I find reasons that make my proposal acceptable to others whom I can expect not to consider the fact that this is my preference to be a sufficient reason for supporting it (Cohen 1989, 33). A public explanation of oneself and one's own reasons 'forces you to report only those reasons that others might plausibly be expected to share' (Goodin 2003, 63).

Deliberative democracy is therefore a way to address controversies through dialogue: when citizens or their representatives disagree morally, they should continue to reason together until they reach mutually acceptable decisions (Gutmann and Thompson 1996). Decisions are legitimate 'to the extent they receive reflective assent through participation in authentic deliberation by all those subject to the decision in question' (Dryzek 2010, 23). Deliberation (or even communication) is based upon the belief that, while not giving up my perspective, I might learn if I listen to the other (Young 1996). While reaching consensus is not always possible, different forms of meta-consensus (on values, beliefs, preferences or discourses) can ensure the functioning of a deliberative arena (Dryzek 2010, 94, 114).

Deliberative forms of democracy have also been advocated as a way to channel the support of critical citizens into democratic institutions by building upon the assumption that contemporary democracies (at the local, national and supranational levels) need to combine representative institutions with other arenas. As Dryzek (2010, 40) noted, 'Democracy does not have to be a matter of counting heads – even deliberative heads. Nor does it have to be confined to the formal institutions of the state or the constitutional surface of the political life. Accepting such confinement means accepting a needlessly thin conception of democracy.' In the past, participation developed especially within political parties, where the reference to common values permitted the formation of collective identities. As mentioned earlier (see chapter 2), the very processes of economic globalization and political transnationalization challenge representative forms of democracy as they have developed within the nation state.

Recently developed partial solutions to the weaknesses of representative democracy appear far from satisfactory. Technocratic models of democracy, based on the assumption of consensual goals (such as economic development) to be reached with the input of experts or public bureaucrats, are accused of disempowering (and alienating) citizens (Sanderson 1999). Media democracy, with legitimation mediated by mass media, has facilitated populist appeals – as commercialization and centralization in the media system have encouraged the trend away from information and critical debate. In this context, interest has risen, among scholars as well as practitioners, in forms of democracy variously defined as deliberative.

Faced with these perceived challenges to representative democracy, the virtues of deliberative democracy are said to include legitimation on the input side and efficacy on the output side: 'Beyond its essential contribution to democracy per se, citizen participation in the policy process can contribute to the legitimization of policy development and implementation' (Fischer 2003, 205). For Bernard Manin, the legitimacy of the decision is the outstanding product of the deliberative theory of democracy: 'A legitimate decision is one that results from the deliberation of all. It is the process by which everyone's will is formed that confers its legitimacy on the outcome' (1987, 351–2). Also for Seyla Benhabib (1996, 69), deliberation 'is a necessary condition for attaining legitimacy...with regard to collective decision-making processes in a polity...what is considered in the common interest of all results from processes of collective deliberation'. And for Amy Gutmann (1996, 344), 'the legitimate exercise of political authority requires...decision-making by deliberation among free and equal citizens'. In this sense, deliberative democracy is 'a normative account of the bases of democratic legitimacy' (Young 2003, 103). Deliberation, as a 'dispassionate, reasoned, logical' type of communication, promises to increase citizens' trust in political institutions (Dryzek 2000b, 64). Indeed, scholars highlighted a 'moralising effect of the public discussion' (Miller 1993, 83) that 'encourages people not to merely express political opinions (through surveys or referendum) but to form those opinions through a public debate' (1983, 89).

In its turn, legitimacy should facilitate the implementation of decisions, and efficiency should increase thanks to the increased information that citizens bring into the process. Among others, Fung and Wright (2001) stated the need to transform democracy in order to improve its capacity to achieve public goods. Deliberation should make people capable of overcoming their own individual interests and participating in the pursuit of a general interest (Cohen 1989, 23–4). In a virtuous circle, deliberative spaces improve citizens' information and decision-making capacity. Research on attempts at extending policy making through deliberative experiments – in the forms of auditing, people's juries and so on – usually focuses attention on the capacity of these instruments to solve problems created, for example, by local opposition to unpopular local land use (Bobbio and Zeppetella 1999, Sintomer 2001).

Deliberative and participatory democracy

A fourth model of democracy developed from some criticism of the original deliberative conception, bridging it with emphasis on deliberation from below. Critics have first of all stigmatized the *exclusionary* nature of the public sphere, especially as conceived in the Habermasian proposal. As Nancy Fraser noted:

> not only was there always a plurality of competing publics, but the relations between bourgeois publics and other publics were always conflictual. Virtually from the beginning, counterpublics contested the exclusionary norms of the bourgeois public, elaborating alternative styles of political behavior and alternative norms of public speech. Bourgeois publics, in turn, excoriated these alternatives and deliberately sought to block broader participation. (1997, 75)

As mentioned in the previous chapter, subaltern counterpublics (including workers, women, ethnic minorities, etc.) actually formed parallel discursive arenas, where counter-discourses developed, allowing for the formation and re-definition of identities, interests and needs (1997, 81). Also, in contemporary societies, a multitude of public spheres offers to those subaltern groups the possibility of forming a collective identity. We can agree with Sheila Benhabib that 'heterogeneity, otherness, and difference can find expression in multiple associations, networks, and citizens' forums, all of which constitute public life under late capitalism' (1996, 84).

Second, and linked to this, liberal deliberative theories are said to tend towards an institutional bias denying that democracy develops (also or mainly) outside of public institutions. Scholars of deliberative democracy disagree in fact about the spheres in which it may take place, some focusing on the institutional public spheres, others on alternative spheres, free from state intervention (della Porta 2005b). Habermas (1996) postulates a double-track process, with 'informal' deliberation taking place outside institutions and then, as public opinion, influencing institutional deliberation. In empirical research, particular attention has been devoted to institutional arenas, from parliaments (Steiner et al. 2005) to administrative committees (Joerges and Neyer 1997), or in the mass media. According to other authors, however, deliberation happens (also or mainly) outside of public institutions. Joshua Cohen (1989) holds that deliberative democracy develops in voluntary groups, in particular in political parties, while John Dryzek (2000) singles out social movements as better positioned to build deliberative spaces, since they keep a critical eye upon institutions. In a similar vein, Jane Mansbridge (1996) stated that deliberation should take place in a number of enclaves, free from institutional power – social movements being among them. As Claus Offe (1997, 102–3) has emphasized, deliberative democracy needs citizens embedded in associative networks, able to build democratic skills among their adherents.

Third, not only does the historical account of the 'bourgeois' public sphere leave aside the 'proletarian' ones, but the very *communicative styles* which are normatively stressed varies. The Habermasian emphasis on the role of reason has been contested by those who pointed instead at the positive role of emotions and narration in public deliberation (Polletta 2006). Research on institutions as well as social movements revealed that different public spheres have different grammars (Talpin 2011; Haug 2010). Habermas has thus been criticized for reflecting elitarian norms: communicative rationality at the expense of story-telling, or politeness instead of passions. The importance of protest action as a complement to discourse was also noted: 'processes of engaged and responsible democratic participation include street demonstrations and sit-ins, musical works and cartoons, as much as parliamentary speeches and letters to the editor' (Young 2003: 119).

Emotions are here considered as important in creating solidarity through closeness and knowledge. As Hannah Arendt observed, a broad way of thinking cannot develop in isolation or solitude, but needs the presence of those others who have to be taken into account in that thinking (Arendt 1972, 282). Rhetoric can perform important functions in bonding and bridging individuals (Dryzek 2010, 69–81). To move beyond individual selfishness, in Iris Young's view too, people must meet, as a 'moral point of view' grows not from solitary reasoning, but from concrete meetings with others, who ask for their own needs, desires and perspectives to be recognized (Young 1990, 106). The need for a deliberation inside counterpublics, or enclaves of resistance, is recognized by the theoreticians of participatory forms of deliberation. Among them Jane Mansbridge stresses that 'democracies also need to foster and value informal deliberative enclaves of resistance in which those who lose in each coercive move can rework their ideas and their strategies, gathering their forces and deciding in a more protected space in what way or whether to continue the struggle' (1996, 46–7).

What is more, social inequality is said to reduce the capacity of oppressed groups to learn the dominant rules of the game, as oppression 'consists in systematic institutional processes which prevent some people from learning and using satisfying or expansive skills in socially recognized settings, or which inhibit people's ability to play and communicate with others or to express their feelings and perspective on social life in contexts where others can listen' (Young 2000, 156). Deliberative democracy, in its original version, is thus accused of favouring (at least reproducing) inequalities:

> Although deliberators will always choose to disregard some arguments, when this disregard is systematically associated with the arguments made by those we know already to be systematically disadvantaged, we should at least reevaluate our assumptions about deliberation's democratic potential. This is all the more problematic as deliberation requires not only equality in resources and the guarantee of equal opportunity to articulate persuasive arguments but also equality in 'epistemological authority', in the capacity to evoke acknowledgment of one's arguments. (Sanders 1997, 349)

Fourth, and most fundamentally, the classical version of deliberative democracy assumes the possibility of reaching consensus through dialogue, thus excluding fundamental conflicts, which are instead parts and parcel of democratic development. It does not therefore help to address a fundamental question: if, as is usually the case, deliberation does not achieve consensus, how should conflicts be addressed (Smith 2009, 11)?

The very plurality of opinions makes conflicts, even bitter ones, all the more likely. As Flybjerg (1998, 229) observed, 'With the plurality that a contemporary concept for civil society must contain, conflict becomes an inevitable part of this concept. Thus civil society does not mean "civilized" in the sense of well-mannered behavior. In strong civil societies, distrusts and criticism of authoritative action are omnipresent as is resulting political conflict.' But, also, exclusion from some spaces of deliberation might produce conflicts. From this point of view, public spheres are conflictual as they are selective: 'If some of the interests, opinions, and perspectives are suppressed..., or if some groups have difficulties getting heard for reasons of structural inequality, cultural misunderstanding, or social prejudice, then the agenda or the results of public policy are likely to be biased or unfair. For these reasons, the public sphere will properly be a site of struggle – often contentious struggles' (Young 2000, 178). The presence of conflicts (that cannot be solved discursively) is particularly important, as mentioned before (see chapter 3), in conceptualizations of radical democracy as based upon agonistic interactions. As Chantal Mouffe wrote, 'taking pluralism seriously requires that we give up the dream of rational consensus which entails the fantasy that we could escape from our human form of life' (2000, 98).

From these criticisms a conception of democracy which is at the same time deliberative and participatory developed. It calls for the formation of public spheres where, under conditions of equality, inclusiveness and transparency, a communicative process based on reason (the strength of the good argument) is able to transform individual preferences and reach decisions oriented to the public good (della Porta 2005a). A deliberative and participatory democracy is first of all inclusive. All citizens have to be included in the process and able to express their voice. Against hierarchy, it 'requires some forms of apparent equality among citizens' (Cohen 1989, 18); in fact, deliberation takes place among free and equal citizens (as 'free deliberation among equals': 1989, 20). This means the deliberative process takes place under conditions of plurality of values where people have different perspectives but face common problems. At least, 'all citizens must be able to develop those capacities that give them effective access to the public sphere', and 'once in public, they must be given sufficient respect and recognition so as to be able to influence decisions that affect them in a favourable direction' (Bohman 1997, 523–4). Deliberation must exclude power – deriving from coercion, but also from an uneven balance of the participants as repesentatives of organizations of different size or influence. In Joshua Cohen's definition, a deliberative democracy is 'an association whose affairs are governed by the public deliberation of its members' (1989, 17). Consensus is, however, possible only if there are shared common values.

Global social movements, public spheres and deliberative democracy

A deliberative model based on participation has been promoted by the social movements that developed at the turn of the millennium claiming global justice. While a participatory emphasis has been pursued by the left-libertarian movements of the 1960s and the following decades, social movement activists have also been aware of the difficulties in implementing direct democracy. The risks of a 'tyranny of the structureless' (Freeman 1970; see also Breines 1989) have in fact brought about an increasing focus on discursive qualities and consensual decision making (Polletta 2002).

Some internal characteristics of this mobilization called for a participatory and deliberative conception. In the global justice movement (GJM), which became visible with the mobilizations against the WTO in Seattle in 1999, characteristics like network organizational structures, plural identities and the presence of a varied repertoire were intertwined with a transnational dimension (della Porta 2007). A plurality of networks active on a variety of issues participated in the protests, including in their ranks organizations and activists with experience in previous movements. New communication technologies – first and foremost the Internet – had not only reduced the costs of mobilization, allowing streamlined and flexible structures, but also facilitated reciprocal interaction between different areas and movements. The social forums represented attempts to create open spaces for meetings of different individuals and groups (della Porta 2009b).

Even though previous social movements also typically had a network structure, the global justice movement emphasized, even more than past movements, its reticular character, presenting itself as 'networks of networks'. Its activists were in fact rooted in an extremely dense network of associations, from Catholic to ecologist associations, from social volunteering to trade unions, from the defence of human rights to women's liberation, often with multiple belongings to associations of different types (Andretta et al. 2002, 184; della Porta et al. 2006; della Porta 2009b; see also della Porta and Caiani 2009). So, for instance, 97.6 per cent of participants interviewed at the anti-G8 countersummit in Genoa in 2001 were (or had been) members of at least one type of organization, 80.9 per cent were (or had been) members of at least two, 61 per cent of at least three, 38.1 per cent of at least four, 22.8 per cent of at least five, 12.6 per cent of six or more (Andretta et al. 2002, 184). Similar results emerged from survey-based research at the first European Social Forum (ESF), in Florence in 2002 (della Porta et al. 2006), and on the fourth ESF in Athens in 2006 (della Porta 2009b; della Porta and Caiani 2009).

The formation of trans-thematic and transnational networks came about 'in action', along with a widening of protest repertoires (della Porta 2008b). From the end of the 1990s, demonstrations against the Millennium Round of the WTO in Seattle sparked a new wave of 'street politics' on global themes. Mass demonstrations had often been called for during countersummits defined as arenas of 'international level initiatives organized during official summits and on the same themes albeit from a critical point of view, raising awareness through protest and information with or without contacts with the official version' (Pianta 2001, 35). Millions of people joined the international day of protest against the war in Iraq on 15 February 2003 (della Porta and Diani 2004; Waalgrave and Rucht 2010).

The campaigns against land mines or the North American Free Trade Agreement (NAFTA) and the Multilateral Agreement on Investments (MAI), the UN-sponsored world conferences and Jubilee 2000 were important occasions for organizational networking, aggregating the more institutionalized organizations – such as development and human rights NGOs, religious and non-religious charities, labour unions and large environmental associations – that had already collaborated in, among other movements, the previous waves of pacifist mobilization. Similarly, the European Marches against Unemployment and Exclusion, the actions in solidarity with the Zapatistas and the Intergalactic meetings (in 1996 in Chiapas and 1997 in Spain), as well the later demonstrations in Prague against the IMF and WB and in Nice and Gothenburg against the EU, constituted moments of interaction among the more radical groups and the critical unions.

Group interviews with activists show a pride in this 'plurality of the movement', whose strength was in fact located in its capacity to network associations and individuals, bringing together

> many situations...that in previous years, especially the last ten, did not come together enough, met around big issues for very short periods, always with a highly emotional impetus, while instead this is, I feel, the first experience I have had in such an alive way of contact and networking where the fact of being in contact and in a network is one of the most important factors...this is the positive thing...the value of the Social Forums. (cited in Del Giorgio 2002, 89)

The network was thus defined as more than the sum of its groups: for it is in the network that the activist 'gets to know people, forms relationships, becomes a community' (2002, 92). As another activist observed,

'A word I feel is key to a different way of doing politics is the concept of relations…the ability to create and amplify relationships counts more than the ability to send them down from above' (in 2002, 252).

The network logic facilitated the bridging of various issues as well. In different countries the different concerns of different movements were connected in a lengthy, although not always very visible, process of mobilization (della Porta 2007). The global justice movement developed from protest campaigns around 'broker issues' that tied together concerns of different movements and organizations. In Switzerland, the campaign against the WTO brought together squatters, human rights activists and labour unionists. In France, the struggle against Genetically Modified food linked peasants and ecologists, while the *mouvements de sans* saw the convergence of the critical unions with organizations of the unemployed, *sans-papiers* and homeless. Jubilee 2000 bridged development NGOs with rank-and-file religious groups. In the anti-Maastricht movement in Spain (and later in the '50 years are enough' campaign), ecologists and pacifists met with critical unionists. In Great Britain, opposition to the Criminal Justice and Public Order Act was a catalyst for the interaction of travellers, squatters, ravers and environmentalists (and in the campaign against dismissals, dockers encountered – even if occasionally –the Reclaim the Street direct action network).

All this diversity needed spaces of confrontation where not only issues but also frames could be bridged. Countersummits and social forums have been important for the construction and exchange of knowledge. The relevance of communication is further confirmed by the importance assumed in the organization of protest, not only by the Internet but also by connected themes, from copyright to censorship (Milan 2009). Competences in counter-expertise are important characteristics of many more formalized associations, but also of think-tanks and alternative media close to protestors. The movement for global justice has in fact developed actions oriented to sensitizing the public on alternative values and cultures. Networking is facilitated by the so-called campaign approach, which foresees the utilization of various forms of protest and information, by wide networks of organizations and individuals, to attain relatively specific, but symbolically significant, demands.

The trans-thematic and transnational nature of the movement constitutes a novelty in an environment which appeared to be characterized by movements' specializations on single themes (from women to the environment, from peace to AIDS). In transnational protests, worries about the environment, women's rights, peace and social inequalities continue as characteristics of the sub-groups or networks involved in the globalization mobilization. The definition of a 'movement of movements' underlines the survival of specific claims, and the non-subordination of one conflict in relation to others. The multiplicity of bases of reference in terms of class, gender, generation, race and religion appears to have led to identities that are, if not weak, certainly composite. In different campaigns, countersummits and social forums, fragments of diverse cultures – secular and religious, radical and reformist, of young and old generations – have tangled together in a wider discourse that has taken the theme of social (and global) injustice as its glue, yet at the same time leaving plenty of space for deepening discussions of different themes. At the transnational level, local and global concerns have been connected to values such as equality, justice, human rights and environmental protection.

Platforms, forums, coalitions and networks have allowed reciprocal knowledge and, often, understanding. Even while pluralism and diversity have been much emphasized, in the movement's discourse a *master frame* has developed around the claim for global justice and another democracy. In parallel, the enemy has been identified in neoliberal globalization, which characterized not only the policies of international financial institutions (the WB, the IMF and the WTO) but also the political choices of national right-wing parties and also left-wing governments. These actors are considered responsible for the growing social injustice, and its negative effects on women, the environment, the global South, etc. Next to social injustice, a common base is the meta-discourse on the search for new forms of democracy. The traditional legitimation of democracy through electoral accountability has been challenged by the development of global governance, but also by the perceived decline in state intervention as a consequence of a global economy. Perceived as hostile to the movement's claims, parties have also been criticized as the carriers of a conception of politics (and democracy) that is limited and exclusive. Distrust of parties reflects the perception shared by some activists that 'politics from below' is a viable alternative to the conception of politics as an activity for professionals defended by the parties (della Porta et al. 2006). The critique of parties – especially those potentially closest to movements – regards their conception of politics even more than their concrete political choices. Stigmatized as the carriers of an idea of professional politics, parties are seen as, at best, interested in electorally exploiting the movement, all the while denying its political credentials. In focus groups, most criticized is the reference made by party leaders to

a *pre-political movement* asking to be listened to and then translated into a political project and programme by those doing politics in the institutional sense of the word, from local institutions to parliaments, and this is extremely dangerous...the very fact that many insist on saying that this is a youth movement...I remember an interview with the mayor of Florence after the Social Forum in which he said 'one cannot ask these young people to express political projects, it is up to us to interpret them'. (cited in della Porta 2007)

This movement's characteristics fuelled in fact a search for alternative conceptions of democracy. Focusing attention on the global justice movement, the research project Demos (Democracy in Europe and the Mobilization of the Society) – covering six European countries (Italy, France, Spain, Germany, Switzerland and Great Britain) as well as the transnational level – showed the increasing relevance of the debate on democracy, inside and outside the movement, confirming, however, that various conceptions of democracy coexist, stressing different democratic qualities (see chapter 1).

Debates tended to develop within the movements on the two main dimensions I used to construct the general typology of models of democracy (see chapter 1). First, participatory conceptions that stress inclusiveness of equals were contrasted with those based upon the delegation of power to representatives. A second dimension referred instead to majoritarian versus deliberative visions, diverging in the decision-making methods. Deliberative aspects have been particularly embedded and valorized by the *method of consensus* that poses an even stronger emphasis on the decision-making process per se than on the outcome of such a process. In the various parts of the Demos research (see della Porta and Reiter 2006; della Porta and Mosca 2006), we have in fact used a typology that crosses these two dimensions of participation (referring to the degree of delegation of power, inclusiveness and equality) and deliberation (referring to the decision-making model and to the quality of communication).

The analysis of the fundamental documents of 244 social movement organizations that have participated in the Social Forum process in Europe has shown that most of them made reference there to democratic values (della Porta 2009b). Participation is one of the most widespread references, mentioned by one-third of the organizations as an internal value and by more than half as a general value. This applies not only to the pure forms of social movement organizations; trade unions and left-wing political parties also referred to participation as a founding principle. However, additional values emerged that specify (and differentiate among) the conceptions of participatory democracy. References to limits to delegation, the rotation principle, mandated delegation, and criticism of delegation as internal organizational values were present although not dominant (each mentioned by between 6 and 11 per cent of our groups). Non-hierarchical decision making was often mentioned (16 per cent), and inclusiveness was even more (21 per cent and 29 per cent). If we group the positive responses on critique of delegation, limitation of delegation, non-hierarchical decision making, and mandated delegation into an index of non-hierarchical decision making, 23.4 per cent had positive scores. Significantly, representative values were mentioned instead by only 6 per cent of our organizations.

With the aim of identifying the visions of democracy, inside and outside the movement, in this document analysis we narrowed them down to four basic conceptions (or models) of internal democracy (della Porta and Reiter 2006). In the *associational model*, the assembly is composed of delegates and – even in those cases in which the assembly consists of all members and is defined as the main decision-making organ – everyday politics is managed by an executive committee; decisions are taken by majority vote. When, according to the selected documents, delegates make decisions on a consensual basis, we speak of *deliberative representation*. When decisions are made by an assembly that includes all members, and no executive committee exists, we have an *assembleary model*, when decisions are taken by a majority; and *deliberative participation*, if consensus and communicative processes based on reason are mentioned together with participation as important values (see table 4.1).

As we can see in table 4.1, half of the 212 organizations we sampled support an associational conception of internal decision making.[1] This means that, at least formally, a model based upon delegation and the majority principle is quite widespread, and indeed expected, given the presence in the global justice movement of parties, unions and NGOs.

Table 4.1 Typology of democratic conception

| | | Participation | |
		High	Low
Consensus	Low	Associational model (%) Visions: 59.0 Practices: 35.6 Norms: 19.1	Assembleary model (%) Visions: 14.6 Practices: 2.5 Norms: 35.9
	High	Deliberative representation (%) Visions: 15.6 Practices: 32.7 Norms: 8.2	Deliberative participation (%) Visions: 10.8 Practices: 29.2 Norms: 36.7

Visions (no. of cases 212), practices (no. of cases 184), norms (no. of cases 1055).
Source: della Porta 2009a, 72.

This is, however, only part of the picture: we classified 14.6 per cent of the organizations as assembleary since, in the documents we analysed, they stressed the role of the assembly in a decision-making process that remained tied to aggregative methods such as voting or bargaining. In an additional quarter (26.4 per cent) of the organizations, the deliberative element came to the fore, with 15.6 per cent of organizations applying consensus within an associational type (deliberative representation) and 10.8 per cent applying it within an assembleary model (deliberative participation).

Consensus is even more prominent if we move, as we did in another part of our research, from the written documents to the accounts of movement practices by representatives of the organizations (della Porta and Mosca 2006). Acknowledging that constitutions and written documents are not always followed in everyday activities, and that praxes are often different from norms, we complemented the information obtained on organizational ideology with interviews on organizational functioning, as perceived and reported by their speakers.[2] In this part we operationalized the dimension of *participation/delegation* by distinguishing groups characterized by a central role of the assembly in their decision-making processes from all other types of organizations (executive-centred, leader-centred, mixed models and so on). On the dimension *deliberation / majority voting*, we separated the groups employing consensus from those employing different decisional methods (simple majority, qualified majority, mixed methods and so on). Here as well, our research testifies to the presence of various types of organizational decision making, confirming that social movements are characterized by 'considerable variation in organizational strength within and between movements' (Klandermans 1989: 4).

Of the 202 out of the overall 212 cases that we could classify, almost one third fall into the deliberative representative category, where the principle of consensus is mixed with the principle of delegation. Another 36 per cent adopt an associational model that is based on majoritarian voting and delegation, while about 30 per cent of the groups bridge a consensual decision-making method with the principle of participation (refusal of delegation to an executive committee); only 2.5 per cent of the selected organizations mix the principle of participation with majoritarian decision making (assembleary model). The fact that interviewees tended to stress consensus more than the organizational documents can be explained in various ways: respondents might be more up-to-date and accurate in describing the actual decision making in their groups, or they may want to give a more positive image of decision making in their organizations. Whatever the explanation, norms of consensus appeared as very much supported by the movement organizations.

Different models of democracy followed from organizational traditions, age, size and self-conception. Reference to consensus was particularly frequent in organizations with smaller memberships and budgets, as well as no paid staff and more reliance on the assembly. There was also some coherence between the search for consensus and horizontal organizational forms, as indicated by the rejection of an executive, the high value given to the assembly, the explicit critique of delegation. Consensual methods were, finally, more widespread in the younger organizations, as well as in the transnational ones (della Porta 2009b).

Similar results also emerged from an analysis of the normative models of democracy proposed by the activists we interviewed at the ESF in Athens (see again table 4.1), although with a greater emphasis on participation. In that sample, the rate of support for associational models of democracy further declined to one-fifth of our population (N = 1,055), and the percentage for deliberative representation reached only 8.2 per cent. From a normative point of view, indeed, the ESF participants appeared equally attracted by either assembleary or deliberative-participative models (about one-third each). Participation and deliberation were considered, therefore, as main values for 'another democracy'.

At the individual level, together with experiences of participation in protest events, at home and abroad, subjective degrees of identification with the global justice movement influenced attitudes towards democracy. In particular, those who identify more with the movement expressed more support for those values that emerged as particularly relevant for the movement organizations – inclusiveness, participation and consensus. Crossing degrees of identification with normative conceptions of democracy, our analysis indicates a statistically significant correlation: with the growth of identification, support for consensual and participatory decision making increased (see table 4.2). Here too, however, the correlation is not particularly strong, indicating quite widespread support for the more participatory and consensual values.

In many of the groups linked to the global justice movement, the positive reference to consensual decision making (often embodied in organizational principles) was therefore quite innovative. Several organizations declared they wanted 'to take decisions that reach the maximum consensus' (RCADE 2001); were 'committed to the principle of consensus decision making' (Indymedia 2002) and experimented with 'an organizational path that favors participation, reaching consensus and achieving largely shared decisions' (Torino Social Forum 2008). In its self-presentation, Attac Germany (2001) stated that the organization is 'a place, where political processes of learning and experiences are made possible; in which the various streams of progressive politics discuss with each other, in order to find a common capacity of action together'.

Table 4.2 Identification with GJM by activists' normative models of democracy

Normative models of democracy	Identification with GJM, %			Total number	% enough or much identified	Mean (value 0–3)
	None or little	Enough	Much			
Associational	21.0	43.0	36.0	200	79.0	2.13
Deliberative representative	12.8	57.0	30.2	86	87.2	2.16
Assembleary	13.7	48.8	37.5	371	86.3	2.23
Deliberative-participative	9.1	49.1	41.8	383	90.9	2.32
Overall %	13.4	48.5	38.2	1,040	86.6	2.24
Measures of association	Cramer's V = .10**				Cr.'s V = .12 ***	ETA = .11**

Source: della Porta 2008a: 76.

Supporting this type of conception, in its 'Criteri di fondo condivisi' (2001), Rete Lilliput defined the 'method of consensus' as a process in which, if a proposal does not receive total consensus from all participants, further discussion ensues in order to find a compromise with those who disagree. If disagreements persist and involve a numerically large minority, the project is not approved (Tecchio, quoted in Veltri 2003, 14). According to the network Dissent!:

> Consensus normally works around a proposal, which, hopefully, is submitted beforehand so that people have time to consider it. The proposal is presented and any concerns are discussed. The proposal is then amended until a consensus is reached. At the heart of this process are principles that include trust, respect, recognition that everyone has the right to be heard and to contribute (i.e. equal access to power), a unity of purpose and commitment to that purpose and a commitment to the principle of co-operation. At these gatherings we seek to reach consensus on most issues, although this is not always possible and often there is no need to reach 'one decision' at the end of a useful discussion. (Dissent! – A Network of Resistance against the G8 2008)

Among the groups most committed to experimentation with consensual methods, specific rules were developed to facilitate horizontal communication and conflict management. Consensus tools included 'good facilitation, various hand signals, go-rounds and the breaking up into small and larger sized groups. These should be "explained by the facilitator at the start of each discussion"' (Dissent! – A Network of Resistance against the G8 2008). Facilitators or moderators were used (for instance, for the Italian Rete Lilliput or the British Rising Tide), with the aim of including all points of view in the discussion as well as implementing rules for good communication, going from the (limited) time allocated to each speaker to the maintenance of a constructive climate (della Porta et al. 2006, 53–4).

Attention to consensual methods as a way to improve communication resonated with the widespread idea of the movement as building public spaces for dialogue. This is illustrated, for instance, by the Spanish Derechos para Tod@s (n.d.), which stressed:

> our goal is to contribute to the spreading of debates, not by narrowing spaces, but by opening them to all those who are critical of this globalization that causes exploitation, repression and/or exclusion...No alternative to the current system can be regarded as the 'true' one. That is, we want to set up a space to reflect and to fight for a social and civil transformation. (Jiménez and Calle 2006, 278)

From the normative point of view, the assumption was that 'The practices of consensus-seeking strengthen bonds, trust, communication and understanding. On the other hand, decision-making based on voting creates power blocks, power games, and hegemonic strategies, excluded and included, hierarchies, thus reproducing the same kind of social relations we are opposing' (London Social Forum 2003).

Consensus was, however, framed differently by different organizations. In a *plural conception of consensus through high-quality dialogue*, which often characterized network organizations, consensus was considered as mainly 'functional for safeguarding the unitary–plural nature of the movement as well as members' demands for individual protagonism' (Fruci 2003, 169). In networks and campaigns, the consensual method was advocated as enabling work on what united the groups, notwithstanding their differences. In this sense, in organizational networks, consensual principles were presented as resonating with a respect for the autonomy of the individual organizations that were part of the federation.

The meaning of consensus was bridged here with a positive emphasis on internal diversity. This was the case, for instance, for Attac Italia, which in its Charter of Intent stipulated that it 'wants to be a democratic and open association, transversal and as much as possible pluralistic, composed of diverse individuals and social forces... it wants to contribute to the renovation of democratic political participation and favours the development of new organizational forms of civil society'. As its national assembly stated, 'We want to continue to build shared associational forms, based on participation and the consensual method, fit for letting diversities meet and work together and develop democratic decisional practices. Because we consider democracy as the most important element of the common good and we want, all together, to re-appropriate it' (ATTAC Italia 2007).

Participation and the method of consensus are, in this sense, considered as the main expressions of democracy 'as a common good'. In particular – but not only – for networks, consensus resonated with an emphasis on the respect for differences, bridged with calls for inclusiveness, within the conception of the organization as an open space – a metaphor often used by our groups. For instance, the Turin Social Forum (2008) presented itself as 'an open place in which even individuals, as well as the organized actors, can meet and work together; a space in which internal differences are accepted and given a positive value'.

A different viewpoint is a *communitarian conception of consensus as collective agreement*, expressed by groups with a deep-rooted 'assembleary' tradition. For instance, the British Wombles declared:

We have no formal membership; all meetings are weekly & open to anyone who wishes to attend. These meetings are where any & all decisions concerning the group are made. The politics we espouse are those we wish to live by – self-organization, autonomy, direct democracy & direct action against the forces of coercion and control... As such, no individual can speak on behalf of the Wombles as all group decisions are made collectively based on consensus. (Wombles 2008)

In this area, consensus resonated with anti-authoritarian, horizontal relations. Accordingly, the French Réseau Intergalactique, which developed around the construction of a self-managed space at the anti-G8 summit in Evian, stated in its Charter: 'there is no dominant voice. It is what we call a horizontal way of functioning: there is no small group that decides. Thus, there is not on the one side thinking heads and on the other side small hands and feet. The aim is to facilitate the integration of each in the discussion and decision-making.'

Consensual methods are here adopted within a prefigurative vision of organizational life. They are linked to the aim of realizing social changes not only though political decisions, but through deep transformations in everyday life and individual attitudes. 'For it is impossible to realize a social transformation through merely political decisions. The activities have to relate to the needs and desires of the people, so that anti-militarism can bring about alternative lifestyles and struggle in a positive way. This would develop by consensus, understood as a process that aims at reaching the agreement which is most satisfactory for all' (Alternativa antimilitarist – MOC.). So, for the London Social Forum, the use of the method of consensus was also linked to the group's self-definition, reflecting in particular the preference for prefigurative politics over effectiveness.

Indignados, *Occupy and deliberative democracy*

A focus on deliberation became all the more central in the most recent movements against austerity. The Arab Spring could be read as yet another testimony that democracy is becoming 'the only game in town'. The effects of the wave of protest that brought about democratization processes in an area of the world traditionally defined as dominated by resilient authoritarian regimes certainly contributed to challenging the idea of a clash of civilization based on the incompatibility of Islam with democracy. Moreover, these protests have shown that, even in brutal dictatorships, citizens do mobilize, and not only on material issues. Interpreting the Arab Spring as merely a call for representative institutions will, however, be misleading. The protestors in the Tahrir Square were calling for freedom, but also practising other conceptions of democracy that are, if not opposed to, certainly different from liberal representative democracy, resonating instead with ideas of participatory and deliberative democracy.

Not by chance, when the ideas of the Arab Spring spread from the MENA (Mediterranean and North-African) region to Europe, they were adopted and adapted by social movements that indeed challenged (neo) liberal democracy. Austerity measures in Iceland, Ireland, Greece, Portugal and Spain were in fact met with long-lasting, mass protests. Directly inspired by the Arab Spring, the Spanish and then Greek *indignados* occupied hundreds of squares in order not only to protest against austerity measures in their respective countries, but also to ask for more, and a different democracy. 'Democracia real ya!' was a main slogan of the Spanish *indignados* protestors who occupied the Puerta del Sol in Madrid, the Placa de Catalunya in Barcelona and hundreds of places in the rest of the country from 15 May 2011, calling for different social and economic policies and, indeed, greater citizen participation in their formulation and implementation. Before this example in Spain, between late 2008 and early 2009, self-convened citizens in Iceland had demanded the resignation of the government and its delegates in the Central Bank and financial authorities, accusing them of collusion with big business. In Portugal, a demonstration arranged via Facebook in March 2011 brought more than 200,000 young Portuguese people to the streets in opposition to their country's political class. The *indignados* protests in turn inspired similar mobilizations in Greece, where opposition to austerity measures had already been expressed in occasionally violent forms. In both countries, the corruption of the government was a central issue of protest, and it remained so when protest moved, as we saw in the beginning of this chapter, to the US and beyond.

The very meaning of democracy was, in all these protests, contested. There is no doubt that the current crisis is a crisis of democracy as well as, or even more than, a financial crisis. As mentioned, neoliberalism was – and, in fact, is – a political doctrine that brings with it a minimalist vision of the public and democracy. It foresees not only the reduction of political interventions oriented to balancing the market (with consequent liberalization, privatization and deregulation) but also an elitist conception of citizen participation (electoral only, and therefore occasional and potentially distorted) and an increased level of influence for lobbies and strong interests. The evident challenges in a liberal conception and practice of democracy have, in this case as well, been accompanied by the (re)emergence of different ones, elaborated and practised by – among others – movements that in Europe today are opposing a neoliberal solution to the financial crisis, accused of further depressing consumption and thereby jeopardizing any prospects for development (whether sustainable or not).

Accused by the centre-left parties of being apolitical and populist (not to mention without ideas) and by the right of being extreme leftists, these movements have in reality placed what Claus Offe (1985) long ago defined as the 'meta-question' of democracy at the centre of their action. The activists' discourse on democracy is articulate and complex, taking up some of the principal criticisms of the ever-decreasing quality of liberal democracies, but also some proposals inspired by democratic qualities other than representation. These proposals resonate with (more traditional) participatory visions, but also with new deliberative conceptions that underline the importance of creating multiple public spaces, egalitarian but plural.

Above all, protestors criticize the ever more evident shortcomings of representative democracies, mirroring a declining trust in the ability of parties to channel emerging demands in the political system. Beginning from Iceland, and forcefully in Spain and Portugal, indignation is addressed towards the corruption of the political class, seen both in bribes (the dismissal of corrupt people from public institutions is called for) in a concrete sense, and in the privileges granted to lobbies and common interests shared by public institutions and economic (often financial) powers. It is to this corruption – that is, the corruption of democracy – that much of the responsibility for the economic crisis, and the inability to manage it, are attributed.

Beyond the condemnation of corruption, the slogan 'they don't represent us' also expresses a deeper criticism of the degeneration of liberal democracy, linked in turn to elected politicians' failure to 'do politics'. The latter are in fact often united in spreading a narrative suggesting that no alternatives are available to cuts in budget and deregulation – a narrative that protestors do not accept. In Spain in particular, the movement asked for proportional reforms to the electoral law, denouncing the reduced weight given to citizen participation inherent to the majority system, where the main political parties tend to form cartels and electors see their choices limited (for this reason, equal weight for each vote was called for). Also in other countries, among other proposals for restoring the importance of citizens are those that call for direct democracy, and which give electors the possibility to express their opinions on the biggest economic and social choices. In this vein, greater possibilities for referendums are called for, with reduced quorums (for signatures and electors) and increased thematic areas subject to decisions through referendums.

Actually existing democracies are also criticized for having allowed the abduction of democracy, not only by financial powers, but also by international organizations, above all the IMF and the EU. Pacts for the Euro and stability, imposed in exchange for loans, are considered as anti-constitutional forms of blackmail, depriving citizens of their sovereignty. Starting in 2011 with the petition Another Road for Europe (www.anotherroadforeurope.org) numerous reforms have been suggested at EU level in order to gain control of financial markets, for example through the introduction of a Financial Transaction Tax, political supervision of banks, the removal of the public role for (private) rating agencies and the creation of public ones, as well as higher taxes on capital, and strategies for economic growth (see also Pianta 2012, chapter 4). More transnational democracy is additionally called for (see chapter 6, this volume).

But in recent mobilizations there is also another vision of democracy, which normative theory has recently defined as 'deliberative democracy', and which the global justice movement has elaborated and diffused through the Social Forums as consensus democracy. This conception of democracy is prefigured by the very same *indignados* who occupy squares, transforming them into public spheres made up of 'normal citizens'. It is an attempt to create high-quality discursive democracy, recognizing the equal rights of all (not only delegates and experts) to speak (and to be respected) in a public and plural space, open to discussion and deliberation on themes that range from situations suffered to concrete solutions to specific problems, from the elaboration of proposals on common goods to the formation of solidarity and emerging identities.

Participatory and deliberative forms of democracy were in fact called for and experienced during these protests. In Spain, as elsewhere, open public spaces facilitated the creation of intense ties. Postill (2012) vividly recalls:

> the strong sense of connection to the strangers I spoke to during that fleeting moment...Under normal circumstances – say, on an underground train – we would have found no reason to talk to one another, but the present situation was anything but normal. The 15-M movement had brought us together, and the sense of 'contextual fellowship'...cutting across divides of age, class and race was very powerful....Many participants later reported a range of psychosomatic reactions such as goose bumps (*carne de gallina*) or tears of joy. I felt as if a switch had been turned on, a gestalt switch, and I had now awakened to a new political reality. I was no longer merely a participant observer of the movement, I was the movement.

The assemblies in the encampments were described by activists as 'primarily a massive, transparent exercise in direct democracy'. So, they declared, 'We feel part of the movement because we contribute to creating it, spreading it, growing it; Internet user and indignado are one and the same person' (@galapita and @hibai 2011, cited in Postill 2012).

Similarly, when the Occupy Wall Street movement started in the United States, quickly spreading to thousands of American cities, the concerns voiced by the protestors addressed the financial crisis, but even more the failure of democratic governments to live up to the expectations of their citizens. The occupations represented not only occasions to protest but also experimentations with participatory and deliberative forms of democracy. Called for by the magazine *Adbuster*, the protest started with a few hundred activists converging on Manhattan on 17 September 2011. A previous protest event had been staged on 2 August by the city group New York Against the Budget Cuts. As a journalist recalled:

> it began as an old-school rally with speeches by lifelong local activists....the dedication was admirable, the rhetoric was antique. We must 'fight back by any means necessary,' said dreadlocked Larry Hales of NYABC....Then hot-tempered Greek student Georgia Sagri shook things up. She took the mic, saying, 'This is not the way that a general assembly is happening! This is a rally!' She continued to blurt out criticisms and piss people off. But a chunk of them, mostly students but also middle-aged folk, joined her in a circle for a radical-consensus general assembly – a mainstay process in countries like Greece and Spain. Then it became something new (Captain 2011)

The style that started to dominate the Occupy Wall Street movement included an emphasis on respect and inclusivity. Moderators tried to assure a racial and gender balance. A consensual, horizontal decision-making process developed – sponsored by the young generations (two-thirds of whom had voted for Obama) and global justice movement activists – based on the continuous formation of small groups that then reconvened in the larger assembly.

The occupation became much entrenched with the very identity of the movement, not just, as for other social movements, an action form among others. Occupied spaces were in fact 'vibrant sites of human interaction that modeled alternative communities and generated intense feelings of solidarity' (Juris 2012, 268). Evictions took away these vital spaces, running the risk of transforming the camps into a sort of fetish, difficult to keep, but also difficult to replace. The clearing of the occupied places by the police in fact created important fractures among activists – for example, between the community of those who were physically occupying and the various circles of those participating virtually and/or intermittently.

Conclusion

Deliberative conceptions of democracy go beyond the traditional criticism of liberal democracy as excluding – or not including sufficiently – the citizens, stressing instead the importance for the very interests and/ or identities that confront each other to be democratically constructed. Democracy is not only a way of counting votes, but especially a way to form preferences through inclusive and high-quality dialogues. If, in their initial versions, deliberative theorists maintained an institutional focus, other scholars have linked participatory and deliberative aspirations. Recent movements, to varying degrees, have done the same, stressing the need to form multiple and open public spheres, to allow the participation of various and plural actors.

Calls for and prefiguration of deliberative democracy follow a vision of democracy profoundly different to that which legitimates representative democracy based on the principle of majority decisions. Democratic quality here is in fact measured by the possibility of elaborating ideas within discursive, open and public arenas, where citizens play an active role in identifying problems, but also in elaborating possible solutions. It is the opposite of an unquestioning acceptance of democracy of the prince, where the professional elected to govern must not be disturbed – at least until fresh elections are held. But it is also the opposite of a democracy of experts, legitimized by the output, for which European institutions have long called. If, especially after the Maastricht Treaty and the introduction of the Euro, calls for this kind of legitimization – which appeals to the capacity to produce, apolitically and on the basis of specialist skills and economic successes – have gradually reduced, it now seems to crumble entirely before the disastrous results of European policies in the recent financial crisis. In protests against the crisis (and the ineffective and unjust responses to it), protestors have started to prefigure, in occupied public spaces, different conceptions of democracy, based on participation and deliberative values.

5

E-Democracy? New Technologies and Democratic Deepening

The so-called Arab Spring was definitely not the product of new technologies, but they certainly helped it to spread. Howard (2010, 201) concluded his analyses of the influence of Internet Communication Technology (ICT) on democratic change from 1994 to 2010 in seventy-five countries with large Muslim communities with these words: 'It is clear that, increasingly, the route to democratization is a digital one.' In addition, he stressed the role of the Muslim diaspora in the West in generating a transnational collective identity through a 'significant amount of politically critical content via mass media such as radio, television, film, and newspapers', that is more and more accessible in Arab countries. So, 'the internet has a causal and supportive role in the formation of democratic discourse in the Muslim communities of the developing world' (2010, 40). In fact, during democratic transitions, an active online civil society emerged as a most important condition for democratization.

It was also through Twitter, Facebook and other social media that protest spread from the MENA region to Europe and then to the United States. In fact, the very characteristics of the technology used by the activists have been said to play an important role in the creation of a participatory ethics that stresses individual involvement over organizational (Juris 2012). In the Occupy movement, 'the combination of Twitter and smartphone, in particular, allows individuals to continually post and receive updates as well as to circulate images, and texts, constituting real-time, user-generated news feeds' (2012, 267).

These examples of the role of new technologies in most recent movements which, as mentioned in the previous chapter, called for different forms of democracy suffice to illustrate how tightly reflections on democracy, communication and social movements are linked. Even if certainly not technologically determined, models of democracy adapt to the means of communication available. The implementation of the central values of each of the mentioned conceptions of democracy requires communicative resources, which are influenced by technologies. Electoral accountability requires some transparency, participation requires interactions, deliberation requires communication: all these are linked to the possibility of transmitting information.

Despite this, social science literatures on social movements, mass media and democracy have rarely interacted. As mentioned before (see chapter 1), research on democracy has tended to focus on representative institutions, pragmatically using 'minimalistic' operationalization of democracy as electoral accountability, and providing structural explanations of democratic developments. Research on the mass media has also tended to isolate them as a separate power, reflecting on the technological constraints and opportunities for communication. Social movement studies have mainly considered democratic characteristics as setting the political opportunities social movements have to address and – more rarely – looked at the constraints that mass media impose upon powerless actors.

More recently, in all three fields of knowledge, some opportunities for reciprocal learning and interactions developed, prompted by some exogenous, societal changes as well as disciplinary evolutions. In this chapter, I would suggest that looking at the intersection of democracy, media and social movements could be particularly useful within a relational and constructivist vision that takes the normative positions of the different actors into account. More broadly, this would mean paying attention to the permeability of the borders between the three concepts, as well as between the three fields they tend to separate. After reviewing the social science literature on the democratic qualities of communication, I shall turn to social movement studies to introduce illustrations of alternative communication practices, inspired by alternative democratic conceptions, in social movements in the new millennium.

What media studies do (and do not) say, on democracy: an introduction

Despite the obvious and growing importance of mass media and social movements for democracy, the debate on their specific contributions to democratic quality has been selective in both fields. Existing research tends to focus on structural conditions, paying limited attention to agency and normative construction.

In media studies, conditions and limits of the media contribution to democracy have not occupied a central place. When addressing the important role of an active and autonomous public sphere, research on political communication has tended instead to stigmatize the commercialization and/or lack of political autonomy of the mass media as a serious challenge to the performance of a 'power of oversight' over the elected politicians. Recent tendencies in the mass media – among which are concentration, deregulation, digitalization, globalization and the pluralization of their publics – have, at best, ambivalent effects on democracy (Dahlgren 2009). While various theorizations have mapped different types of public spheres (Gerhard and Neidhardt 1990), and, traditionally, research on political communication has stressed the role of different filters between the media-as-senders and the citizens-as-receivers (e.g. Deutsch 1964), recent research on political communication has mainly focused on the mass media as a separate power. The debate on democracy and the media has mainly been addressed by looking at the effects of institutional settings on media freedom and pluralism (e.g. Gunther and Mughan 2000).

Some more attention to democracy developed around the new media. Research on the Internet addressed the potential improvements that digital communication could bring about in democratic quality. In fact, attention to the relations between the Internet and democracy grew together with the rapid spread of related technologies: from 40 computers connected with each other in research centres in the US in 1972 to the 93 million hosts in 2000 (Zittel 2003, 2).

So important are the expected effects of electronic communication considered to be that new concepts have been proposed, including e-participation (as the possibility of expressing political opinion online), e-governance (as the possibility of accessing information and public services online), e-voting (or e-referendum, with the possibility of voting online) or, even more broadly, e-democracy, defined as the increasing opportunities for political participation online (Rose 2005). As for other technologies, opinions on advantages and disadvantages have been polarized between sceptics and enthusiasts. The potential of the Internet in improving democratic quality has been indeed discussed, with reference to the different conceptions we have analysed in the previous chapters.

As for *liberal* democracy, the use of the Internet has been seen as improving communication between citizens and elected politicians, with increasing accessibility to information, occasions for feedbacks and transparency. E-governance is supposed to reduce the discretionality of public administrators, by improving public access.

The Internet has been said to impact on democratic *participation* as well. As a horizontal, bi-directional and interactive technology, it is expected to favour a multiplication of information producers (Bentivegna 1999; Warkentin 2001), as well as of information available for consumption (Ayers 1999; Myers 2001). In fact, 'The open and accessible character of the net means that traditional centers of power have less informational and ideational control over their environment than previously' (Dahlgren 2009, 190).

As for the *deliberative* dimension of democracy, the Internet is said to increase the quality of communication, by improving not only the number of sources of information, but also their pluralism (Wilhelm 2000). In general, 'The powerful have been spying on their subjects since the beginning of history, but the subjects can now watch the powerful, at least to a greater extent than in the past. We have all become potential citizen journalists who, if equipped with a mobile phone, can record and instantly upload to the global networks any wrongdoing by anyone, anywhere' (Castells 2009, 413). Multiplying the spaces for exchange of ideas, the Internet should also improve mutual understanding by allowing for the development of multiple, critical public spheres.

As with other technologies, opinions on the advantages and disadvantages of the Internet are split, however (for a review, della Porta and Mosca 2005). In research on its use in representative politics, concerns have been expressed especially about the unidirectional (top-down) use of new technologies by politicians and administrators alike (Zittel 2003, 3), as well as the risks for the security and privacy of their users that the very generative characteristics of PCs – that is, their openness to reprogramming by anyone – brings about (Zittrain 2008, 19). The potential egalitarian effects are denied by scholars who stress instead the presence of a digital divide which increases rather than reduces inequalities, being the lack of access to the Web tendentially cumulated with lack of access to other resources, at both individual and country levels (Margolis and Resnick 2000; Rose 2005; Norris 2001). As for its deliberative quality, concerns have been expressed not only with reference to the plurality of information, but also to the very quality of communication online (Schosberg, Zavestoski and Shulman 2005). The e-public spheres have been defined as 'partial', elitarian and fragmented (Sunstein 2001).

Additionally, despite the increasing attention, the discussion on the improvement of democratic politics on the Web tends to remain either highly normative or quite technical, with even some nuances of technological determinism. Even though interest in the Internet and democracy is growing exponentially, the field of studies is still perceived as dominated by 'technomaniacs' and 'utopian dreamers' (Zittel 2004, 2).

These gaps in the reflections on communication and democracy have not been fully filled by social movement studies. Paradoxically, notwithstanding their obvious relevance for democracy (and vice versa), social movement research has been rarely concerned with the movements' democratic functions. Usually, democracies have been considered as the context of social movements, and some of the characteristics of representative institutions (especially territorial and functional division of power) have been seen as particularly important in favouring 'healthy' (intense but moderate) protest (della Porta and Diani 2006, ch. 8). Also a little frequented area, research on social movements and the media has traditionally addressed especially the limited capacity of social movements to influence the mass media, characterized by selectiveness but also by descriptive biases when covering protest (Gamson and Modigliani 1989; Gamson 2004).

Media are certainly important for social movements. As Gamson (2004, 243) observed, 'the mass media arena is the major site of contest over meaning because all of the players in the policy process assume its pervasive influence – either it is justified or not'. Control of the media and of symbolic production therefore becomes both an essential premise for any attempt at political mobilization and an autonomous source of conflict. Even though the extent to which protest events are first of all 'newspaper demonstrations', i.e. oriented mainly at media coverage (Neveu 1999, 28ff.) is debatable, media are indeed the most obvious shaper of public sensitivity (Jasper 1997, 286). The success of protest action is influenced by the amount of media attention it receives, and this also affects the character of social movement organizations (Gitlin 1980). Pluralism in the media would therefore facilitate that participation of the less-advantaged groups that normative theorists have considered as extremely important for democratic quality.

Traditionally focused on the interaction between the mass media and social movements, research has repeatedly singled out the media bias against social movements endowed with little social capital – in terms of relations with the press and reputation as reliable sources – to be spent with journalists.

Social movements have in fact been described as weak players in the mass-media sphere, and the relationships between activists and journalists as competitive (Neveu 1999). General tendencies (journalistic preference for the visible and dramatic, for example, or reliance on authoritative sources of information) and specific characteristics of the media system (a greater or lesser degree of neutrality on the part of journalists, the amount of competition between the different media) both influence social movements. Recent evolutions towards depoliticization of the journalistic profession, or increasing commercialization (Neveu 1999), further reduce activists' access. When they have been effective in producing newsworthy events, social movement organizations and activists have been said to do so at high cost, in terms of adaptation to the media logic. In his influential volume *The Whole World is Watching*, Gitlin (1980) described different steps in relations with the media, going from lack of interest to cooptation. Beyond the media, discursive opportunities in the broader public are quoted as determining movements' relative success in agenda setting.

As Charlotte Ryan observed long ago (1991), the focus on inequality in power between the different actors who intervene in the mass media has been useful in counterbalancing some naive assumptions of the (then-dominant) gatekeeper organizational model, which underestimated the barriers to access to the news faced by weak actors. At the same time, however, it risks underestimating the capacity for agency by social movement organizations as well as the active role of audiences in making sense of media messages and their capacity to democratize communication.

Summarizing, both media studies and social movement studies have paid limited and selective attention to democracy. Democratic institutions tended to be considered mainly as the independent variable, that is the context that influences the qualities of media and social movements' chances for mobilization. While in media studies, the debate on the potential democratic functions of the Internet remained focused on its technological potential, social movement studies, in their turn, pointed at the selectivity of the mass media towards non-institutional actors.

As I am going to argue in the next section, research on alternative media has instead focused attention on social movements as agents of democratic communication following participatory and deliberative visions of democracy. Given recent changes in the technological and cultural opportunities, scholars in this field tend to stress more and more the blurring of the borders between senders and receivers, producers and users.

Social movements as agents of democratic communication

If mass media assets have been considered as structural constraints for a democracy from below, attention to agency is stronger in research on the media close to the movements, variously defined as alternative, activist, citizen radical, autonomous, etc. (for a review, Mattoni 2012). In Downing's definition (1984, 3), 'radical alternative media constitute the most active form of the active audience and express oppositional strands, overt and covert, within popular cultures'. They are 'media, generally small scale and in many different forms, that express an alternative vision to hegemonic policies, priorities and perspectives' (1984, v). With their activities, they improve the democratic capacity of control, but also search for ways to democratically construct and spread news.

Studies on alternative, or radical, media stress especially the differences in the ways in which they produce news, as well as in the public they address. In general, they look, at a micro level, at both the product and the (decentralized) practices of news production. In this approach, radical alternative media are social movement organizations of a special type, constructing a public sphere for the movement. Their *raison d'être* is in the critique of the established media (Rucht 2004) and the promotion of the 'democratization of information' (Cardon and Grandjou 2003). In this way, they play an important role for democracy, by expanding the range of information and ideas available, by being more responsive to the excluded, and by impacting on participants' sense of the self.

Doubts are expressed, however, about their capacity to go beyond those who are already sympathetic to the cause, and to reach the general public. Social movements do indeed develop different movement strategies to address the media: from abstention to attack, alternative and adaptation (Rucht 2004). Meso-media, circulating information between the activists, have also to perform the uneasy task of reaching the mass media, if they want their message circulated outside movement-sympathetic circles (Bennett 2004).

Some recent reflection and research on social movements and their communication practices also challenged a structuralist view, focused on the media as institutions, and a conception of alternative media as separated from the broader media field, and have looked more at their relations, norms and vision. Research on alternative media started indeed to stress the agency of social movements and their communicative practices, as well as the integration of (or at least overlapping between) different actors and fields of action in media, seen as arenas (Gamson 2004). Characteristics of these media are not only their critical, counter-hegemonic contents, but also their capacity to involve normal citizens in news production as well (Atkinson 2010). Given their horizontal links with their audience, participatory activists contribute to blurring the borders between audience and producers, readers and writers, through co-performance (2010, 41).

Some recent trends appear to have facilitated this blurring of the borders between producers and receivers. Not only are citizens active processors of media messages, but, as Lance Bennett observed, 'People who have long been on the receiving end of one-way mass-communication are now increasingly likely to become producers and transmitters' (2003b, 34). This increased capacity of normal citizens and activists to produce information has been seen as a consequence of post-modern individualization, with an increasing fluidity and mobility of political identities (2003b), but also of specific changes in the media field, such as:

1. New ways of consuming media, which explicitly contest the social legitimacy of media power;
2. New infrastructures of production, which have an effect on who can produce news and in which circumstances;
3. New infrastructures of distribution, which change the scale and terms in which symbolic production in one place can reach other places. (Couldry 2003, 44)

In fact, as part of the new trend in 'communication power', Manuel Castells has noted that 'the production of the message is self-generated, the definition of the potential receiver(s) is self-directed, and the retrieval of specific messages or content from the World Wide Web and electronic communication networks is self-selected' (2009, 55). In this way, 'The media audience is transformed into a communicative subject increasingly able to redefine the process by which societal communication frames the culture of society' (2009, 116).

Communication is becoming more and more relevant for some contemporary movements, and not only because of its instrumental value. As mentioned, research on democracy inside the global justice movement pointed at the growing attention to values related to communication in an open space: respect for diversity, equal participation and inclusiveness (della Porta 2009a). The importance of conceiving social movement organizations as spaces for *networking*, with a positive emphasis on diversity, is present in particular in the World Social Forum, as well as in the macro-regional and local social forums. This has been nurtured under the conception of an 'open space method' of internal democracy, that strives to produce strength from diversity.

In recent reflections linking communication and participatory democratic quality, the focus of attention is not so much (or no longer) on the abstract 'power of the media', but more on the relations between media and publics: the ways in which 'people exercise their agency in relation to media flows' (Couldry 2006, 27). Media practices therefore become central, not only as the practices of the media actors, but more broadly as what various actors do in relations with the media, including activist media practices. Not only is 'reading media imagery...an active process in which context, social location, and prior experience can lead to quite different decoding' (Gamson et al. 1992, 375), but also people participate more and more in the production of messages.

Research has looked not only at the permeability of the borders between media producers and media consumers, but also at the important effects of the symbolic and normative construction of the relations between media and social movements, journalists and activists.

Web 1.0, social movements and democracy

Attention not only to agency but also to norms seems to increase as well in research on social movements and deliberative media, in particular in reflections on the democratic potential of new communication technologies. A main recent innovation has been the conceptualization of a media environment (similar to Bourdieu's field) in which not only different spokespersons intervene, but also different types of media interact. In Mattoni's definition (2012, 33), a media environment is an 'open, unpredictable and controversial space of mediatization and communication, made up of different layers which continuously combine with one another due to the information flows circulating within the media environment itself'. As she observed (2012, 34), 'in complex and multilayered media environments individuals simultaneously play different roles, especially in particular situations of protest, mobilization and claims making'. A continuous flow of communication between what Bennett (2004) conceptualized as micro-, meso- and macro-media also makes the boundaries between news production and news consumption more flexible.

Attention to agency and normative (and social) construction has been growing in research on social movements and the Internet that has stressed its potentials for social movement communication. New media have transformed the ambitions and capacity for *communication* of social movements. In particular, the Internet is exploited for online mobilization and the performance of acts of dissent: the term 'electronic advocacy' refers to 'the use of high technology to influence the decision-making process, or to the use of technology in an effort to support policy-change efforts' (Hick and McNutt 2002: 8). Also, in part thanks to the Internet, transnational campaigns have grown to be longer, less centrally controlled, more difficult to turn on and off, and forever changing in term of networks and goals (Bennett 2003a). Given their greater flexibility, social movement organizations have emerged as more open than earlier movements to experimentation and permeable to technological changes, with a more innovative and dynamic use of the Internet. Given the low costs of computer-mediated communication, the new technologies offer cheap means of communication beyond borders. Moreover, the Internet has facilitated the development of epistemic communities and advocacy networks (Keck and Sikkink 1998) that produce and spread alternative information on various issues. This has been particularly important for the mobilization of transnational campaigns.

Beyond their instrumental use, the new technologies have been said to resonate with social movements' vision of democracy at the normative level. Fast and inexpensive communication allows for flexible organizational and more participatory and deliberative structures (Smith 1997; Bennett 2003a). More generally, the Internet

> fits with the basic features of the kind of social movements emerging in the Information Age...To build an historical analogy, the constitution of the labor movement in the industrial era cannot be separated from the industrial factory as its organizational setting...the internet is not simply a technology: it is a communication media, and it is the material infrastructure of a given organizational form: the network. (Castells 2001, 135–6)

The use of the Internet is thus 'shaping the movement on its own web-like image', with hubs at the centre of activities, and the spokes 'that link to other centers, which are autonomous but interconnected' (Klein 2002, 16).

The Internet has also been said to multiply public spaces for deliberation, therefore allowing for the creation of new collective identities (della Porta and Mosca 2005). In various campaigns and protest actions, online forums and mailing lists have hosted debates on various strategic choices as well as reflections on their effects, a demonstration's success or failure among 'distant' activists. Virtual networks have shown themselves capable of developing a sense of community (Freschi 2002; Fuster 2010).

Research on contemporary movements has confirmed the importance of social movement agency in determining the use of new technologies, as well as the blurring borders between news production and news consumption. First of all, there are differences, and even tensions, in the use of new technologies by various organizations and activists, reflecting different conceptions of democracy and communication even within the same social movement. Most of the 266 Web sites that referred to the global justice movement that we analysed during the Demos project (della Porta 2009a and 2009b) provided a significant amount of information, improving opportunities for political education through articles, papers and dossiers (90 per cent of the cases), conferences and seminar materials, and news sections (78 per cent). Web sites served broadly as means for self-presentation to the outside, being used as sort of electronic business cards that had to represent the identity, through information on past history and current activities, of the organization. A large majority (about 80 per cent) of those social movement organizations also provided information on their Web site on the physical existence and reachability of the organization (80 per cent); and published the statute (or an equivalent document) of their organizations, thus improving the transparency of their internal life. The potential for *mobilization through the Web* was also widely exploited, especially for *offline protest*, with the publication of one's own calendar (60 per cent) but also of initiatives by other organizations, as well as by providing concrete information (through handbooks or links to useful resources) on offline forms of action (36 per cent). About two-thirds of Web sites advertise the participation of their organization in a protest campaign.

Much less used, however, were some of the most innovative opportunities offered by new technologies. First, only about one-third of the sampled Web sites provided instruments for *online protest*, such as e-petitions, netstrikes and mailbombings. Second, *open spaces* for discussion were offered through the presence on a Web site of specific applications like forums, mailing lists, blogs or chat lines, that allow for multilateral interactivity, in only about one-third of the Web sites.

Some differences in the use of the Internet also emerge from the survey with the representatives of social movement organizations. While most of them indeed tended to frame new media as crucial (della Porta 2009b), a more limited number stressed the peculiar capacity of the Internet to promote participation and deliberation, highlighting that new technologies can facilitate the spreading and sharing of power and considering Internet tools such as mailing lists as (potentially at least) 'permanent assemblies'. Open publishing and open management systems were employed only by a few groups in order to widen participation in the group life and to democratize the organization, avoiding the concentration of power in the hands of a few technologically skilled individuals.

The Demos survey of participants in the fourth ESF in Athens (in May 2006) confirmed that the Internet represented a fundamental means of communication among activists of the global justice movement (see also della Porta and Mosca 2005, 171, on the first ESF in Florence in 2002). In particular, a very high percentage of respondents (between 75 and 85 per cent) used the Web to perform moderate forms of online protest (less than one-third employed more radical ones such as net-strikes); to exchange information with their own group; to express political opinions online. With very high frequency (by almost half of respondents at least once a week), the Internet was used as an instrument to exchange information with one's own group, and very often it was also used for petitioning and campaigning. Occasions to express political opinions online were, however, exploited less frequently (Mosca and della Porta 2009).

Conceptions of democracy inside and outside the groups tend to filter the technological potentials of such innovations, thus pointing at different genres (Vedres, Bruszt and Stark 2005) or styles (della Porta and Mosca 2005) in the politics on the Web. This confirms that 'deterministic assumptions are challenged by an awareness that technology is not a discrete artifact which operates externally to impact upon social relations' (Pickerill 2003, 23).

Contextual and organizational characteristics in fact helped to explain the strategic choices made by social movement organizations. In an adaptation to national cultures, they tended in fact to privilege transparency and provision of information in some of the countries that we covered in our research (Germany, Great Britain and Switzerland), and identity building and mobilization in others (France, Italy and Spain). But also different social movement organizations tended to exploit a variety of technological opportunities, producing Web sites endowed with different qualities that apparently reflect diverging organizational models. In particular, those oriented towards more formal and hierarchical structures seemed to prefer a more traditional (and instrumental) use of the Internet, while less formalized groups tended to use more interactive tools available online in identity building, as well as various forms of computer-mediated protest. Movement traditions as well as democratic conceptions also played some role in influencing the different qualities of the Web sites. Overall, these data show that less resourceful and newer social movement groups tended to develop a more innovative use of the Internet, while more resourceful and older groups tended to use it as a more conventional medium of communication (Mosca and della Porta 2009).

Research at the individual level also confirmed the importance of political commitment in influencing the use (and type of use) of the Internet. Surveys of activists in the global justice movement have in fact indicated that, while gender and education have no relation to the frequency and forms of Internet use, use was related with the interviewees' level of activism, as the more mobilized population also used the Internet more intensively and in more innovative ways. The various uses of the Internet all increased with identification with the movement, multiple organizational memberships, participation through protest and in other forms (2009). As already noted elsewhere (della Porta and Mosca 2005), offline and online protests emerged therefore as strongly related and reinforcing each other. The more activists identified with the movement, the more they used the Internet to take part in moderate forms of action online and to express their political opinions, both in their own group and outside of it. The higher the number of groups in which activists were involved, the more they used the Internet as an instrument for political protest and expression of political opinions. Similar trends can be noted if we consider the level of mobilization, as measured by participation in protest events and multiple repertoires of action.

Once again, the use of the Internet cannot be conceived in isolation from communication by other means. New media are part of the broader media environment. Many interviewees underlined that face-to-face relationships were very important for the construction of virtual nets, which do not emerge spontaneously. In addition, the Internet was often considered as something adding to existing relations, rather than as an alternative to them.

Summarizing, protest campaigns indeed affected activists' perceptions of the media (Couldry 2000) and different social movements' uses of the media were influenced more by normative assessments than by instrumental constraints.

Arab spring, *indignados* and (very) new technologies

While the previously mentioned research on the global justice movement focused on its use of new technologies such as Web sites or mailing lists, most recent studies of the wave of protest that started with the Arab Spring paid particular attention to the social media and their effects on conceptions and practices of democracy. While recognizing that media alone do not make social movements, Juris has pointed at the different organizational frames which are facilitated by the two types of technologies. As he noted, 'whereas the use of listservs and websites in the movements for global justice during the late 1990s and 2000s helped to generate and diffuse distributed networking logics, in the #Occupying movements social media have contributed to powerful logics of aggregation' (2012, 260–1). While the logics of networking aims at connecting diverse collective actors, the logics of aggregation involve the assembling of diverse individuals in physical spaces.

Research on these contentious politics thus confirms that social movements have a strong capacity to quickly adapt to the evolving communication technologies. Rather than networks of networks, social media facilitate a mass aggregation of individuals (2012, 267). Cheaper and easier to use than the previous Internet instruments of communication, the social media allow for more subjective intervention that extends beyond traditional activist communities, but also a more submerged and fragmented form of communication.

Social networks certainly played an important role in the recent move-ments for democracy in the Arabic countries. As Postill (2012) noted, 'the combination of a politicized pan-Arab TV network (Al Jazeera), widely available mobile phones with photo and video capabilities, and the rapid growth of social media such as Facebook and YouTube since 2009, has created a "new media ecology" that authoritarian regimes are finding very difficult to control'. The information cascade generated through the social media was impossible for the authorities to stop, as simultaneous and multi-channel feeds spread 'virally'.

The Arab Spring has been defined as being characterized by 'the instrumental use of social media, especially Facebook, Twitter, YouTube, and text messaging by protestors, to bring about political change and democratic transformation' (Khamis and Vaughn 2011, 1). New media facilitated the development of free spaces, networking and planning. They allowed 'citizen journalists' to document the protest activity as well as to denounce police repression. As an activist declared, 'To have a space, an online space, to write and talk [to] people, to give them mes-sages which will increase their anger, this is my favorite way of online activism. This is the way online activism contributed to the revolution. When you asked people to go and demonstrate against the police, they were ready because you had already provided them with materials which made them angry' (in Aouraght and Alexander 2011).

The technological support came from a rapidly increasing availability of new tools (in Egypt, there were at the time 23 million broadband Internet users and 80 per cent of families had mobile phones), as well as some freedom in using the media arena. While satellite television chan-nels had already introduced some media pluralism, the Internet allowed for broader – if not equal – citizen participation through peer-to-peer communication between users and online networking. In fact, here as elsewhere, most of the user-generated content spread through social media (Khamis and Vaughn 2011).

The role of new media was particularly relevant before and during the Egyptian uprising, when they enabled 'cyberactivism, which was a major trigger for street activism; encouraging civic engagement, through aiding the mobilization and organization of protests and other forms of political expression; and promoting a new form of citizen journalism, which provides a platform for ordinary citizens to express themselves and document their own versions of reality' (Khamis and Vaughn 2011).

Different new media were used in different ways. Facebook allowed for the spreading of information from (virtual) friend to (virtual) friend as it is a social network enabling the sending of messages to thousands of people, 'with the added benefit that those receiving the messages were already interested and trusted the source' (Idle and Nunns, 2011, 20).

'We Are All Khaled Said', founded by Google executive Wael Ghonim and named after a young Egyptian activist killed by the police, had a Facebook page with over 350,000 members already before 14 January 2011. The National Coalition for Change used Facebook, Twitter and YouTube to send text messages, such as 'Look what is happening in Tunisia.' As Ghonim invited 'We Are All Khaled Said' Facebook members to protest on 25 January, within three days more than 50,000 people responded that they would attend. Within Facebook, the April 6 Youth and the Kolona Khaled Said groups' pages, as well as pages of high-profile individuals (such as Mohamed al-Baradei, Aida Seif-al-Dawla or Hossam el-Hamalawy), not only were meeting points particularly instrumental in mobilizing youth, but also contributed to the circulation of many SMSs, e-mails, Tweets and Facebook posts (Aouraght and Alexander 2011, 1348). In a virtuous circle, the use of social media increased during the mobilization

> Facebook became something one had to have. Egypt gained more than 600,000 new Facebook users between January and February 2011 alone. On the day the Internet switched back on (February 2), 100,000 users joined this social networking space and it became the most accessed website in the country (followed by YouTube and Google), and aljazeera.net saw an incredible increase in page views and search attempts. (Aouraght and Alexander 2011, 1348)

The blogging service Twitter (with 175 million registered users in 2010) allowed participants to post their comments, and 'tweet' about specific subjects, including hashtags (such as #Jan25 for Egypt or #sidibouzid for Tunisia) that permitted launching as well as following protest events. In the very first week of the protest, as many as 1.5 million Egypt-related tweets were counted (Aouraght and Alexander 2011), in many case allowing for contacts between activists and foreign journalists (Lotan et al. 2011). The #Jan25 hash tag produced up to twenty-five tweets per minute during the day of the protest (2011).

Digitally encoded video, audio or text were uploaded onto the Internet, and were aggregated by topic and by type. YouTube, for instance, allowed people to upload user-created content, among which were amateur videos. Particularly influential was the call to action from a YouTube video posted by Asmaa Mahfouz that stated: 'If you stay home, you deserve all that's being done to you, and you will be guilty before your nation and your people. Go down to the street, send SMSes, post it on the 'Net, make people aware' (Wall and El Zahed 2011).

Materials produced by activists were also collected and made public. An activist recalled:

We built a media camp in Tahrir Square. It was two tents, and we were around five or six technical friends with their laptops, memory-readers, hard disks. We had all physical means with us and we hung a sign in Arabic and English on the tent itself saying, 'Focal point to gather videos and pictures from people in the street'. And we received a huge amount of videos and pictures and then we go back online and keep posting them online. In the first few hours, I gathered 75 gigabytes of pictures and videos from people in the streets. (in Aouraght and Alexander 2011)

Social media were also used to reduce the risks of repression (e.g. through the use of tools such as Hotspot Shield and Tor, which protect the anonymity of the user), and to spread information about how to improve security and calling for attention when in danger (Eltantawy and Wiest 2011, 1215). Creative responses were developed to the regime's ban on Internet and mobile phone access (from 28 January 2011 for about five days): by tweeting the Web sites of proxy servers; setting up FTP (file transfer protocol) accounts to transmit videos to international media; 'using landlines to connect to internet services in neighboring countries by calling international numbers with older dial-up modems'; even resorting 'to using Morse code, fax machines, and ham radio to get the word out about events on the ground'. The Web site of the group We Rebuild transcribed transmissions from Egyptian amateur radio stations; resources for circumventing the blackout were published; there was smuggling of 'satellite phones and satellite modems into Egypt, which did not depend on Egypt's infrastructure to function' (Khamis and Vaughn 2011). Blogs gave advice about how to use dial-up on mobile phones and laptops, also suggesting connecting to the Internet service provider Noor that was left operational as it was used by the Egyptian stock exchange and Western companies. To facilitate communication by protestors, some of its subscribers even removed their passwords for wi-fi access. When the Al Jazeera television channel in Cairo was closed down, people started watching Al Jazeera via Hotbird and Arabsat. Citizens also continued to tweet by calling friends abroad and asking them to tweet their messages or by using the 'speak to tweet' tool – provided by some engineers from Twitter, Google and SayNow – which transformed voice messages into Twitter messages (Eltantawy and Wiest 2011). With some irony, one blog stated: 'great news, blackout not affecting morale in Cairo, veteran activists from 60s and 70s living advice on how to do things predigital #Jan25' (Jamal 2012).

Thanks to the combination of old and new communications techniques, information overcame borders, as 'Egyptian activists were supported by the flow of information coming to them from abroad, while simultaneously influencing international public opinion abroad, through their own coverage of the Egyptian uprising and the information they provided on it'. When the mobilization began, messages from Tunisian protestors spread on the Egyptian blogs: they 'advised their Egyptian counterparts to protest at nighttime for safety, to avoid suicide operations, to use media to convey their message for outside pressure, to spray-paint security forces' armored vehicles black to cover the windshield, and to wash their faces with Coca-Cola to reduce the impact of tear gas' (Eltantawy and Wiest 2011). They also advised 'Put vinegar or onion under your scarf for tear gas', and brainstormed with their Egyptian counterparts on how to evade state surveillance, resist rubber bullets, and construct barricades (Khamis and Vaughn 2011).

Influenced by the Arab Spring, the protest of the Spanish *indignados* was also highly mediated. Not by chance, at its origin was the campaign No Les Votes (Don't Vote For Them) asking people not to vote for any of the three major parties responsible for a hotly contested bill accused of aiming at curtailing copyright infringement by Internet users, and of attacking digital freedom in favour of media lobbies (as documents published by WikiLeaks confirmed). Network organizations emerged during this campaign, among them Youth Without a Future (Juventud Sin Futuro) and Real Democracy Now! (Democracia Real Ya! DRY).

Following its roots in campaigns on media rights, the Spanish movement of the *indignados* showed strong skills in the use of new technologies. As Postill (2012) well described: 'The key role played in the inception and coordination of the movement by hackers, bloggers, micro-bloggers, technopreneurs and online activists is hard to overestimate.' In fact, 'What is striking about 15-M nanostories is how successfully leading activists used Twitter in the build-up towards the 15 May protests across Spain. By means of Twitter hashtags such as #15M or #15mani (#15mdemo), DRY supporters were able not only to rally protesters at short notice but also to set the changing political and emotional tone of the campaign.' In the words of two activists: '[T]he direction (el sentit) is created mostly on Twitter. Hashtags serve not only to organise the debate but also to set the collective mood: #wearenotgoing, #wearenotafraid, #fearlessbcn, #awakenedbarrios, #puigresignation, #15mmarcheson, #closetheparliament' (2012). Indeed, 'The nanostories being shared about specific protests or power abuses may be short-lived, but over time they add up to a powerful sense of common purpose amongst hundreds of thousands of people. Together, they form a grand narrative of popular struggle against a corrupt political and economic order.'

Postill's partial lists of media use that made the movement go viral included:

- Web forums, e.g. Burbuja.info had 17,000 posts by 20 May
- Blogs, e.g. top blogger Ignacio Escolar's received 10,000 visits per hour
- Collaborative documents such as manifestos, press releases and directories
- Pedagogical materials on Spain's electoral system
- Analogue versions of digital media forms, e.g. post-it tweets on square kiosks
- Cartoons published online as well as in print form
- Mainstream and alternative radio phone-ins
- Citizen photography, including Flickr group Spanish Revolution
- Videoclips, e.g. 40-second aerial view of Puerta del Sol by an independent media company viewed 275,000 times in less than 24 hours
- Live streaming by small alternative media
- Aggregators and link recommendation sites, especially Meneame, experienced unprecedented traffic growth
- Facebook – by 10 June the DRY Facebook group alone had 400,000 members
- Twitter users linked to 15-M numbered just over 2,000 users on 25 April and 4,544 users on 15 May; by 22 May this figure had expanded tenfold to 45,731. DRY had over 94,000 followers by 22 August. (2012)

There are nevertheless limits to the use of new media. First, new media are available for social movements, but also for their opponents. In reciprocal outbidding, the decentralized, 'leaderless' model of the Tea Party has been supported by the Internet. As a member said, 'I use the term open-source politics. This is an open source movement': open to constant modification (Rauch 2010, 1). This has been seen as an adaptation to Barack Obama's electoral campaign, combining skilful multichannel online reach, through Web sites, social media, political blogs, e-mails and mobile phones, for communication, fundraising and mobilization (Delany 2009). Additionally, regimes also adapt to new technologies, using them for control and repression. In particular, dictators learn from each other: what failed in authoritarian Egypt was, instead, successful in authoritarian Syria.

The logic of aggregation of masses of individuals in some public space, sometimes powerful, also has some shortcomings. As already observed about demonstrations called through mobile phones and social media – such as the protest in Spain after the terrorist attacks – mobilization can be very successful in terms of number, but tends to be more volatile and intermittent than in the past (Sampedro 2005). Mobilization through social media, moreover, implied until now mainly an alternative use of market-oriented platforms, which were built to make profit. The building of alternative platforms is still an ongoing challenge.

Conclusion

Democracy, media and social movement are closely interlinked. While the commercialization of mass media is seen as reducing space for pluralism, as well as for the voice of less powerful groups, research on social movements' media stresses their capacity to spread alternative information. They are vital, in fact, for that 'counterdemocracy' which allows for control of the governors, but also to improve chances of participation and deliberation as well. Social movements have shown much creativity in the use of new communications technology, exploiting the chance of reduced costs and global reach. Quickly changing technologies present opportunities, but also challenges, for democracy, as they influence modes of participation. This is the case, for instance, with the adding of Web 0.2 social media to the existing Internet instruments provided by the Web 0.1, which has created the potential for fast mobilization of individuals, offering instruments for improving internal democracy, but needs to be integrated with other instruments of communication, both during the peak of mobilization and during its decline. The impact of technologies is in fact filtered through normative conceptions of democracy.

6

The Challenge of
Global Governance

*During a speech at the European University Institute on 11 November
2011, Herman van Rompuy, president of the European Council, after
declaring that Italy 'needs reforms, not elections', presented his conception of democracy thus: 'There is the time of parliamentary democracies: of legislative procedures, of votes, the work to get a
majority.... There also is the time of public opinion, which needs to
be convinced, taken along a road. There finally is the time of implementation, of executing the measures once they are agreed.' Ph.D.
students from all over Europe showed posters with 'Democracy?'
written on them. In a document they distributed they charged that
'the office of President of the European Council is the symbolic incar-
nation of the ever more blatant, democratic deficit at the heart of the
European Union. The unelected and unaccountable head of a European people whose popular consent in the appointment was deemed
superfluous...However, the crisis of democracy in the European
Union is much more insidious than the simple appointment of a
presidential figure head. The undemocratic ethos has infiltrated the
very structures of the Union, evident in its consistent disregard for
the expressed popular will of its citizens. As the EU becomes ever less
accountable to the people of Europe, it has hastened its drift away
from its core founding values.' This deficit notwithstanding, they
declared: 'we are of the view that another Europe is possible...Our
Europe can and will once again be rooted in its founding values of
human dignity, freedom, equality and solidarity, constructed upon and
protected by accountable and truly democratic political institutions.'
Among their '95 theses', two read as follows: 'No common currency*

without a common democracy!' and 'You can't balance the budget with a democratic deficit!'

This is just a recent, quite vivid, illustration of how the debate on the financial crisis and ways to address it is, in Europe as in the American occupied parks and squares, intertwined with that on the competing visions of democracy, their forms and legitimation. Attention to participation and deliberation, as well as to the role of 'counter-democracy' emerges as particularly relevant in the social science reflection on global democracy. A development of democracy at the transnational level emerges as all the more urgent, as the international system based on sovereign nation states seems to have evolved into a political system composed of overlapping multi-level authorities with little functional differentiation and scant democratic legitimacy. While 'the discovering of interdependence reduces sovereignty' (Badie 1999, 297), globalization brings about a 'transnationalization' of political relationships. If the national political context still cushions the impact of international shifts on national politics, growing economic interdependence goes hand in hand with a significant internationalization of public authority associated with a corresponding globalization of political activity (Held and McGrew 2007). Globalization has indeed increased the awareness of 'global commons' that cannot be defended only at the national level, and undermined a hierarchical model based on territorial control (Badie 1999, 301). While the liberal democracy model is challenged by the shift of power towards electorally unaccountable bodies, the extent to which participatory and deliberative models of democracy are able to incorporate a transnational dimension is a question I am going to discuss in this chapter.

Globalization and democratic deficit: an introduction

The effects of globalization on democracy are ambiguous at the very least. As Dryzek (2010, 120) noted:

Political theory in general has long proceeded on the assumption that the main locus of political authority demanding attention is the sovereign state. Democratic theorists have generally concurred, specifying in addition that the state must be accompanied by a well-defined demos, the people in whose name rule is exercised... Yet this image captures only a subset of politics in today's world. Arguably this subset is declining.

In fact, international organizations have contributed to the spread of international regulations and norms that in some cases supersede national sovereignty. As has often been pointed out, 'no official authority controls states in the contemporary world system, but many are subject to powerful unofficial forces, pressures and influences that penetrate the supposed hard shell of the state' (Russett and Starr 1996, 62). On the other hand, this new situation has contributed to the creation of supranational norms that, in the case of human rights, support the defence of some citizens' rights, especially against authoritarian regimes.

If global governance implies the development of global norms, the area covered by international public law is, however, still limited; particularly in the economic sphere, a private law based on contracts proliferated. Law in the European tradition is seen as command of political power; the international juridical order is instead based on the privatistic logic of the contract (Ferrarese 2000; see also Allegretti 2002). A new *lex mercatoria* emerged with the increasing role of law firms specializing in corporate law, but also with societies for bond rating and debt security, arbitration and similar methods of dispute resolution (Sassen 2001). Growing numbers of lawmakers implies opacity of rules, with the development of a law *à la carte* designed around the global firms' needs (Delazay and Garth 1996). In this transnational private legal regime, norms are reactive, ad hoc, often unwritten and always negotiated (Ferrarese 2000, 138). Globalization implies, therefore, an increasing fragmentation and opacity of sovereign power with alternative legalities, either overlapping, complementary or antagonistic (Beck 1999). The power delegated to rating agencies and their lack of transparency is at the centre of the debate on the political responsibility for the financial crisis.

The debate on global democracy started with the observation of a lack of democratic accountability and even transparency in many intergovernmental organizations (IGOs) with competences extending beyond the negotiation of treaties. In parallel to the acquisition of power by numerous IGOs, criticism centred on the manifest deficit of democracy that characterizes these organisms which are mainly non-elective and un-transparent in their way of functioning (Held and McGrew 2007). In Europe the era of 'permissive consensus' on the EU appears to have ended, given an increasingly demanding public opinion. The growing tendency of national governments to justify unpopular decisions such as budget cuts as following from restrictions imposed by the process of European integration has increased the critical attention paid to choices made by European institutions. The conflict over European integration has been described as a 'sleeping giant', still mainly unstructured within party systems but ready to explode when political entrepreneurs are ready to come forward and represent it. Although 'at the moment in most countries the electorate is willing to freeze their preferences with regard to the EU, and choose parties on the basis of other considerations', the question has been asked of 'how long this can last' (Franklin and van der Eijk 2004, 47). In fact, in many European countries, opposition to integration has been channeled through euro-sceptic parties of different strengths, and made visible especially during the referendums on the EU Constitutional Treaty (della Porta and Caiani 2009).

Even less democratic legitimacy has been accorded to those informal networks that, like the G7, the G8 or the G9, link together those states that consider themselves to be superior in terms of economic and other powers. Especially criticized has been the self-referentiality of these nets, as well as their capacity to strengthen the power of the few over the many, militarily and/or economically dependent countries. Strong criticism was also addressed to the international financial institutions like the WB, the IMF and the WTO, accused of implementing neoliberal policies to the advantage of some powerful states thanks to their increasing power.

Not only the lack of elected officials, but also the unequal power of the states in some IGOs has been critically discussed. In the United Nations, the role of the superpowers is evident in the Security Council and the veto power recognized for some states; as for the WB, the five largest shareholders (the USA, Japan, Germany, France and the UK) appoint an executive director each. In the WB and IMF, the influence of the most powerful countries is recognized according to the principle 'one dollar, one vote'.[1] The many economic crises of the last decade have also shaken the legitimation of institutions whose aim is to promote economic and social development; for example, the fact that as many as fifty countries remained for twenty years clients of the IMF and WB does not reflect output success (Mueller 2002, 113).

In international relations, important steps have been taken towards recognizing the political nature of the international politics of states as well as international organizations. First, constructivist approaches challenged the idea that states act on their inherent interests, focusing on the many ways in which interests (as identities) are indeed constructed. Recent attempts to go beyond (rigid) perspectives towards eclectic ones recognize the need to investigate empirically the actual relevance of material interests, norms, and perceptions thereof (Sil and Katzenstein 2010). Those who have brought the transnational dimension back into international relations have also pointed at the complexity of international decisions that involve not just states, but also interest organizations and principled actors (Risse, Ropp and Sikkink 1999).

What is more, a debate on the politicization of international organizations has developed from the observation that, especially since the 1980s, the Westphalian principle of national sovereignty has been challenged: 'In addition to violations by major powers, international institutions have developed procedures that contradict the consensus principle and the principle of non-intervention. Some international norms and rules create obligations for national governments to take measures even when they have not agreed to do so. Moreover, in some cases, decisions of international institutions even affect individuals directly' (Zürn, Binder and Ecker-Ehrhardt 2010, 2). The politicization of the discourse on international organizations is indeed reflected in a growing attention to their democratization: while 'until twenty years ago, very few international relations textbooks paid any attention to the problem of democracy across borders.... Over the past twenty years, the intellectual landscape has changed considerably' (Archibugi, Konig-Archibugi and Marchetti 2011, 1).

A main challenge for global democracy is in the construction of global identities and global institutions. Normative theories of democracy reflect in particular on the changing definition of 'relevant political communities'. If, in a communitarian approach, democracy is seen as difficult to apply in culturally heterogeneous communities (Archibugi 1998, 206), for others the weakening of the reference to a 'pre-political community of shared destiny' makes political participation all the more important. In Habermas' words, in postnational constellations 'the strength of the democratic constitutional states lies precisely in its ability to close the holes of social integration through the political participation of its citizens...Basic human rights, and rights to political participation, constitute a self-referential model of citizenship, insofar as they enable democratically united citizens to shape their own status legislatively' (Habermas 2001, 76–7).

Building democratic institutions is also difficult as, many believe, 'the liberal democratic state does not provide any applicable model for global democracy' (Dryzek 2010, 177). Common to reflections on global democracy is 'the vision of a system of global governance that is responsive and accountable to the preferences of the world's citizens and works to reduce political inequalities among them' (Archibugi, Konig-Archibugi and Marchetti 2011, 6). While one can agree that 'either democracy is global or it is not democracy' (Marchetti 2008, 1), the search for institutional reforms with a view to a democratization of supranational institutions is still at an initial stage. The understanding of what global democracy should be changes, moreover, in different theorizations, which stress either liberal, participatory or deliberative qualities.

Three ideal types have in fact to be distinguished (2008). *Confederalist* views rely on democracy inside each state and maintain the right of each government, democratically elected, to represent its citizens when voluntarily participating in international organizations. *Polycentric* views see a multilevel system of global governance with institutions accountable to the specific stake-holders that are affected by their decisions (Macdonald 2008). Criticizing the stake-holder approach from normative (as in democracy all citizens express their views on all issues) and empirical (as it is impossible to define who has a stake and who not in complex systems of government) points of view, *federalist* views defend instead the right of world citizens to be represented as such in international organizations of world government directly (Archibugi, Koenig-Archibugi and Marchetti 2011, 7–9). The inclusion of all citizens of the world, regardless of whether they are directly affected by the decision made, is a main principle in this view of democracy, that stresses, in fact, participatory qualities (Marchetti 2011). Similarly, the normative proposal developed around the concept of 'cosmopolitan democracy' postulates a direct participation of citizens in institutions of global democracy (Archibugi, Held and Koehler 1998, 4). Cosmopolitan democracy implies, in fact:

> the development of administrative capacity and independent political resources at regional and global levels as a necessary complement to those in local and national politics...A cosmopolitan democracy would not call for a diminution per se of state power and capacity across the globe. Rather it would seek to entrench and develop democratic institutions at regional and global levels as a necessary complement to those at the level of the nation-state. (Held 1998, 24)

As a project oriented to the development of democracy within and among states, but also at the global level, federal visions of global democracy imply the existence of global institutions where citizens are seen as individual 'inhabitants of the world' rather than as part of a nation state. The basic assumption is that 'if some global questions are to be handled according to democratic criteria, there must be political representation for citizens in global affairs, independently and autonomously of their political representation in domestic affairs' (Archibugi 1998, 211–12). Global institutions should therefore enable 'the voice of individuals to be heard in global affairs, irrespective of their resonance at home' (Archibugi 2003, 8).

Numerous theorists therefore suggest that a global democracy requires democratic states, but also democratic supranational institutions. Proposals for short-term reforms of existing international organizations include the reorganization of leading UN institutions such as the Security Council, in order to increase the power of developing countries; the creation of a second UN chamber; the use of transnational referendums; compulsory submission to the jurisdiction of an International Human

Rights Court; and the establishment of an effective and accountable international military force. Other proposals have addressed the presence in the UN General Assembly of delegates of both national governments and opposition groups, as well as directly elected delegates; limitation or abolition of veto power; opening to regional organizations; a consultative vote for representatives of NGOs; and an elective parliamentary assembly with consultative power (Archibugi 1998, 221). The subordination of international financial institutions to the UN General Assembly has been suggested as a way to make them more transparent and accountable, as well as the reform of IGOs on the basis of 'one state, one vote'. In the long term, proposed reforms include the creation of a global parliament, the strengthening of international legal systems embracing criminal and civil laws, and a Charter of global rights and obligations (Held 1998, 25).

The federalist conception of global democracy stresses even more the need to maximize citizens' participation at all different layers of political decision making as the only way to overcome 'the crucial pathology of political exclusion', by addressing especially transnational exclusion (Marchetti 2008, 2). In systems that attenuate the links between the decision makers and those who bear the costs of those decisions, citizens' participation in institutions of global democracy reflects not only the fundamental notion of democratic inclusion of choice-bearers in the control of choice-makers, but also notions of interaction-dependent justice (2008, 21ff.). Pointing at the need for a deliberative reform, Dryzek (2010, 124) suggested the creation of a mini-public at global level as a solution that would overcome the objective difficulty in electing a global parliament, developing a post-Westphalian, post-liberal and post-electoral thinking. In his proposal, he stresses discursive representation as more easily obtained at global level than representing persons through elections (2010, 192).

These proposals may appear too moderate to some, too utopist to others; they signal, however, the perceived need to respond to the challenges of globalization with a democratization of international institutions. More generally, they indicate that the economic, cultural, and social processes of globalization produce political conflicts whose outcomes will affect the legitimacy and efficacy of democratic institutions.

A global civil society?

Beyond institutional reforms, the weaknesses of liberal democracy at supranational level make the building of spaces for participatory and deliberative democracy all the more urgent. Civil society organizations have played an important role of control and advocacy. In a more and more politicized system of international relations, criticism of neoliberal forms of globalization and demands for 'another globalization' entered the mass-media public sphere, especially with the protests against the WTO summit in 1999 – as the American weekly *Newsweek* wrote (13 December 1999, 36), 'one of the most important lessons of Seattle is that there are now two visions of globalization on offer, one led by commerce, one by social activism'.

The globalization processes in economics, culture and politics have been reflected in the emergence of a global civic society – a much-used and much-debated term to indicate a civil society that 'increasingly represents itself globally, across nation-state boundaries, through the formation of global institutions' (Shaw 1994, 650; see also Anheier, Glasius and Kaldor 2001). Part of the global civil society, formal international non-governmental organizations (INGOs) have grown in numbers, members and availability of material resources. The same can be said of transnational social movement organizations (TSMOs), a term coined to define transnational organizations active, often through protest, within networks of social movements. While social movements developed with the growth of national politics, the formation of TSMOs has been seen as a response to the growing institutionalization of international politics (Smith 1995, 190).

From the beginning of the twentieth century to its end, the number of INGOs grew from 176 in 1909 to 15,965 in 1997 (Deutscher Bundestag 2002, 427; Princen and Finger 1994, 1; cf. also Held and McGrew 2007, 35). Some of them have been highlighted as having not only increased their membership, but also strengthened their influence in various stages of international policy making (Sikkink and Smith 2002). Their assets include their increasing credibility in public opinion and consequent availability of private funding, as well as their rootedness at the local level. Their specific knowledge, combined with useful contacts in the press, make many INGOs seem particularly reliable sources of information. With a professional staff on hand, they are also able to maintain a fair level of activity even when protest mobilization is low. Independence from governments, combined with a reputation built upon solid work at the local level, enables some INGOs to perform an important role in mediating inter-ethnic conflict. They may not only contribute to broadening participation in global policy making, but also improve the accountability of powerful global actors. Additionally, 'the deliberative qualities of global civil society actors may contribute to the emergence of a global public sphere' (Tallberg and Uhlin 2011, 212).

Civil society organizations are said to perform their functions, in part at least, through participation in international policy making. In particular in the UN, the number of INGOs with consultative status increased from 41 in 1948 to about 2,870 today (2011, 215). United Nations conferences on issues such as environment, development or gender rights have seen much participation 'from below'. Even traditionally closed international organizations, such as the WTO, now accept NGOs as observers (more than 700 participating in its ministerial conference in 2005). Besides their consultative role, civil society organizations are also important in the implementation of decisions. So, for instance, the percentage of projects financed by the WB involving civil society organizations grew from 21 per cent in 1990 to 72 per cent in 2006 (2011, 215).

The debate on the democratic qualities and effective influence of a global civil society is, however, still open. Many INGOs are in fact considered as not really autonomous from their own governments and/or donors, elitist and hierarchical in their internal organization, ineffective and too tamed in their intervention (see, e.g., Betsill and Corell 2008; Steffen, Kissling and Nanz 2008; Scholte 2011). The global civil society has been defined as stemming from the taming process of the social movements of the pre-1989 period as well as the decline of old civic associations (such as unions) and the transformation of the former into NGOs: professionalized, institutionalized and organized around particular causes (Kaldor 2003). Especially since the 1980s, transnational social movement organizations developed, in part due to disillusionment with the effects of moderate strategies, and adopted more contentious attitudes. Here as well, however, doubts about the extent to which they are really cosmopolitan have been expressed, and their (Western-centred) ethnocentrism, and also their single-issue nature, have been critically noted.

Social movements and global democracy

Faced with transformation in the relations between different territorial levels of power, recent waves of protest on global issues have been interpreted as reflecting the 'politicization' of a supranational level of governance, which had traditionally been conceived (if considered) as highly technical and legitimated 'by the output' (della Porta 2009a and 2009b). Moreover, they emerged from the disappointment with previous, tamed forms of mobilization at transnational level.

In various ways, international organizations have provided opportunities for the development of transnational networks of protest and global frames, acting, as Sidney Tarrow (2005) suggested, as a coral reef for movements beyond borders (see also della Porta and Caiani 2009). While some of them (especially the international financial institutions) have been seen as main targets for protest, others, however contested, have also offered some discursive and political opportunities to social movement organizations. The latter, in their turn, became active in the democratization of international organizations and politics, first of all by practising a democratic surveillance on their actions, but also by developing specific criticisms of their democratic deficit and proposals for reform.

This is particularly visible in the debate on one of the most powerful and most contested of the international organizations: the EU. The qualitative analysis of the organizational documents of about 250 social movement organizations involved in the European Social Forum (ESF) points at some main elements of criticism and, sometimes, proposals for democratization of public institutions (della Porta 2009a and 2009b).

A general complaint by the activists of the ESF is that the EU uses its competences on market competition and free trade to impose neoliberal economic policies, while the restrictive budgetary policies set by the Maastricht parameters are stigmatized as jeopardizing welfare policies. The privatization of public services and increasing flexibility of labour are criticized as worsening citizens' wellbeing and job security. Under the slogan 'Another Europe is possible', various proposals were tabled at the first ESF, including 'taxation of capital' and a Tobin Tax on financial transactions. In particular, the proposed Constitutional Treaty was feared as the 'constitutionalization of neoliberalism'. A participant at the seminar 'For a democratic Europe, a Europe of rights and citizenship', held during an ESF, claimed that 'everything is subordinated to competition, including public services, the relations with the DOM-TOM [Domaines d'outre mer, Territoires d'outre mer], and the flow of capital (something that, by the way, makes any Tobin Tax impossible)'.

Criticisms of the conceptions of democracy at EU level also address security policies, with a call for a Europe of freedoms and justice as opposed to a Europe 'sécuritaire et policière'. At the first ESF, the EU stance on foreign policy was considered to be subordinate to the US, environmental issues as dominated by the environmental-unfriendly demands of corporations, and migration policy as oriented towards building a xenophobic 'Fortress Europe'. In particular, EU legislation on terrorism was criticized as criminalizing such categories as the young, refugees and Muslims. EU immigration policies were defined as obsessed with issues of security and demographic needs. Activists from solidarity groups denounced the role of European states and corporations in Haiti, Latin America and Africa, and expressed disapproval of aggressive EU trade policies and asymmetric negotiation of commercial treaties. In terms of defence policies, proposals tabled during the second ESF range from 'a Europe without NATO, EU and US army bases' to multilateralism, from the refusal of a nuclear Europe to provision of more resources to the UN and the request for inclusion in the Constitution of the refusal of war as an instrument of conflict resolution

Beyond concrete policy choices, criticisms are also addressed at the secretive, top-down ways in which these policies are decided. In particular, the activists criticize the lack of democratic accountability: while decisions move up to higher levels, 'at the local level we have very little influence on the decision-making process, but our influence becomes null when it comes to questions such as the European constitution or the directives of the WTO or the IMF. We are even criminalized when we attempt it.' The Assembly of social movements at the third ESF asked for, among other things, more participation 'from below' in the construction of 'another Europe':

> At a time when the draft of the European Constitutional treaty is about to be ratified, we must state that the peoples of Europe need to be consulted directly. The draft does not meet our aspirations. This constitutional treaty consecrates neo-liberalism as the official doctrine of the EU; it makes competition the basis for European community law, and indeed for all human activity; it completely ignores the objectives of an ecologically sustainable society. This constitutional treaty does not grant equal rights, the free movement of people and citizenship for everyone in the country they live in, whatever their nationality; it gives NATO a role in European foreign policy and defence, and pushes for the militarization of the EU. Finally it puts the market first by marginalizing the social sphere, and hence accelerating the destruction of public services.

Similarly, groups like Attac criticized the democratic deficit, linked to the lack of parliamentary control over the executive, but also promoted a 'democratic constitutive European process that starts from the peoples', rejecting the 'neoliberal process of a Europe of the powerful and the governments' (*Il movimento e la politica*, 17 October 2003).

In sum, social movement organizations have expressed concerns about the accountability of international organizations. Their lack of transparency, the internal inequalities among states, as well as the lack of citizens' involvement have been criticized. At the same time, however, there has been an interest by those very organizations in the construction of institutions of global governance, perceived as indispensable for controlling the negative effects of economic globalization.

The orientation towards strengthening the institutions of global governance, but at the same time democratizing them, is in fact especially visible in the attitudes towards the UN or the EU. In particular, the international campaign 'Reclaim our UN' promotes a reform of that

institution, based upon values of multilateralism, international cooperation, strengthening of international law, creation of democratic international institutions, subordination of the international financial institutions
to the UN, extended competences for the International Court of Justice,
establishment of an international judiciary police, development of world
citizenship with 'responsible participation of every citizen within a grassroots globalization', and increased access for the civil society to decision-
making institutions. If this trust in the 'reformability' of the UN is not
shared by all the groups I have analysed, there is a widespread demand
for transnational governance of economic processes and a return to
politics as opposed to the dominance of the market.

Similarly, institutions of macro-regional governance – among them the
EU – are considered to be necessary in order to reduce the damage from
economic globalization. So, for instance, the Seattle to Brussels Network,
after denouncing the undemocratic nature of EU decision making on
trade ('EU trade policy-making...is opaque, non transparent and deeply
undemocratic': European NGO Statement: 12 key demands to the EU in
the run-up to the 6th WTO Ministerial Conference), asked the EU to
'promote enhanced transparency and democratic participation and
accountability in EU trade policy making', including consultations with
parliaments and civil society groups (cited in Zola and Marchetti 2006).
At the same time, calls for the defence of a European social model as an
alternative to the American one are voiced, especially by trade unions
(see Reiter 2006, 249). Typically, Attac promoted a social Europe, a
Europe of civic and social rights for all residents, a Europe of the citizens,
a Europe that promotes peace – as opposed to a Europe of the market, of
trade, of the elites, of the governments, undemocratic, subject to the US.

Although critical of existing institutions, the global justice movement
seemed, however, aware of the need for supranational (macro-regional
and/or global) institutions of governance. At one of the plenary assemblies of the second ESF, Italian activist Franco Russo stated: 'There is a
real desire for Europe...but not for any Europe. The European citizens
ask for a Europe of rights: social, environmental and peaceful. But does
this Constitution respond to our desire for Europe?'

The image of 'another Europe' (instead of 'no Europe') is often stressed
in the debates. During the second ESF, the Assembly of the Unemployed
and Precarious Workers in Struggle stated that 'For the European Union,
Europe is only a large free-exchange area. We want a Europe based on
democracy, citizenship, equality, peace, a job and revenue in order to
live. Another Europe for another World'. In this vision, the building of
'another Europe imposes putting the democratic transformation of
institutions at the centre of elaboration and mobilization. We can,
we should have great political ambition for Europe... *Cessons de*

subir l'Europe: prenons la en mains' (http://workspace.fse-esf.org/mem/
Act2223, accessed 20 December 2006). Unions and other groups active
on public services proclaimed 'the European level as the pertinent level
of resistance', against, among other issues, national decisions to cut
services and subsidies. The 'No to the Constitutional draft' is combined
with demands for a 'legitimate European constitution', produced through
a public consultation, 'a European constitution constructed from below'.
And many agree that 'the Europe we have to build is a Europe of rights,
and participatory democracy is its engine'. In this vision, 'the European
Social Forum constitutes the peoples as constitutional power, the only
legitimate power'.

Social movement organizations in the ESF thus perceived their role as
important in the creation of a European public space. Criticizing the
failure of the Convention for the Constitutional Treaty to involve (at
least part of) the civil society, the Italian Attac declared that:

> In the last two years a new public sphere was born in Europe; it has
> been promoted not by the consensus-hunters sent by the commission
> to look for some dialogue with the civil society, but by the oppositional
> movements....It would be a mistake, however, if, faced with the
> myopia of the European governments and their frequent factual con-
> nivance with imperial policies, one were to look back, feeding the
> illusion that the nation states are the terrain on which the movement
> can develop its democratic instances. (*La Convenzione Europea e i
> movimenti sociali*, 20/11/2002)

Even the most critical organizations called for 'another Europe', constituting free space where the issues of what Europe is, and of what it
should be, are discussed. Among them, EuroMayDay proclaimed: 'We
are eurogeneration insurgents: our idea of Europe is a radical, libertarian,
transnationalist, antidystopian, open democratic space able to counter
global bushism and oppressive, exploitative, powermad, planetwrecking,
warmongering neoliberalism in Europe and elsewhere. Networkers and
Flextimers of Europe unite! There's a world of real freedom to fight for'
(EuroMayDay 2004). Also the ESFs have been spaces where ideas of
'another Europe' have developed. This is well illustrated by the Declaration of the Assembly of the Movements of the Fourth European Social
Forum (ESF) in Athens on 7 May 2006, which stated: 'We reject this
neo-liberal Europe and any efforts to re-launch the rejected Constitutional Treaty; we are fighting for another Europe, a feminist, ecological,
open Europe, a Europe of peace, social justice, sustainable life, food
sovereignty and solidarity, respecting minorities' rights and the self-
determination of all peoples.'

Concrete proposals to improve the quality of democracy at EU level were in fact developed during the ESF. They ranged from the establishment of an annual day of action devoted to media democracy to the building of alternative media (workshop titled 'Reclaim the Channels of Information: Media Campaigns and Media Protest'), from the reduction of import taxes on medicines to an increase in the use of unconventional medicines (seminar on 'Health in Europe: Equity and Access'), from the introduction of the right to asylum in the European constitution to the regularization of all undocumented migrants (workshop on 'Right to Migrate, Right to Asylum'); from a European social charter that recognizes the right to decent housing to the occupation of empty buildings (workshop on 'Housing Rights in Europe: Towards a Trans-European Network of Struggles and Alternatives'); from the dialogue with local authorities to participation of the people in international experiences of cooperation (workshop on 'Decentralized Cooperation: A Dialogue between Territories as a Response to Global Challenges'); from quality control on hard drugs to the liberalization of soft ones (workshop on 'Perfect Enemies: the Penal Governance of Poverty and Differences').

Countersummits and ESFs have certainly networked a broad set of organizations and individuals that expressed dissatisfaction with European institutions. Especially after the French constitutional referendums, the position of movement organizations such as Attac has been highlighted as a sign of the (re)emergence of a left-wing-leaning Euroscepticism, after years in which research after research had noted more support for the EU on the left than on the right end of the political spectrum. These criticisms did not, however, imply a call to go back to the nation state. First, the social movement criticisms addressed not the existence of an EU level of governance but more specific policy choices and different aspects of the democratic deficit. What is more, the very fact of organizing at the EU level, instrumentally oriented at first, has contributed to the development of European identity and, indirectly, promoted critical Europeanization. In this sense, protest such as the EU countersummits and the ESFs had a strong cognitive and affective impact.

In the course of the countersummits, alongside an increase in the number of organizations involved and the structuring of the protest network, the definition of what was at stake also evolved: from an initial focus upon unemployment to a broader range of EU policies, and participation of activists from various movements. This shift accompanied the development of a European identity that the various ESFs contributed to strengthening. The analyses of the ESFs have in fact shown the emergence of a European social movement that is innovative in terms of the development of identity, strategies and organizational structure that go beyond the boundaries of the nation states, addressing the institutions of the multilevel European governance. Although critical of the European institutions, activists promoted, through their action and campaigns, a European identity.

Social movement activists as critical cosmopolitans

Similar tensions between the criticism of existing EU institutions and the perceived need to create supranational levels of governance emerge also from the analysis of surveys of activists at transnational protest events. Among those who protested against the G8 in Genoa, trust in representative institutions tended to be low, with, however, significant differences regarding institutions at different territorial levels (see also della Porta et al. 2006). In general, some international organizations (especially the EU and the United Nations) were seen by activists as more worthy of respect than their national governments, but less so than local bodies. Research on the activists at the first ESF confirmed that mistrust of the institutions of liberal democracy was spread cross-nationally, although particularly pronounced where national governments were either right-wing (Italy and Spain at the time), or perceived as hostile to the claims of the global justice movement (as in the UK). Not even national parliaments, supposedly the main instrument of representative democracy, were trusted, while there was markedly greater trust in local bodies (especially in Italy and France), and, albeit to a somewhat lower degree, in the United Nations. The EU scored a trust level among activists which is barely higher than that for national governments. Similar data on the second and the fourth ESF confirm the general mistrust in representative democratic institutions, especially in national governments, followed by the EU and then the UN, with some more trust in local institutions (much less, however than in the first and second ESF), although with some qualification (della Porta 2007). Among other actors and institutions, we notice a very low level of trust in the church and mass media, as well as in the unions in general (considering the type of demonstrator), and a similarly low trust in the judiciary and (even lower) in political parties (table 6.1). Activists continue to trust social movements instead (and, a bit less, NGOs) as actors in a democracy from below. In sum, in seeking 'another Europe', one central feature is mistrust of parties and representative institutions. The common location of activists on the left of the political spectrum is blended with a high interest in politics, defined as politics 'from below', but mistrust in the actors in institutional politics. It should be noted that mistrust is higher among the activists surveyed in 2006 than among those surveyed in 2002 and 2003.

Table 6.1   Trust in institutions among ESF participants in Florence, Paris, and Athens (valid cases only)

Type of institution*	Florence 2002		Paris 2003		Athens 2006	
	%	N	%	N	%	N
Local institutions	46.1	2365	43.1	2034	26.6	1122
National government	6.1	2451	11.6	1997	11.5	1126
National parliament	14.9	2428	–	–	20.5	1130
European Union	26.9	2444	17.3	2002	14.5	1141
United Nations	29.6	2444	31.7	1985	18.1	1136
Political parties	20.4	2423	23.0	2007	21.2	1120
Unions	16.1**	**	57.5	2025	49.0	1122
Social movements	–	–	90.0	2067	85.7	1139
NGOs	–	–	77.3	2002	66.8	1132
Both the above	89.4	2464	–	–	–	–
Church	17.2	2441	15.5	1987	9.1	1135
Mass media	12.4	2449	9.3	2010	3.9	1142
Judiciary	36.7	2429	–	–	33.8	1136
Police	7.3	2454	–	–	10.7	1132

*The degree of trust was translated into a dichotomous variable in the following way: 'not at all' and 'little' = 'no'; 'a fair amount' and 'a lot' = 'yes'.
** The data refer to respondents to the non-Italian survey, N = 417. In the Italian version respondents were asked about their trust in specific unions, with the following results: trust in Cisl/Uil: N = 229, 8.9%; trust in Cgil: N = 1104, 42.8%; trust in grass-roots trade unions N = 990, 38.4%.
Source: della Porta 2009a, 89

Activists present at the various ESFs were in fact critical of EU politics and policies. At the first ESF, interviewees from different countries stated that the European Union strengthens neoliberal globalization and were sceptical about the capacity of the EU to mitigate the negative effects of globalization and safeguard a different social model of welfare (table 6.2). While Italians expressed greater trust in the EU, and British activists were more sceptic (followed by the French and Spanish activists), the differences were, however, altogether small. Comparing the distributions on these items of the Italians at the ESF in 2002 with those of the anti-Bolkestein marchers in Rome we can see that opinions remained stable, and constantly pessimistic.

When moving from the assessment of existing institutions to the imagined ones, the activists of the first ESF expressed, however, strong interest in the building of new institutions of world governance: 70 per

Table 6.2 'How much do you agree with the following statements?' (equilibrated sample)

	Italy	France	Germany	Spain	UK	Total ESF	Rome 2005
(a) The European Union attempts to safeguard a social model that is different from the neoliberal one							
not at all	46.7	50.7	47.4	51.4	68.3	53.7	42.4
a little	43.7	35.8	43.6	38.5	26.1	36.8	37.7
some	8.9	8.2	7.7	6.4	4.2	7.0	11.7
very much	0.7	5.2	1.3	3.7	1.4	2.5	4.0
Total	100%	100%	100%	100%	100%	100%	100%
N	135	134	78	109	142	598	410
(b) The European Union mitigates the most negative effects of neoliberal globalization							
not at all	31.7	50.0	29.7	44.0	59.4	44.4	41.8
a little	51.1	27.9	48.6	40.4	21.7	36.6	40.5
some	15.1	13.2	14.9	10.1	5.6	11.5	11.7
very much	2.2	8.8	6.8	5.5	13.3	7.5	1.5
Total	100%	100%	100%	100%	100%	100%	100%
N	139	136	74	109	143	601	410
(c) The European Union strengthens neoliberal globalization							
not at all	3.6	3.0	2.4	1.5	6.1	3.6	4.6
a little	18.7	6.0	4.9	6.3	5.4	8.6	11.8
some	43.2	32.8	35.4	38.7	15.0	32.3	31.7
very much	34.5	58.2	57.3	53.2	73.5	55.5	48.2
Total	100%	100%	100%	100%	100%	100%	100%
N	139	134	82	111	147	613	410

Source: della Porta 2009a, 92

cent of the respondents were quite or very much in favour of this, including strengthening the United Nations, an option supported by about half our sample (table 6.3). Furthermore, about one-third of activists agreed that, in order to achieve the goals of the movement, a stronger EU and/or other macro-regional institutions were necessary (with higher support for the EU among Italian activists, and very low support among the British activists). Respondents in Athens in 2006 confirmed a widely shared scepticism that strengthening the national governments would help in achieving the goals of the movement (only about a quarter of the activists responded positively). Between the first and the fourth ESF the belief in the need for building (alternative) institutions of world governance became almost unanimous (93 per cent of the respondents), with instead a lower per cent in Athens in support of a strengthening of the EU (from 43 per cent to 35 per cent) and/or the UN (from 57 per cent to 48 per cent).

The activists at the first ESF expressed also quite a high level of affective identification with Europe: only 18 per cent felt not at all attached, 34 per cent felt little attached, 37 per cent moderately and 11 per cent very much. This means that about half of the activists

Table 6.3 *Opinion of ESF participants in Florence and Athens about which institutions should be strengthened to achieve global social movements' goals (valid cases)* *

Type of institution* *	Florence 2002		Athens 2006	
	%	N	%	N
National governments	22.0	2362	25.6	1066
European Union***	43.2	2383	34.9	1073
United Nations	56.6	2405	48.4	1056
Institutions of world governance to be built****	64.6	2400	92.5	1127

*Question in the Florence questionnaire: 'In your opinion, to achieve the goals of the movement it would be necessary to strengthen...'; question in the Athens questionnaire: 'In your opinion, what should be done to tame neoliberal globalization? Strengthen...'.
**The level of disagreement/agreement was translated into a dichotomous variable in the following way: 'strongly disagree' and 'disagree' = 'no'; 'agree' and 'strongly agree' = 'yes'.
***The Florence questionnaire asked for the strengthening of EU or other international supranational institutions.
****The Athens questionnaire asked about the building of new institutions that involve the civil society on the international level; the Florence questionnaire asked about the building of new institutions of world governance.
Source: della Porta 2009a, 94

felt a moderate or strong attachment to Europe (with also in this case less support from British and Spanish activists and more from French, Germans and Italians). The activists at the ESFs therefore do not seem to be Eurosceptics, wanting to return to an almighty nation state, but 'critical Europeanists' (or 'critical globalists'), convinced that transnational institutions of governance are necessary, but that they should be built from below. Activists from various countries expressed, therefore, strong criticisms of the actual politics and policies of the EU, but they also showed strong identification with Europe and a certain degree of support for the European level of governance (della Porta 2002a).

Although we have discussed protest at the EU level as an example of critical Europeanism, Europe does not seem to be an exception. Transnational waves of protest have in fact been said to create critical cosmopolitans, and the mobilization over transnational issues to fuel the development of cosmopolitan identities (Tarrow 2005).

Conclusion

With the increasing competences of international organizations, the issue of their democratic accountability came forcefully onto the agenda of scholars and committed citizens alike. Reflections addressed the tensions between the normative need to build institutions of global democracy and the empirical difficulties in the implementation of those projects. The most ambitious models of a global federation are at the same time the ones that promise to increase the participatory and deliberative quality of democracy, but also the ones that appear to be more difficult to realize in practice. However, the increasing power of international organizations also brought with it some seeds for the development of a global civil society and some promises of democratization of international politics from below: transnational social movement organizations in fact not only intervene (in more or less contentious forms) in institutional decision making by international organizations and develop proposals to democratize them but also form global public spheres that increase the transparency of international organizations.

As we saw, looking especially at the EU, transnational activists emerge as critical cosmopolitans. Looking at the frames and discourses of these activists, as well as those of their organizations, we observe the development of a form of 'critical Europeanism' that is fundamentally different from the traditional 'nationalist' Euroscepticism on which research on Europeanization has focused so far. In actions, through the organization of transnational campaigns, they contribute to building organizational and symbolic resources for a (more) democratic global politics.

Networking during protest campaigns was in fact instrumentally important in increasing the influence of each organization and individual. In what was less a scale shift process (Tarrow 2005; Tarrow and McAdam 2004) than a scale multiplication one, during transnational campaigns activists began to identify as part of a European or even a global subject. Action in transnational networks also enabled the construction of transnational identities through the recognition of similarities across countries.

7

Democratization and Social Movements

As it is usually told, the story of the Arab Spring starts when Moham-mad Bouazizi had his goods confiscated for illegal street selling; when he protested he was slapped in the face by a police woman. A jobless college graduate and then fruit seller Bouazizi immolated himself in front of the local city council in Sidi Bouzzid. Even before his death, a few weeks later, popular protests spread, soon reaching Tunis, target-ing the authoritarian regime led by Zine El Abidine Ben Ali, who fled to Saudi Arabia. As Teije Donker observed, however, 'The above account is as simplified as it is misleading (and sometimes plain wrong: Bouazizi was no college graduate and the police woman later denied ever hitting him); social mobilization had been mounting for years, the protests in Sidi Bouzzid were exceptional but not unheard of, and the self-immolation of Mohammad Bouazizi in itself not the final nail in the coffin of Ben Ali. Collective mobilization during the 2010–2011 uprising built on previous ones: from numerous strikes and protests in the regions since 2005, and a six-month-long uprising in Gafsa in 2008, to more recent protests in mining regions at the beginning of 2010. Without these earlier uprisings the Tunisian revolution would not have emerged' (Donker 2012, 2).

The successful example of Tunisia inspired protests for democracy in Egypt. Here as well, we have a conventional narrative which sets the beginning of the successful, peaceful revolution as the demonstra-tion against torture and police brutality called for by the Facebook group 'We are all Khaled Said' for 25 January, the National Police Day. The call was immediately supported by members of various youth group associations, such as the 6 April movement. In Warkotsch's reconstruction, 'On the day itself, what was expected to be a larger than usual demonstration, but nonetheless a singular event, for the first time managed to gather huge masses oftentimes spontaneously from the neighborhoods, which they passed through. In between the 25th and the 28th, protests erupted in a number of Egyptian cities, which turned fiercely violent in the case of Suez, where battles with the police ensued for days to avenge the death of protesters' (Warkotsch 2012, 3–4). Taken aback, the authoritarian regime tried different repressive tactics, including a blocking of the Internet and mobile phones. All attempts were unsuccessful though as, 'on the 28th of January, in Cairo alone, hundreds of thousands of protesters marched on the streets, chanting the by now well-known slogan that united their demands, from the economic to the political – "the people want the overthrow of the regime"' (2012). It is on this day that Tahrir Square was occupied by the protestors, and held until 11 February 2011, when President Mubarak stepped down. Here as well, the events mobilized different social and political groups that had grown in opposition to the dictatorship over a period of many years.

While the recent events of the Arab Spring were celebrated as the citizens conquering democracy – or at least, fighting for it – the social sciences have been quite silent on these processes of democratization from below, as democratization studies focused on the elites, and social movement studies on established democracy. In this chapter, I am going to address this paradox, as well as reflecting on how a social movement perspective can help us to understand transitions to democracy, their successes and their limits. I shall do this by first looking at the gap in the social science literature on democratization, which has focused either on structural preconditions or on elites' predispositions. I shall then look at social movement studies for inspiration on concepts and data on actual processes of democratization from below. The political opportunities, especially in terms of characteristics of the repressive regime, as well as the material and symbolic resources available for the opposition and the emergent dynamics of eventful protest, will be discussed as potential explanations of social movement participation in democratization processes.

Democratization studies and the (neglect of) social movements

While, in both normative and empirical literature, the importance of civil society (especially in the form of social movement organizations) in the construction of democracy is more and more emphasized, democratization literature has focused on elites. As Nancy Bermeo (1997) stated, in general, literature on democratization accords much less attention to popular organizations than to political elites. An empirical linkage between social movements and democratization processes has, however, been established. Among others, Charles Tilly has observed 'a broad correspondence between democratization and social movements' (Tilly 2004, 131). When looking at the impact of social movements on democracy, the empirical evidence is, however, mixed, as social movements differ in their willingness, as well as in their capacity, to support democracy. Beyond a social movement's propensity to support democracy, democratization processes might follow different paths, being more or less influenced by the mobilization of social movements.

Notwithstanding the practical and theoretical relevance of the topic, the interactions between social movements and democratization have rarely been addressed in a systematic and comparative way. On the one hand, social movements have been far from prominent in the literature on democratization, which has mainly focused on either socio-economic preconditions or elite behaviour. On the other hand, social movement scholars, until recently, have paid little attention to democratization processes, mostly concentrating their interest on democratic countries (especially on Western European and North American experiences), where conditions for mobilization are more favourable.

Studies on democratization have traditionally assigned a limited role to social movements and protest. Within *modernization* theory, Lipset's (1959) pioneering work associated the chances for the emergence of a democratic regime with economic development. Although powerful in explaining the survival of established democracies, modernization theory tended to ignore the role of social actors and movements in *crafting* democracy, leaving the timing and tempo of democratization processes unexplained. When scholars within this approach did examine the role of organized and mobilized actors in society, they tended – as in Huntington (1965; 1991) – to consider mobilization, in particular of the working class, as a risk more than an asset.

There is, however, in this approach a useful attention to social conditions for democracy, and therefore the role of social classes in producing democratization. In particular – but not only – in traditional Marxist approaches, democracy has often been presented as the typical political form of capitalism. As Dietrich Rueschemeyer, Evelyn Huber Stephens and John D. Stephens (1992, 1) summarized, 'in this view capitalism and democracy go hand in hand because democracy, while proclaiming the rule of the many, in fact protects the interests of capital owners...The unrestrained operation of the market for capital and labour constitutes the material base of democracy.' Even though capitalism might also prosper without democracy, 'virtually all full-fledged democracies are associated with capitalist political economics' (1992, 2).

If the link between democracy and capitalism has often been stressed, different trends in the research on social structures and democratization offer different conclusions. Quantitative research, based on large-N comparison, consistently found a positive correlation between economic development and democracy; small-N comparisons have instead limited this relationship to specific – and even rare – historical conditions. Already Lipset (1959) had stated that the economically better off a country is, the higher are the chances that it is a democracy. Education, with related values of tolerance and moderation, as well as the development of a middle class are considered as main causal mechanisms. Generous provision of social security, by satisfying the needs of the population, increase support for the status quo.

Comparative historical investigations point instead at the capitalist interest in authoritarian regimes, especially in dependent countries. Among others, O'Donnell (1979) stressed an 'elective affinity' between bureaucratic authoritarianism and capitalist development. It has also been suggested that the development of capitalism favoured the development of democracy only for earlier economic development (and first democratization), while late-comers (especially at the periphery) had more chances of being ruled by autocrats. As mentioned (chapter 2), Barrington Moore (1973) influentially singled out different paths to development, with a fascist path dominated by powerful landowners and a bourgeoisie that needs protectionist support by the state. Additionally, democracies offer asymmetrical chances to articulate interests, privileging some social groups over others.

In this tradition, Barrington Moore (1973), R. Bendix (1964) and T.H. Marshall (1992) all recognized the impact of class struggles in early democratization (cf. chapter 3). While the usual focus has been on the middle class as promoters of democratization, more recently, Dietrich Rueschemeyer, Evelyn Huber Stephens and John D. Stephens (1992) have pointed to the role of the working class in promoting democratization in Southern Europe, South America and the Caribbean. According to them (1992, 6), 'one would have to examine the structure of class coalitions as well as the relative power of different classes to understand how the balance of class power would affect the possibilities for democracy'. As classes have some specific tendencies in defining what benefits and losses democracy can bring them, the analysis should focus on the structure of class coalitions, under the assumption that 'those who have the most to gain from democracy will be its most reliable promoters and defenders' (1992, 57). While for some scholars democracy can fit

various social structures, for Rueschemeyer et al. there is a mutual rein-
forcement between democracy and capitalism, given that capitalist development 'transforms the class structure, strengthening the working and
the middle-class and weakening the landed upper class. It was not the
capitalist market nor capitalists as the new dominant force, but rather
the contradictions of capitalism that advanced the cause of democracy'
(1992, 7).

In contrast to Barrington Moore's approach, they stated in fact that
'The working class was the most consistent democratic force' (1992, 8).
Noting the irony in liberal historians and orthodox Marxist ones converging in defining the bourgeoisie as *the* protagonist of democracy, they
counter that 'it was the subordinated classes that fought for democracy',
so that 'the chances of democracy, then, must be seen as fundamentally
shaped by the balance of class power' (1992, 46–7). The middle class
played instead an ambivalent role, pressing for their inclusion, but only
occasionally (when weak) allying with the working class, in order to
extend democracy to them as well. The peasantry and rural workers
played different roles, according to their capacity for autonomous organization and the influence of dominant classes upon them. In particular,
small independent family farmers tended to be more pro-democracy than
peasants from large landholdings (1992). The counter-hegemonic growth
of working classes is therefore pointed out as critical for the promotion
of democracy as 'a dense civil society establishes a counterweight to the
state, so favouring democracy' (1992, 50).

In short, some of the main works in historical sociology linked democratization to class relations, stressing the importance of the working class
as promoter of democracy. Although recognizing a path of democratization from below, these studies still tended to explain it mainly on the
basis of structural conditions. In fact, class accounts that acknowledge
the role of workers tend to adopt a structural perspective, predicting
democratization when democracy-demanding classes (especially the
working class) are stronger than democracy-resisting ones (Foweraker
and Landman 1997).

A structuralist bias is criticized by the so-called *transitologist* approach,
that stresses agency instead, as well as a dynamic and processual vision of
democratization, focusing on elite strategies and behaviour (O'Donnell
and Schmitter 1986; Higley and Gunther 1992). While civil society is
supposed to play an important role in promoting the transition process,
these 'resurrections of civil society' are seen as short disruptive moments
when movements, unions, churches and the society in general push for the
initial liberalization of a non-democratic regime into a transition towards
democracy. In particular, research on Latin America pointed at the need
for revision of structuralist perspectives, indicating that 'there may be no

single precondition that is sufficient to produce such an outcome. The search for causes rooted in economic, social, cultural/psychological, or international factors has not yielded a general law of democratization, nor is it likely to do so in the near future despite the proliferation of new cases' (Karl 1990, 5).

Literature in the transitology perspective tends indeed to downplay the role of structural conditions, which had received much attention in the past, stressing instead the role of leadership. For O'Donnell and Schmitter transitions from authoritarian rule are illustrations of 'underdetermined social change, of large-scale transformations which occur when there are insufficient structural or behavioral parameters to guide and predict the outcome' (1986, 363). Structural interests, therefore, need to receive less attention than elite dispositions, which are seen as determining whether democratization occurs at all.

It is in fact elites who count. As Ruth Collier noted, much of the latest literature on recent democratization processes 'emphasizes elite strategic choices, downplaying or ignoring the role of labour in democratization' (Collier 1999, 5). In this narrative, the heroism of the few drives the process, as it is the action of exemplary individuals that tests the capacity of the regime to resist (Bermeo 1990, 361). Stress is thus put on the role of opposition leaders, often individuals, who are considered to be especially relevant in periods of high uncertainty and indeterminacy, and approaches are extremely state-centric, with privileged roles accorded to institutional actors. The attention paid to elite behaviour is not 'class analysis by another name' as material interests are not the primary determinant of their dispositions but rather their 'concern for future reputation' (1990, 361). Class also tends to stay out of the picture, as strategies are analysed in game-theoretical terms as incumbents and challengers, soft-liners and hard-liners.

The role of the civil society is instead considered to be marginal. In their seminal work, O'Donnell and Schmitter (1986, 53–4) observed that:

> In some cases and at particular moments of the transition, many of these diverse layers of society may come together to form what we choose to call the popular upsurge. Trade unions, grass-roots movements, religious groups, intellectuals, artists, clergymen, defenders of human rights, and professional associations all support each other's efforts toward democratization and coalesce into a greater whole which identifies itself as the people.

Although this is a moment of great expectations, 'regardless of its intensity and of the background from which it emerges, this popular upsurge is always ephemeral' (1986, 55–6; for a similar view, Huntington 1991, 605). As Ulfelder (2005, 313) summarized, even though mass mobilization is recognized as important in pushing to expand the limits of mere liberalization and partial democratization, it is seen as 'an "ephemeral" process vulnerable to elite co-optation, manipulation, exhaustion, and disillusionment'.

Within transitology, more systematic attention to civil society in democratization processes can be found in Linz and Stepan's (1996) model of extended transition, which addresses Eastern European cases. Contrasting it with a political society composed of elites and institutionalized actors, they suggested that 'A robust civil society, with the capacity to generate political alternatives and to monitor government and state, can help transitions get started, help resist reversals, help push transitions to their completion, help consolidate, and help deepen democracy. At all stages of the democratization process, therefore, a lively and independent civil society is invaluable' (Linz and Stepan 1996, 9). They, however, did not pay much empirical attention to it. Rather, transitology tended to consider movements and protest actors as manipulated by elites and focusing on very instrumentally defined purposes (see Przeworski 1991, 57; for a critique, Baker 1999). Even though the dynamic, agency-focused approach of transitology allowed for some interest in the role played by movements in democratization to develop (Pagnucco 1995), it did not focus attention on them.

As, in this wave of reflection, the *reforma pactada / ruptura pactada* in Spain was considered (explicitly or implicitly) to be the model for successful democratization, the ephemeral life of the civil society tended to be perceived as not only inevitable, given the re-channeling of participation through the political parties and the electoral system, but also desirable, in order to avoid frightening authoritarian soft-liners into abandoning the negotiation process with pro-democracy moderates.

In traditional approaches, in order to succeed, transitions are expected to be smooth, and actors to moderate their aims. Samuel P. Huntington (1991) has been one of the strongest supporters of this moderation view. Moderation is seen as a positive evolution in the attitudes and goals of the various actors. In his 'Guidelines for democratizers', his recommendation is to: 'Make particular efforts to enlist business leaders, middle-class professionals, religious figures, and political party leaders, most of whom probably supported creation of the authoritarian system. The more "respectable" and "responsible" the opposition appears, the easier it is to win more supporters' (1991, 607). The moderates in the opposition are thus warned against the 'masses': 'Be prepared to mobilize your supporters for demonstrations when these will weaken the partners in the government. Too many marches and protests, however, are likely to strengthen them, weaken your negotiating partner, and arouse middle-class concern about law and order' (1991, 616).

Like Huntington, O'Donnell and Schmitter (1986, 27) also pointed at the importance of tactical moderation. They warned indeed that 'If the opposition menaces the vertical command structure of the armed forces, the territorial integrity of the nation state, the country's position in international alliances, or the property rights underlying the capitalist economy or if widespread violence recurs, then even bland regime actors will conclude that the costs of tolerance are greater than those of repression.' Democratizing actors are therefore advised to avoid explosive redistributive issues, moderate their aims and queue requests, circumscribing the agenda. Parties – not movements – are considered to be pivotal in these efforts at moderation, acting as instrument of social and political control, as well as of effective demobilization. As Bermeo (1990, 369) summarized, the main message of the series of studies edited by O'Donnell and Schmitter is that 'political party leaders are the key players in the transition gamble. They set the stakes; they work out the compromises; they act as the forces for moderation that the successful transition process requires. In Venezuela, Spain, or Peru, political parties negotiated pacts, mediated conflicts and sedated revolts.'

This assumption is also disputed, however. In particular, Nancy Bermeo criticized the claim 'that too much popular mobilization and too much pressure from below can spoil the chances for democracy', suggesting instead that 'in many cases, democratization seems to have proceeded alongside weighty and even bloody popular challenges' (Bermeo 1997, 314). In particular, the Portuguese transition, which began in April 1974:

> violated most of the cautionary parameters set out by the literature on democratization. The laboring classes were far from docile. Capitalist property rights were challenged successfully on a very broad scale. The country's position in international alliances was the subject of strenuous debate, and decolonization shattered the territorial integrity of the state. The vertical command structure of the armed forces was completely transformed. Nevertheless, democracy muddled through. (1997, 307)

But the moderation argument is not even valid for the most celebrated cases, such as the Spanish one, where elites did form pacts, but in a situation in which radical conflicts developed. The persistence of contention has been seen in fact as relevant not only in producing liberalization, but also in steering the transition process, and influencing democratic consolidation.

Democratization in social movement studies

The relevance of contention is stressed by social movement studies, which, however, flourished in (and on) established democracies, with less than rare attempts to look at social movements in phases of democratization (for a review, Rossi and della Porta 2009). Even in established democracies, the relations between movements and democracy have mainly been looked at in terms of institutional opportunities for protest, rather than of the attitudes towards and practices of democracy by activists and their organizations (della Porta 2009a, 2009b; della Porta and Rucht forthcoming).

If a systematic analysis of processes of transition from below is lacking in both disciplines, there has, however, been some recent convergence of attention on the questions of social movements and democratization. The emergence of the global justice movement pushed some social movement scholars to pay more attention to issues of democracy, as well as to social movements in the global South. Some pioneering research aimed at applying social movement studies to authoritarian regimes, from the Middle East (Wiktorowicz 2004; Hafez 2003; Gunning 2007) to Asia (Boudreau 2004) and the former Soviet Union (Beissinger 2002). More generally, recognizing the structuralist bias of the political process approach, a more dynamic vision of protest has been promoted, with attention paid to the social mechanisms that intervene between macro-causes and macro-effects (McAdam, Tarrow and Tilly 2001). Recently, some scholars within this approach proposed the reformulation of the transitology perspective, taking into account the role played by contentious politics (2001; Schock 2005; Tilly 2004). Similarly to the transitology approach, they have stressed agency as well as the importance of looking at democratization as a dynamic process.

There are, additionally, several case studies on democratization processes and social movements, as well as protest. As Ulfelder (2005, 313) synthesized, 'Various subsequent studies of democratic transitions have afforded collective actors a more prominent role, allowing for the possibility that mass mobilization has a substantial impact on the transition process and is sometimes the catalyst that sets a transition in motion.' Understanding participation of social movements in the democratization process requires exploring different meanings of the term 'from below'. Following Ruth Collier (1999), one might refer to the power of certain actors, distinguishing insiders and outsiders; one can refer to the social background of those actors, distinguishing e.g., between upper and lower classes; and one can refer to the arenas where the conflicts take place, distinguishing institutional versus protest ones. Additionally, we can easily assume that the balance of both participation by outsiders and contention varies in empirical cases.

Case studies have indicated that democratization is often linked to contentious dynamics, such as pro-democratic cycles of protest, and waves of strikes (cf. Foweraker and Landman 1997; Collier 1999; McAdam, Tarrow and Tilly. 2001). They can affect different steps of the democratization process.

Protests (especially, strikes) often constitute precipitating events that start *liberalization*, spreading the perception among the authoritarian elites that there is no choice other than opening the regime if they want to avoid an imminent or potential civil war or violent takeover of power by democratic and/or revolutionary actors (e.g. Bermeo 1997; Wood 2000). During liberalization, civil society organizations publicly (re) emerge in a much more visible fashion (O'Donnell and Schmitter 1986): trade unions, left-wing parties and urban movements, mainly in shanty-towns and industrial districts, have often pushed for democracy (Slater 1985; Collier 1999; Silver 2003; Schneider 1992, 1995; Hipsher 1998a), sometimes in alliance with transnational actors (e.g. in Latin America, as well as in Eastern Europe; Keck and Sikkink 1998; Glenn 2003).

During the *transition* to democracy, old (labour, ethnic) movements and new (women's, urban) movements have often participated in large coalitions asking for democratic rights as well as social justice (Jelin 1987; Tarrow 1995; della Porta, Valiente and Kousis forthcoming). The importance of protest in transition processes has been observed in Africa (Bratton and Van de Walle 1997), Latin America and Southern Europe (Collier and Mahoney 1997). The mobilization of a pro-democracy coalition of trade unions, political parties, churches and social movements has often been pivotal in supporting the movement towards democracy in the face of contending counter-movements pushing for the restoration of authoritarian/totalitarian regimes. The bargaining dynamic among elites interacts then with the increased intensity of protest (Casper and Taylor 1996, 9–10; Glenn 2003, 104).

Social movements are also active during *consolidation*, a step that is generally considered to start with the first free and open elections, the end of the uncertainty period and/or the implementation of a minimum quality of substantive democracy (Linz and Stepan 1996; O'Donnell 1993, 1994; Rossi and della Porta 2009 for a review). In some cases, this is accompanied by a demobilization of civil society organizations as energies are channelled into party politics; in others, however, demobi-lization does not occur (e.g., on Argentina, Bolivia and the Andean region, Canel 1992; Schneider 1992; Hipsher 1998a). In fact, social movement organizations mobilized during liberalization and transition rarely totally disband; on the contrary, democratization often facilitates the development of social movement organizations (for example the women's movement in Southern Europe: della Porta, Valiente and Kousis forthcoming). The presence of a tradition of mobilization, as well as movements that are supported by political parties, unions and religious institutions can facilitate the maintenance of a high level of protest, as in the Communist party's promotion of shantytown dwellers' protests in Chile (Hipsher 1998b; Schneider 1992, 1995); the Partido dos Trabalhadores (PT) and part of the Roman Catholic Church with the rural movements and unions in Brazil (Branford and Rocha 2002; Burdick 2004); or the environmental movements in Eastern Europe (Flam 2001). In this stage, movements might claim the rights of those who are excluded by 'low intensity democracies' and ask for a more inclusive democracy (i.e. for peasants, employment, indigenous people's and women's rights) and the end of authoritarian legacies (Eckstein 2001; della Porta, Valiente and Kousis forthcoming). Furthermore, movements' networks play an important role in mobilizing against persistent exclusionary patterns (Yashar 2005). Keeping elites under continuous popular pressure after transition can facilitate a successful consolidation (Karatnycky and Ackerman 2005). What is more, movements' alternative practices and values help to sustain and expand democracy (Santos 2005).

The exogenous dimension: Attribution of political opportunities

If we want to understand when social movements have good chances to become important actors in democratization processes, we might first of all look at political opportunities, especially as they are perceived by the different actors. As mentioned, structuralist approaches have investigated external conditions that might explain paths of democratization. Democratization studies have looked at economic development and class structure, while social movement studies have focused attention on political dimensions, defined with reference to stable characteristics, such as the functional and territorial distribution of power, political culture and the cleavage structure, as well as more dynamic ones such as the positions of potential allies and opponents. The basic assumption in this approach is that the more opportunities a political system offers for social movements, the more moderate, single-issue and open-structured they will be. Previous research on democracies has indicated that political opportunities influence mobilization levels (Kriesi 1991; Tarrow 1989; Kriesi et al. 1995), strategies (Eisinger 1973; Kitschelt 1986), ideologies/framing and behaviour (della Porta and Rucht 1995; Kriesi et al. 1995) and organizational structures (Kriesi 1996).

Among the political opportunities that affect protest are the *characteristics of the authoritarian regime* the movements address. In general, 'The authority patterns, elite bargains, and corporate interests on which different types of autocracy are based make those regimes differently vulnerable to different kinds of public challenge' (Ulfelder 2005: 326–327).

Linz and Stepan (1996) suggested that the type of non-democratic regime influences the potential for the democratization path. In *totalitarian* regimes, which are the most repressive, the development of autonomous organizations and networks that could then be the promoters of democracy is particularly difficult. *Sultanistic* (or personalistic) regimes, due to the high personalization of power, include the manipulative use of mobilization for ceremonial purposes and through para-state groups, discouraging and repressing, however, any kind of autonomous organization that could sustain resistance networks. *Authoritarian* regimes, thanks to their higher degrees of pluralism, do instead generally experience the most massive mobilizations, and the best-organized underground resistance based on networks that either pre-dated the regime or were formed later.

Developing a similar typology of authoritarian regimes, Barbara Geddes (1999) has looked at strategies of cooperation and conflict among elites in military, single-party and personalistic autocracies, linking their characteristics to the dynamics of their breakdown. As she suggested (1999, 1):

> Different forms of authoritarianism break down in characteristically different ways. They draw on different groups to staff government offices and different segments of society for support. They have different procedures for making decisions, different characteristic forms of intra-elite factionalism and competition, different ways of choosing leaders and handling succession, and different ways of responding to society and opposition...These differences...cause authoritarian regimes to break down in systematically different ways, and they also affect post-transition outcomes. (Geddes, 1999, 6)

In general, personalistic regimes are not very vulnerable to internal splits, but are instead to the death of the leader and/or economic crisis; single-party regimes show high degrees of resilience, thanks to diffuse incentives for party cadres to cooperate; military regimes are the most fragile, given different visions of the proper role of the army.

Ulfelder's research, based on event history analysis of riots, general strikes and anti-government demonstrations, shows that contention has no relevant effects on personalistic regimes, while single-party and military regimes are more likely to break down following non-violent anti-government protests, and military regimes are less likely to break down in the case of violent protest. He notes that, 'These distinct patterns highlight key differences in the underpinnings of different kinds of autocracy, and thus their vulnerabilities to contentious collective action. The durability of personalistic regimes depends largely on bargains among cliques with no claim to grass roots, so ruling elites are freer to ignore popular challenges or to suppress them vigorously when they occur' (2005, 314).

The idea that personal regimes are more resilient to protest has, however, been contested, even before the Arab Spring. Michael Bratton and Nicolas van de Walle (1994) have concluded from comparative research on Sub-Saharan Africa that, as neopatrimonial elites fragment over access to material resources and pacts among the elites are unlikely, transitions are mainly driven from below. As they summarized,

> the practices of neopatrimonialism cause chronic fiscal crisis and make economic growth highly problematic. In addition, neopatrimonial leaders construct particularistic networks of personal loyalty that grant undue favor to selected kinship, ethnic, or regional groupings. Taken together, shrinking economic opportunities and exclusionary patterns of reward are a recipe for social unrest. Mass popular protest is likely to break out, usually over the issue of declining living standards, and to escalate to calls for the removal of incumbent leaders. ... Endemic fiscal crisis also undercuts the capacity of rulers to manage the process of political change. When public resources dwindle to the point where the incumbent government can no longer pay civil servants, the latter join the antiregime protesters in the streets. Shorn of the ability to maintain political stability through the distribution of material rewards, neopatrimonial leaders resort erratically to coercion which, in turn, further undermines the regime's legitimacy. The showdown occurs when the government is unable to pay the military. (1994, 460)

Beyond regime types, the *strength of the state* – its resources but also its cohesiveness – might play a relevant role in shaping democratization from below. Social movement studies have long implicitly assumed that there is no opportunity for mobilization in authoritarian regimes. Decisions by the state to repress are complex, as the state is diversified and different groups have different visions and interests. In all of them, dictators have to guess how much repression will suffice to control dissent without producing backlash effects. But 'calculations will change as the events progress and context changes', with, e.g., increasing international pressure, opposition, elite defection or economic crises (1994, 128–9).

The very strength of the state might be path-dependent on how it was formed. Social movements have been considered as conditioned by the type of regime they challenge, but one has to consider also the opposite relation in addressing the question of how regimes change. Analysing 'Why [some regimes] are more prone to act collectively in some political systems?', Dan Slater (2010, 4–5) suggested that it depends upon 'historically divergent patterns of contentious politics'. In fact, the risk of the challenge, as perceived by the elites, defines the 'ordering power' as the command of a steady flow of resources towards the Leviathan, so that it can apply coercion in a sufficient and targeted manner. It is not only the amount, but also the type, of contention that explains the specific forms authoritarian regimes took. The central idea is in fact that

> How well authoritarian leaders fare at capturing the strategic resources that elite groups possess depends on the types of contentious politics that presage the birth of the authoritarian Leviathan. Where such conflicts are widely perceived as endemic and unmanageable...authoritarian regimes enjoy an excellent opportunity to craft a protection pact: a pro-authoritarian coalition linking upper groups on the basis of shared perceptions of threat. (2010, 15)

Beyond the type of regime and its strength, the *style of repression* is a particularly relevant dimension. In his in-depth comparison of Burma, Indonesia and the Philippines, Vincent Boudreau noticed that both repression – as 'coercive acts of threats that weaken resistance to authority will' (2004, 3) – and collective memory of repression emerge as relevant in explaining how changing collective actors are able to bring down an authoritarian regime. Some modes of repression marginalize all activists, pushing them to build coalitions, while others distinguish between forms and actors; some eliminate activists, others let them survive. In all three countries he studied, democratic movements developed, led by charismatic women, flourishing in periods of economic crises, opposing a regime more and more isolated. Their forms and dynamics change, however, as they are influenced by a long history of contention, and its repression. In general, the stronger the repression, the more difficult it was to sustain movements for democracy.

The specific national histories (including colonial domination and anti-colonial struggles) played a role in the forms that mobilization for democracy assumed, as well as in its outcomes. State repression in fact affected protest:

> State repression killed, bruised, imprisoned and terrified citizens, but seldom indiscriminately. Most focused on specific targets, and so

shaped the material and organizational resources that survived, promoting political forms that escaped the state's most direct proscription. Often, forms that authorities judge least threatening survived – as with student protests in the 1970s in Indonesia. Elsewhere, forms survived because the authorities had had neither the capacity nor the will to defeat them – as with insurgencies in both the Philippines and Burma. Activist forms and organizations, however, do not exist independently of activists. Repression shapes the duration, direction and intensity of activist careers in ways that profoundly influence political contention. Where activist forms and organizations survive state attack, generations of experienced dissidents bring their accumulated wisdom and leadership to the struggle, and provide a thicker and more complex network of support for new protest. Elsewhere, authorities may eliminate entire activist generations and deprive new claim makers of experienced leaders. (2004, 10–11)

The specificities of the regime go beyond repressive tradition, however. In particular, the complex *political culture* and societal networks of the 'real existing socialism' have been analysed in order to explain the specific dynamics of contention during democratization. As Valery Bunce observed, some characteristics of Eastern European socialism influenced regime development. The very first one was the ideological mission of the ruling elite: 'Unlike most dictatorships, which tend to be concerned with stability, if not a version of cultural class nostalgia, and which operate within a capitalist economic framework, socialist regimes were future-oriented, avowedly anticapitalist and premised on a commitment to rapid transformation of the economy, the society, and, following that, in theory at least, the polity as well' (1999, 21). These ideological concerns brought to the extreme the late-developer model, and import substitution towards autarkic economies depressed agriculture and consumption, while increasing savings. In parallel, growth became a fetish, and production was concentrated on the markers of modernization. Linked to this was the construction 'of a conjoined economic and political monopoly that rested in the hands of the Communist Party' (1999, 22). Party and the state were also fused, as the state relied on the party for its personnel as well as for its resources. The result was an extraordinary penetration of the state by the party, and a very powerful elite.

This strength was temporary, however, as those characteristics fuelled a vicious circle: 'Over time and certainly by accident, the institutional framework of socialism functioned to deregulate the party's monopoly and to undermine economic growth. This set the stage for crisis and reform – and, ultimately, for the collapse of all of these regimes' (1999, 26). This happened especially through inter-elite conflicts along vertical and horizontal lines, which peaked in periods of succession. These were intensified by a stress on planned and rapid transformations, with high rates of turnover in elites, but also the need to mobilize resources at the base. In their turn, conflicts among elites strengthened the role of the society, with 'a robust correlation between instances of intraparty conflicts and outburst of public protest' (1999, 27), which happened in the German Democratic Republic (GDR) in 1953, in Hungary in 1956, in Poland in 1956, 1968, 1970–1 and 1980–1.

The fusion of state and party also tended to create a broad potential base for the opposition, through the creation of a large and homogeneous group of discontent, as 'The party's economic, political, and social monopoly, its commitment to rapid socioeconomic development, limited wage inequalities, and stable prices for consumer items, its preference for large enterprises and large collective forms, and its creation of consumer-deficit societies all worked together to give publics in the European socialist systems a remarkably uniform set of experiences' (1999, 28). Faced with a potentially unified challenger, the all-powerful party functioned, in its turn, as a unified target, as fusion of functions also meant convergence of claims. In fact,

> the party did not just orchestrate elite recruitment, attendance at rallies, and the content of the mass media. It also functioned in the economy as the only employer, the only defender of workers' rights (through party-controlled unions), the only setter of production norms, and the only allocator of vacation time (while being the builder and maintainer of vacation retreats). At the same time, the party allocated all goods and set all prices. Finally, it was the party (sometimes through enterprises) that was the sole distributor of health care, transportation, and opportunities for the leisure-time activities. (1999, 28)

A bias towards systemic uniformity also contributed to this convergence as shared experiences produced uniform interests and a shared definition of the target.

Given all these contextual differences, different *transition paths* can also offer different opportunities to social movements. Linz and Stepan (1996, ch. 2) singled out the specific challenges of multiple simultaneous transitions, where regime changes are accompanied by changes in the economic system and/or in the nation state arrangement. It is important not only whether the previous regime was authoritarian or totalitarian, but also whether it was a capitalist or a communist one (Stark and Bruszt 1998). Especially when there is a triple transition, the problem of nation-state building is reflected in the emergence of nationalist movements mobilizing in the name of contending visions of what the *demos* of the future democracy should be (Beissinger 2002). The moderation versus radicalization of claims for autonomy/independence has been traditionally mentioned as favouring versus jeopardizing, respectively, the transition to democracy (among others, Oberschall 2000; Glenn 2003).

Finally, the *international system* has long been the missing variable in democratization studies. In fact O'Donnell and Schmitter's firmest conclusion was that democratization was largely to be explained in terms of national actors and their calculations. The international dimension of democratization processes has been considered as having little influence. In the 1990s, however, attention developed on the role of international variables, including the potential support or lack thereof by international institutions and superpowers. Recent research addresses instead some major *transnational* influences linked to the evolving interstate rules that define the global normative context for action by states and parties engaged in violent conflict, as well as the development of transnational epistemic communities linking states and civil society organizations against human rights violations (Keck and Sikkink 1998; Chiodi 2007). The Helsinki Treaty as well as Gorbachev's liberalization politics in the Soviet Union have been quoted as most influential for the 1989 transitions in all of Central Eastern Europe.

The endogenous dimension: mobilization of resources

Some (even if very limited) free space, outside of state control, tends to survive as 'locales that lie outside the scrutiny of the regime and its agents' (Johnston 2011, 113). Usually secretive, these spaces grant, however, some freedom to express one's own opinion. They are 'small islands of free thoughts and speech' (2011, 103) which include – as in the case of Yemen (Carapico 1998) – social gatherings, neighbourhood associations, unions and study groups. Some groups, such as recreational, intellectual or religious organizations, assume a duplicitous character, allowing for the development of sites of opposition. They are politicized under brutal violations of human rights and religious freedom. In particular, intellectual dissidents are supported by reputation and international ties and act through open letters, petitions, dissemination of information. Campaigns of protest on peace, or women's, labour, nationality or neighbourhood issues are sometimes not repressed 'for ideological reasons, for reasons of international politics or to provide a safety valve to reduce more direct antiregime protest' (Johnston 2011, 124). Early-riser groups might also have the function of building oppositional networks. Developmental studies often make reference to a variety of grass-roots NGOs as alternative developmental agencies, that work as something between modern associations and more traditional groups – and often interact with the state (reciprocal influence).

Their activity takes different forms. One of them has been defined by Johnston as the oppositional speech situation: 'Oppositional talk in repressive society is marked by double entendre, symbolism, monitoring of participants, specific rules of speech, that is, what it is appropriate to say, how to say it, and to whom. A common element is underground humor' (2011, 115). In particular, jokes work as escape valves for anxiety (2011, 116). Protests are often hit-and-run: graffiti, clandestine placement of flags or crosses in symbolic places (2011, 121), event seizure of official events (e.g. singing of prohibited songs at concerts or sporting events, or diversion of funerals) but also strikes. Various electoral repertoires have been singled out in the so-called 'Orange revolutions', especially in Eastern Europe and the former Soviet Union.

Underground networks of resistance often undermine the legitimacy of, and the (national and international) support for, authoritarian regimes (on the Latin American cases, see Jelin 1987; Corradi, Weiss Fagen and Garretón 1992; Escobar and Álvarez 1992). Human rights movements, trade unions and churches promote the delegitimation of the authoritarian regime in international forums such as the United Nations, and in clandestine or open resistance to the authoritarian regime at the national level. The resilience of resistance networks under the impact of repression often leads to splits in the ruling authoritarian elites (Schock 2005). Among the social movement organizations that have played a pro-democratic role are church-related actors (see Lowden 1996 on Chile; Burdick 1992; Levine and Mainwaring 2001 on Brazil; della Porta and Mattina 1986 on Spain; Glenn 2003; Osa 2003 on Poland); human rights networks, sometimes in transnational alliances (Brysk 1993; Brito 1997; Sikkink 1996; Keck and Sikkink 1998, ch. 3); cultural groups (Glenn 2003 on Czechoslovakia); as well as, very often, the labour movement, sometimes in alliance with 'new social movements'. Social networks of various types have emerged as fundamental, especially for some paths of mobilization under authoritarian regimes (Osa and Cordunenanu-Huci 2003).

Following social movement studies, we can assume that three sets of characteristics in these networks can affect their role in democratization processes: their frames on democratic issues, organizational structures and action repertoires (on these concepts, see della Porta and Diani 2006).

Some social groups are particularly likely to build mobilizing structures against the authoritarian regimes. In his comparison of Iran, Nicaragua and the Philippines, all similarly having high rates of development and an authoritarian regime supported by the US, Parsa (2000) focused in particular on the role of students', clerics' and workers' organizations. *Students* are main actors in most political transformations. As Parsa (2000, 94) summarized:

> Students in developing countries have been at the forefront of revolutionary struggles and have revealed an intense interest in fundamentally transforming the social structures ... They have enjoyed immense prestige and have often played a very significant role in the revolutionary process. Highly concentrated in colleges and universities, students possess extensive communication networks, which facilitates their collective action. Students in higher education often benefit from the university's relative autonomy – where it exists – and academic freedom, which provide them, at least theoretically, with immunity and insulation from state repression. (2000, 94)

Especially when university education expands, students are often the first social group to engage in collective action, and those who do it more often.

The *clergy* has often been considered conservative, but also sometimes becomes politicized and struggles for change, catalysed by the end of the alliance between the church and the state. In fact, 'The clergy's relative immunity and control of a social space safe from government interference enable them to play an important part in political mobilization' (Parsa 2000, 131). Clerics were involved in all three cases Parsa studied, but mainly moderates, even in Iran where only a minority supported Khomeini. The role of the low clergy in support of workers' and nationalist protest and in criticism of the Catholic hierarchy's support for the dictator has often been mentioned in the Spanish case, while the role of Evangelical circles from below emerged in the GDR. Religious groups played an important part in denouncing human rights abuses and social inequality in cases as different as the Philippines and Chile.

But it is especially workers' organizations that have played a most important role in democratic transitions. Workers' organizations were fundamental in several episodes of mobilization for democracy. A clear case in which the workers had a strong mobilization capacity and impact was Spain where, as Maravall (1982) noted:

> popular pressure from below, especially that coming from the workers' movement, played a crucial part in the transition. It was a causal factor in the Francoist crisis, in the non-viability of any mere 'liberalization' policy, in the willingness on the part of the 'democratic right' to negotiate the transition and carry through reform up to the point of breaking with Francoism, and in the initiative displayed by the Left up to the 1977 elections.

The importance of the mobilization of labour in Latin America has been particularly stressed by Collier and Mahoney (1997), who concluded their comparative analysis:

> In initial stages of democratization, labor mobilization in the pattern of destabilization/extrication contributed to divisions among authoritarian incumbents, who previously had no transitional project. During relatively early stages in the transitions game labor protest for democracy helped to derail the legitimation projects of incumbents. In later stages of the transition labor mobilization had two effects. First, depending on the pattern, protest provoked or quickened the transition and kept it on track. These effects were the consequence of pressure exerted to the very end. Our case evidence thus calls into question the perspective that labor restraint during the final transition phase contributes to democracy by convincing elites that democracy can lead to social and political order, thereby facilitating elite negotiations.... Second, mobilization and protest won labor-based parties a place among the negotiators and also in the successor regimes. (1997, 299–300)

High levels of labour mobilization in Peru, Brazil, Uruguay and Argentina not only contributed to the breakdown of the regimes but also won the representation of the workers a place in the elites' negotiations towards the establishment of a new regime. In sum, 'The collective action of labour movements thus played a key democratic role not only in propelling a transition, but also in expanding political space and the scope of contestation in the new democratic regime' (1997, 300).

Framing democratization from below

Beside organizational resources, action frames, that is the schemata of interpretation that enable individuals to locate, perceive, identify and label occurrences within their life space as well as the world at large (Snow et al. 1986, 464), count. As mentioned, social movement framings about democracy vary. Past research indicated that the labour movement was often divided in its positions on representative democracy. Even if it tended to support the various stages of (initial) democratization, cross-national differences were relevant (Marks, Mbaye and Kim 2009). Beyond support for democracy in general, specific conceptions of democracy are relevant, as these interact with other organizational characteristics that also affect the role of civil society in democratization processes.

First and foremost, social movements developed grass-roots' conceptions of mobilization. In Brazil, the urban popular movements, that developed with the liberalization of the 1970s, played an important role. Even if they were fragmented along class lines (middle class versus popular classes), related with social and political identity rather than individual material interests, and were at risk of being co-opted into clientelistic networks, they were particularly influential in introducing a participatory ethos rather than as an enlightened vanguard. As Mainwaring (1987, 149) noted, 'The movement has helped redefine the parameters of political discourse in subtle but significant ways. Perhaps most important has been the change in discourse, away from the technocratic elitist discourse that permeated all sides of the political spectrum in the late 1960s and first half of the 1970s, to a new discourse that emphasized popular participation.' Showing a similar emphasis, in Poland, the KORs renamed themselves the Committee for Social Self-organization (from Workers' Defence Committees) (Ash 2011).

The relevance of participatory and even deliberative models of democracy in the opposition is particularly visible in Eastern Europe, where it was embodied in a conception of civil society. There informal 'microgroups' allowed for the spread of a 'horizontal and oblique voice', with 'the development of semantically coded critical communication'. As Di Palma observed:

> Voices are horizontal because they offer an alternative to 'vertical voice,' that is, to the communication of petition and command that dictatorships prefer. They are oblique because they are coded. Coding, though, is more than just a way of hiding from the authorities. Particularly in Eastern Europe, the aspiration to reject the system's opacity, to be public and transparent, was powerful. Coding created an emotional and cognitive bond among opponents of the regime, who came to recognize that they were not alone. (1991, 71)

An embodiment of this conception was the *samizdat*, that is, clandestine publications. Di Palma stresses three of their features, linking them to a specific conception of civil society:

> First, the publications – typically, personal political and parapolitical testimonials – were authored, reproduced, and circulated through self-generated, improvised networks, in which the authors and the disseminators at each step were often single individuals. Second, this meant that in certain cases, though the publications were illegal and alternative, they were not strictly clandestine. Full clandestinity would have defeated the testimonial function. Third, the individual nature of

samizdat also meant that organizational infrastructures to sustain publication were, strictly speaking, not necessary. (1991)

So, dissent 'kept intellectual mobilization alive, chose transparency over conspiracy, laid bare the deadening effects of communist normalization, and made the recovery of truth its banner'. This explains why the organized opposition chose the form of civic forums, which were conceived as broad in scope and ambition, as 'They aimed at defining postcommunism by an alternative (though nonetheless traditional) set of shared civic values and at consolidating a public sphere, a critical public opinion (that is, a civil society), as the core of a transparent democratic order' (1999). As Ulrich Preuss noted, the 1989 movements did not try to impose a common will of the people, but rather promoted a principle of self-government, based upon 'the idea of an autonomous civil society and its ability to work on itself by means of logical reasoning processes and the creation of appropriate institutions' (1995, 97). In this sense, the democratic opposition expressed a criticism of liberal democracy, stressing instead participatory and deliberative democratic qualities (Olivo 2001, 2–3). In fact, while not aiming at conquering state power, the democratic opposition aimed at building autonomous spaces in which to develop what they defined as 'a culture of dialogue', 'a culture of plurality and the free public domain' (cited in 2001, 14). In these free spaces (or 'parallel polis', in Havel's words), as dissident Ulrike Poppe put it, 'members learned to speak authentically and to relate to each other...to engage in social matters and to put up resistance' (in 2001). So, here, the groups that formed the citizen's movement in the GDR were characterized by 'openness and publicity... grassroots democracy, rejection of patriarchal, hierarchical, and authoritarian structures, non-violence, spirituality, unity of private and public consciousness' (2001, 88). The citizens' movement (calling for 'democracy now') aimed at constituting public forums for deliberation, open to all citizens, self-organizing, with a commitment to participatory democracy (2001, 92). Local round tables and citizens' committees reflected this conception.

If this framing helped mobilization against the regime, it also appeared, however, problematic to sustain mobilization after transition to democracy. As Dryzek (2010, 141) noted:

breakdown of democratic regime is more likely to yield a democratic replacement when there is a deliberative capacity present under the old regime...If opponents of the old regime come from a deliberative public space as opposed to (for example) a militarized resistance movement or a network of exiles involved in strategic machinations, then they can bring to the crisis some clear democratic commitment that stems from abiding by deliberative precepts.

Nevertheless, for activists accustomed to deliberative and participatory conceptions and practices of democracy, the liberal ones that tend to prevail at institutional level tend to be disappointing.

Conceptions of democracy have also been linked to repertoires of action. An emphasis on protest brings about a 'logic of membership' that favours participatory democratic models (della Porta 1995). More participatory and deliberative values tend to foster opposition, increasing participation and providing arenas for plural, inclusive coalitions during phases of liberalization and transition, as well as allowing for more civil society mobilization in the successive periods. However, as Baker rightly noted, the radical view of the civil society that had developed in the opposition in Eastern Europe (as in Latin America) was 'tamed' after the transition, when a liberal conception of democracy prevailed. As he summarized, 'For the opposition theorists of the 1970s and 1980s, civil society was an explicitly normative concept which held up the ideal of societal space, autonomous from the state, wherein self-management and democracy could be worked out. That is, the idea of civil society was political and prescriptive' (Baker 1999, 2). Civil society theorists, such as Michnik and Kuron in Poland, Havel and Benda in Czechoslovakia, and Konrad, Kis and Bence in Hungary:

> also saw civil society originally in the more positive, or socialist, terms of community and solidarity. Indeed, for many such theorists civil society indicated a movement towards post-statism; for control of power, while not unimportant, would be insufficient for the fundamental redistribution, or even negation, of power itself. If this was to be achieved, self-management in civil society was necessary. (ibid.)

These theorists considered self-organized structures from below to be fundamental loci for and of democracy:

> workplace and local community self-government, based on personal contact, exercised daily, and always subject to correction, have greater attraction in our part of the world than multi party representative democracy because, if they have their choice, people are not content with voting once every four years...When there is parliamentary democracy but no self-administration, the political class alone occupies the stage. (Konrad, in Baker 1999, 4–5)

This happened, indeed, during the consolidation of a model of democracy which was based on a liberal conception, which was focused on elected elites and excluded civil society from the true construction of politics and democracy, which had, rather, to be mediated through political parties. Procedural, liberal democracy obscured the substantive claims of the radical conception of civil society, contributing to reducing the participation of the citizens.

The power of action

If political opportunities tend to influence the forms protest takes during transition (with bloody repression fostering radicalization), and mobilizable resources influence the degree of participation of civil society in transition processes, one should not forget that protests themselves produce opportunity and resources. As Beissinger rightly observed, protest events tend to cluster in time: 'They are also linked sequentially to one another across time and space in numerous ways: in the narrative of the struggles that accompany them, in the altered expectations that they generate about subsequent possibilities to contest, in the changes that they evoke in the behavior of those forces that uphold a given order, and in the transformed landscape of meaning that events at times fashion' (2007, 16–17). This happens cross-space, so that what is initially constrained by structures becomes potentially a causal variable in a further chain of events. As tides have a catalytic effect of one movement upon the other, the tide of nationalism emerged from broader mobilizational cycles.

Democratization in fact involved waves of protest that also spread cross-nationally. There is indeed, between proximate units, what Beissinger (2002) defined as a tipping model, with a rapid spread through active promotion as well as contagion, based upon the power of conformity. For those who were successful, the attempt to reproduce themselves was also a way to consolidate support as well as of expressing their ideological belief in the rightness of their own behaviour. But there was a mutual empowerment too, again shaped by some structural preconditions, such as some economic growth, a middle class, education, political rights and a robust political culture of opposition (see Foran 2005 on revolutions). So, 'Essentially, as a modular phenomenon proceeds, increasing numbers of groups with less conducive structural preconditions are drawn into action as a result of the influence of the previous successful examples' (Beissinger 2002, 266).

During the 1989 wave, cross-nationally, the examples of the earlier risers reduced the costs for the later comers. As Kuran (1991, 39) observed:

The success of antigovernment demonstrations in one country inspired demonstrations elsewhere. In early November, Sofia was shaken by its first demonstration in four decades as several thousand Bulgarians marched on the National Assembly. Within a week, on the very day throngs broke through the Berlin Wall, Todor Zhivkov's thirty-five-year leadership came to an end, and his successor began talking of radical reforms.

So, 'In the days following the fall of Czechoslovakia's communist regime, a banner in Prague read: "Poland – 10 years, Hungary – 10 months, East Germany – 10 weeks, Czechoslovakia – 10 days".' The implied acceleration reflects the fact that each successful challenge to communism lowered the perceived risk of dissent in the countries still under communist rule. In terms of our model, as revolutionary thresholds in neighbouring countries fell, the revolution became increasingly contagious. Had this banner been prepared a few weeks later, it might have added 'Romania – 10 hours' (1991, 42).

Changes in action affect the elites' calculus as well. Even in the most authoritarian regimes, the exclusivist ideology of the regime creates resentment that can be mobilized by the opposition. As Wood (2000, 11) stated:

> In oligarchic societies, the exclusivist ideology of economic and regime elites (whether racially coded or not) toward subordinates (indeed, its explicit disdain for members of subordinate groups), together with the experience of repression, fuels deep resentments that can be mobilized by an insurgent group, providing a collective identity based on their claim to common citizenship that lessens the costs of collective action and contributes to the emergence of its leadership as an insurgent counter-elite.

Even if the elites are recalcitrant, insurgency can, however, change their strategic calculations as 'the accumulating costs of the insurgency (and the various counterinsurgency measures) transformed the interests of economic elites, eventually convincing substantial segments "that their interests could be more successfully pursued by democratizing compromise than by continued authoritarian recalcitrance"' (2000, 5–6).

While no new elite might emerge, prolonged insurgency alters elites' perceptions, as it 'may affect the proximate determinants of investment in any one of three ways. It may depress present profit rates (because of extended strikes or subsequent wage increases, for example), dampen expected profit rates (if mobilization is seen as likely to recur), or render expectations so uncertain that investors suspend investment' (2000, 151). Protest thus fuels itself: 'Rather than simply responding to new political opportunities extended by the state, the insurgent social movements create and expand the structure of political opportunity through their interim victories and ongoing struggles' (2000, 12). Insurgents, in their turn, faced with the exclusionary nature of the regime, learn to value democratic participation.

Conclusion

The Arab Spring can be read as yet another proof of the (potential and actual) relevance of social movements in processes of regime change. Although not always as visible, and often unsuccessfully, social movements on human rights, workers' rights, students' rights have in fact struggled for democracy, contributing to weakening dictators. As the democratization literature focused on the elites and social movement studies on established democracy, a growing body of research reviewed in this chapter indicates the relevance of national and international opportunities in influencing pro-democratic protests, their forms and effects. Moreover, it confirms that even authoritarian regimes still leave free spaces, which social movements use to mobilize resources for their collective struggles. What is more, protests are 'eventful' in their capacity to change the structural opportunities and enrich resources. In contrast to essentialist, deterministic and reductionist understandings, it is therefore important to stress temporality, interconnection and agency in what Beissinger (2002) called 'noisy politics'.

8

Restricting Citizens' Participation: The Policing of Protest

Genoa, July 2001, G8 countersummit. In addition to installing high bar-
riers to protect the so-called 'red zone' around the summit meetings, the
airport, railway stations and motorway exits were closed, and suspected
activists were taken back to the city limits. The entire first day of the
summit, events followed a similar pattern: after the Black Bloc's attacks,
the police force responded by setting upon those in or near peaceful pro-
tests, including doctors, nurses, paramedics, photographers and jour-
nalists. Above all, the fight with the so-called 'disobedients', encircled
and repeatedly charged, started in this fashion. After the police charge,
some groups of demonstrators reacted by throwing stones, and the
police used armoured cars. During one incursion, a carabinieri (an
Italian militarized police force) jeep became stuck and its occupants
were attacked by demonstrators. One of the carabinieri inside opened
fire, killing a 23-year-old Genovese activist, Carlo Giuliani. Within the
red zone, the police used water cannon laced with chemicals against
demonstrators from ATTAC and left-wing and trade union groups, who
were banging on the fences and throwing cloves of garlic. On the
evening of 21 July, the police burst into the Diaz School, where the
Genoa Social Forum (GSF, the coordination of social movement groups
that organized the protest), its legal advice team, the Indymedia press
group, and a dormitory for protestors were based, searching for weapons
and Black Bloc activists. The press described the behaviour of the police
as particularly brutal – a description which members of parliament who
were present concurred with. Of the ninety-three persons detained and
arrested in the building, sixty-two were referred to hospital with varying
medical diagnoses. In the days that followed, various testimonies were

published recounting civilians' mistreatment in the Bolzaneto barracks, where a centre for identifying detainees had been set up. Many witness statements, a large number of them from foreigners, described physical and psychological assaults. Using tear-gas and truncheons, and forcing detainees to stay on their feet for hours, police compelled those being held to repeat fascist and racist slogans. In 2012, various police officers were sentenced for the violent aggressions towards activists at the Diaz School and the Bolzaneto barracks, and suspended from work – none of them went to prison, though. Very severe sentences (of up to twelve years in prison) were, on the other hand, passed against ten demonstrators, accused of 'sacking and devastation' (della Porta et al. 2006).

15 October 2011, a global day of action, called for by the Spanish indignados, *saw around 300,000 protestors converging on Rome for a national march. One of the largest, the Roman event was, however, one of the most problematic, as it was disrupted by violent protests and the authorities' lack of will or capacity to protect the peaceful demonstrators. The police decided to build a large no-go area in the city centre, protecting the so-called 'palaces of power', while leaving the other areas practically unpatrolled. In the words of a protest organizer: 'This is a police approach that definitely goes back to before Genoa in 2001, in particular with the use of red zones – from Seattle to 17 March in Naples, let's say that this type of model has persisted. It was there at the beginning of the 2000s, it was there in 2005 when there was an attempt to reach the Senate [Upper House of Parliament] and in 2008 when there was an attempt to get to Montecitorio [Lower House of Parliament] and it was present throughout all of 2010. I mean the police forces arrange themselves – how can I say it – they organise themselves to maintain public order at some street demonstrations by exclusively defending certain symbolic places which in this country represent the power of the state. Everything else is absolutely excluded from public order concerns. In my opinion, 15 October, at least regarding the city of Rome, witnessed the most striking example of this approach.... On 15 October the police concentrated all of its forces behind the barriers that marked the area inaccessible to the demonstrators. Therefore, the area from the Imperial Fora to the Parliament, the Chamber of Deputies, on a day in which all these institutions, in most cases, were closed, empty, therefore – how can I put it – all of this is questionable' (cited in della Porta and Zamponi 2012). It was in fact outside of the patrolled 'red zone' that small groups of protestors burned cars and broke windows, without police intervention until demonstrators – peaceful and otherwise – reached the final destination: Piazza San Giovanni. The police charged them with water cannon and tear gas, and street battles lasted for hours. On 16 October the main headline on the front page of the daily* La Repubblica *was 'The Black Bloc Devastates Rome. Seventy wounded, among them ten officers. Carabinieri's van burned. Critics of the police handling of public order. City put to fire and sword, 5 hours of guerrilla war. The* indignati *rebel against the violent ones', while the lead picture showed demonstrators throwing rocks at a burning carabinieri van.*

The policing of protest at the anti-G8 countersummit in Genoa is one (admittedly extreme, but in several aspects also quite typical, as in Rome 2011) example of the policing of protests in the new millennium, especially of protests that mainly address international targets *and* involve a substantial number of protestors from different countries. In this chapter, I will look at recent transformations in the control of protest, and the challenges they pose to the development of high-quality democracy. After introducing the concept of protest policing, I shall present empirical illustrations of its recent evolution, discussing how the democratic transformations we have discussed in previous chapters seem to affect it, challenging democratic qualities.

Social movement and the policing of protest: an introduction

Social movements do challenge the power of the state, establishing a (temporary) counterpower. They do not limit themselves to asking for specific policy changes: relying mainly on protest as a means to put pressure upon decision makers, they challenge the power of the state to impose its monopoly on the use of legitimate force. Taking to the streets, often forcing their presence beyond the legal limits in order to get their voice heard, they directly interact with the police, who are supposed to defend law and order. In their interventions, the police forces have therefore to realize an uneasy balance between the defence of state power through the implementation of laws and regulations and the recognition of rights to demonstration. The intervention of the police in case of violations is in fact not automatic: with regard to public order, indeed, many minor violations are tolerated in order to avoid major disorders. While sometimes the government sends specific orders (or, at least, signals) about the type of intervention required (or desired) at political demonstrations, the police enjoy, at different hierarchical levels, broad margins of discretionality. Most decisions are taken on the spot, and determined by the assessment of the specific situation as well as by interactive dynamics.

The way in which the government and the police use the power to repress the opposition has relevant, though complex, effects on the protest (Lichbach 1987; Opp and Rohel 1990; Gupta, Singh and Spargue 1993; Francisco 1996; Moore 1998). Increasing the costs of protesting, it might reduce the individual availability to participate. However, the sense of injustice, as well as the creation of intense feelings of identification and solidarity, prompted by repression can increase the motivation to participate (Davenport 2005; Francisco 2005; della Porta and Piazza 2008). As mentioned in the previous chapter, police control tends to impact on the repertoires of protest, through a reciprocal adaptation (or, sometimes, escalation) of police and demonstrators' tactics (della Porta 1995). And it might also influence the organizational forms used, for instance by spreading a sense of mutual mistrust through the use of infiltration (e.g. Fernandez 2008).

Quantitative research, often based upon broad cross-national comparisons, has singled out some causal determinants of police styles (e.g. in terms of violation of human rights, misconduct, etc.) (Davenport 1995; Poe and Tate 1994; Poe, Tate and Camp Keith, 1999). Ethnographic research and case studies have for their part led to understanding of the motivations for the different police styles in dealing with different social and political groups (e.g. Waddington 1994; Waddington 1992; Critcher and Waddington 1996; Waddington and Critcher 2000; Waddington, Jones and Critcher 1989).

The forms state power takes have a clear impact on the policing of protest. If repression is much more brutal in authoritarian than in democratic regimes (e.g. Sheptycky 2005 on Latin America; Uysal 2005 on Turkey), even authoritarian regimes vary in the amount of protest they are ready to tolerate, as well as in the forms in which they police the opposition (see also chapter 7). Moreover, variations do exist also in democratic regimes, with some countries considered to be traditionally more inclusive, others more exclusive (della Porta 1995). In both types of regime, the police strategies in addressing the demonstrations reflect some more general characteristics of state power. In this sense, it is to be expected that the change in the balance of state powers related with the various transformations described all through this volume have an impact on the styles of protest policing. In particular, the wave of transnational protests that marked the turn of the millennium seems indeed to have challenged some well-established police strategies and structures (e.g. della Porta, Petersen and Reiter 2006).

Even if in a selective way and with frequent inversions, the policing of protest in democratic regimes has been characterized by some trends towards a growing publicization, nationalization and demilitarization. First of all, the task of policing is at the core of the definition of a Weberian state power that claims the monopoly of force. Second, the process of state building brought about the assumption by the central state of the control of public order. Even if the degree of centralization in the police structures clearly varies, and local police bodies often maintain specific profiles and styles (see, e.g., Wisler and Kriesi 1998 on Switzerland and Winter 1998 on Germany), there has, however, been a progressive orientation of protest and its policing towards the national level. Third – here, as well, with cross-country differences – there has also been a progressive transfer of public order control from the military to the police. Especially since the 1980s, research on the policing of protest in European democracies and the United States has singled out a reduction of strategies of control based on an escalation of force – with low priority given to the right to demonstrate, and an increase in mistrust of a negotiated control – with a broader recognition of the right to demonstrate (McPhail, Schweingruber and McCarthy 1998, 51–4; della Porta and Fillieule 2004).

If we look at the evolution of the policing of protest nowadays, with particular attention to the control of transnational protests, these trends seem to have met some (more or less brisk) reversals. Although public order policing had never been exclusively under public control (see, e.g., private policing on university campuses or in the factories, but also the use of organized crime to intimidate unionists and protestors), the privatization and semi-privatization of spaces such as shopping malls, as well as the outsourcing of police functions to private companies (e.g. in the airports, but also universities), has recently increased and made more visible the role of private police bodies in the control of protest. Additionally, the control of more and more transnational protests brought about a growing coordination of police units from different countries. Third, since the 1980s, processes of militarization of public order have been noted even in countries, such as Great Britain, once considered to be the best examples of 'citizens' policing'. This militarization, including equipment, training, organization and strategies, has been tested in the fight against organized crime, but also street crimes and football hooliganism, migrating then to the control of protest. Finally, negotiated strategies were not consistently implemented in the control of transnational protests, where priority has been often given to security concerns (della Porta, Petersen and Reiter 2006). Escalations in the interactions between demonstrators and protestors developed here from the use of coercion against demonstrators, with the building of fences and no-go areas to isolate diplomats and heads of government from the very sight of the protest. The example of 15 October 2011, mentioned in the incipit of this chapter, as well as several instances in the policing of recent anti-austerity protests, indicate a return of those police styles.

Militarization, fortification and intelligence-led control

Are we witnessing the re-emergence of the escalated force model, or the development of a new repressive protest-policing style? Can we observe a definite break with the de-escalating, negotiated model of protest policing that dominated in the 1980s and well into the 1990s? Or is the control of transnational countersummits an exception in a policing of protest that remains mainly negotiated? Negotiated management signified a considerable departure from the protest-policing style dominant in Western democracies prior to the 1960s and 1970s. The traditional escalated force strategy was, in fact, based on a presumption of irrational crowd behaviour (Le Bon 1895) and rooted in intolerance of direct forms of political participation. Highly suspicious of any gathering, its supporters gave low priority to demonstration rights and foresaw the massive use of force to suppress even small violations of laws and ordinances. During the '1968' protest cycle, attempts to stop unauthorized demonstrations and a law-and-order attitude towards the 'limited-rule-breaking' tactics that spread from the US civil rights movement to the European student movement (McAdam and Rucht 1993) and then to new social movements pushed the police to adapt their strategies of control. The prevailing police strategy after the 1980s was instead designed to reduce coercive interventions. Limited lawbreaking, implicit in non-violent, civil disobedience forms of protest, tended to be more or less tolerated by the police, with peacekeeping considered more important than law enforcement.

In the new millennium, in recent transnational protest events *coercive strategies* returned as a prominent aspect of protest policing, apparently recalling the 'escalated force' style, although with adaptations to new protest repertoires, police frames and technologies. in particular, clear signs of militarization were observed. A massive police presence, usually with high visibility, has been noted at numerous transnational protest events in North America and Europe. In most of the cases considered in comparative research on the policing of transnational protests (della Porta, Peterson and Reiter 2006), police officers donned heavy anti-riot gear and, above all, special units were deployed for coercive intervention against 'troublemakers'. The army often intervened, as did paramilitary bodies (such as SWAT in the US: Fernandez 2008).

Before and during countersummits, militarization has been visible in the number of police, their attitudes, their equipment. As Starr, Fernandez and Scholl (2011, 43) observed: 'It is not hyperbole to say that the space becomes a war zone, with officers dressed in sophisticated military gear and accompanied by armored vehicles. The closer to the actual meeting location, the more militarized the space becomes.' In fact, as they summarized:

> weapons used by police at protests include striking weapons, chemical weapons, electric weapons, projectiles (plastic, rubber, and wooden bullets), water cannons (sometimes with pepper spray in the water, which has a high rate of dispersal and which, unlike tear gas, is invisible), and concussion and shock grenades (the former meant to make a scary explosive sound, the latter used to simultaneously create a disturbing flash or light; both have been linked to severe injuries when they land on or close to people). (2011, 84)

Live ammunition was used in the anti-EU summit in Gothenburg in June 2001 (three demonstrators wounded) and in Genoa (one demonstrator killed). So-called non-lethal arms were also often misused, contrary to instruction: e.g. projectile weapons aimed above the waist, gas in close spaces, *tonfa* batons (with an iron part inside) handled upside-down.

These developments emerge as significant departures from the protest-policing styles dominant in the 1980s and 1990s. Admittedly, the advent of negotiated management did not signify the disappearance of coercive intervention. Research has frequently stressed the selectivity of police intervention and the survival of harsh modes of protest policing in the 1980s and 1990s (della Porta 1998; Fillieule and Jobard 1998). However, antagonistic interventions with a 'show of force' attitude and a massive, highly visible police presence were generally reserved for small extremist groups or football hooliganism. In the case of transnational protest events organized by the global justice movement, these features have been observed instead in conjunction with mass demonstrations of tens of thousands, if not hundreds of thousands, of participants. Massive use of force as a strategy for maintaining public order, however, was effective only with a favourable police/demonstrator ratio (as in Canada or Copenhagen; for New York City, see Vitale 2005). In cases of massive demonstrations, with large numbers of peaceful demonstrators and small (but highly mobile) groups of radical Black Bloc, shows of force and undiscriminating intervention produced escalation: police brutality against non-violent participants has often been denounced in numerous transnational protest events, and, as in Gothenburg and Genoa, police charges have triggered violent reactions even by previously peaceful groups of protestors.

Deterrence of demonstrators – both in general and in specific areas – has been a main strategic element in the policing of transnational protest events. As Fernandez recently observed, 'The closing of public spaces to activists is a growing tactis in policing dissents' (2008, 86). As far as the European Union is concerned, border controls were routinely reintroduced during international demonstrations within the Schengen area, and numerous potential participants (also EU citizens) were refused entrance, often on a questionable legal basis. In Quebec City as well as in Genoa, checkpoints were set up at the city borders, and railway stations were closed and/or heavily patrolled.

Especially after 2000, summits were called in places difficult to reach and hostile to protest (as was the case, for instance, for the WTO summit in Quatar in 2001, the G8 summit in Kananaskis in 2003, and those in Gleaneagles in 2005, and Heiligendamm in 2007). In fact, 'The selection of a summit location is an important aspect of the geography of global governance and mirrors the contestation of global power relations' (Starr, Fernandez and Scholl 2011, 29). Not only are locations chosen in order to discourage protest, but 'Once a location is selected, authorities start to reorganize the surrounding area by rating spaces on a "danger scale".'

Above all, the 'fortification' of summit sites and, in general, police measures aimed at their protection are difficult to reconcile with a negotiating strategy. Fences were built in Seattle and (increasingly sophisticated and impenetrable) in Windsor, Washington, Prague, Quebec City, Gothenburg and Genoa. Special trains transporting activists to Prague were blocked at the borders. This process has the intent of channelling dissent into pre-established zones, far away from the actual gatherings, 'in order to secure the operational flows involved in a summit meeting and to control dangerous objects identified beforehand' (Starr, Fernandez and Scholl 2011, 35). In fact, fences grew from 2.5 km long in Quebec City for the Free Trade Area of the Americas (FTAA) summit in 2001 to 12.5 km long around Heiligendamm in 2007. Moreover, 'the construction of the fence has been steadily improved and is standardized according to the security handbooks of transnational police agencies. Fences are higher, more massive, with cement foundations, and are often equipped with movement detectors and surveillance cameras' (2011, 36). Two levels of security zone (red and yellow) were imposed in Genoa, three at the Strasbourg NATO summit in 2009. To the fences, mobile blockades are added, made of police vehicles, or even with the bodies of policemen themselves.

Transnational protests called for international policing. In Genoa functionaries of the German federal criminal police, directly connected with their data banks, were present as liaison officers. At the Evian G8 in May 2003 police units from different countries intervened together in the streets. Among EU member states, the transnational control of protest involved the networks of police cooperation that had developed as a form of intergovernmental collaboration outside the EU institutions, like TREVI (since 1976 directed above all against terrorism) or Schengen (the 1985 agreement between a group of member states to gradually abolish internal border controls, which became effective in 1995).

During the prelude to the summit meetings, the police forces in various countries also employed coercive measures not aimed at protecting the official summit, but offensively directed against movement activists and their protest. In Genoa, in Copenhagen and elsewhere, police officers were accused of harassing young people who looked like movement activists, employing continuous identity checks and body searches during the days and nights prior to the protest events. Heavy patrolling was used as an instrument of intimidation in countersummits, in Genoa as in Washington DC, Cancun and Miami (see also Fernandez 2008). Preventive arrests targeted against specific protest actions, as well as those considered to be the movement leaders, as well as the confiscation of propaganda material like puppets or banners were denounced in Seattle and afterwards. Police were reported to have entered and searched demonstrators' headquarters, independent media centres and legal assistance offices (including those located in premises offered by the local authorities), for example in Washington, Prague, Gothenburg and (with the most dramatic consequences) in Genoa.

In addition, an array of legal provisions (from city regulations and national codes) against vandalism, trespassing, failure to disperse, disobeying a lawful order, but also traffic laws, and laws on use of fire in public (e.g. to prohibit the burning of flags), have been used in order to repress protest. In fact, 'Temporary ordinances, creative use of old laws, and legal permits are now common ways to control the protest' (Fernandez 2008, 166). In the United States, before the summit of the World Economic Forum, the New York City police department called for zero tolerance against violent protestors, implementing arrests against any interference with traffic (following an edict of 1845 prohibiting three or more people from assembling in a public space wearing masks). In the same vein, fire regulations and public health ordinances have been used in order to prevent the preparation of protest. Regulations against meeting in public parks are implemented to prohibit protests. Protest permits have been used to reduce the movements of protestors and restrict them to inconvenient areas. The housing of demonstrators has been actively boycotted (as e.g. in Calgary, where the authorities refused to host protestors, and out-bid an offer by the protestors to lease land from the Stoney First Nation) (Fernandez 2008, 87). Similarly, in Europe and the US, regulations on health and public safety have been used to 'disoccupy' the parks and squares occupied during anti-austerity protests.

In the policing of transnational countersummits, there has been, in general, a much stronger emphasis on isolating political leaders and dignitaries from the risks of contact with demonstrators than on negotiating with organizers to define spaces and limits of protest. In some cases (as in Gothenburg and Genoa) serious negotiations started late and were more or less haphazard. While negotiations did precede several protest events, in many cases little care seems to have been taken to ensure open communication lines during demonstrations, one of the cardinal points of negotiated management; in fact, contacts between authorities and organizers were often interrupted, as in Seattle, Prague, Quebec City, Gothenburg and Genoa, among others. This trend continued in recent protests, such as the one previously mentioned in Rome.

Intimidation includes mass arrests, but also mistreatment during arrests. Mass arrests, sometimes far from the demonstration venue, have been observed at transnational protests in Seattle, Washington, Prague, Quebec City, Gothenburg and Genoa. Most of these arrests were not approved by judicial authorities. There has also been criticism of intimidating conditions during mass arrests, with several cases in which 'protesters are deprived of their legal rights to counsel, same-sex searches, phone calls, access to bathrooms, blankets, heat, beds, timely arraignment and release... They are also subject to cruel and unusual punishment while in custody, such as denial of medical care, excessively tight hand-cuffs, beatings, sexual abuse, death threats, and being held at gunpoint' (Starr, Fernandez and Scholl 2011, 81). While most people arrested before and during protests are released without charges, there are some cases of very high sentences for minor illegal acts of dissent, as 'trespassing and property damage, traditionally areas of civil disobedience, are being recast as severe and violent crimes or even terrorism' and conspiracy (Starr, Fernandez and Scholl 2011, 87).

Coercion and deterrence strategies were linked to information strategies. The literature on protest policing has underlined the significance of technical innovation and the influence of advanced surveillance, information processing and communications technologies on the way policing is organized. New terms such as 'strategic', 'pro-active', and 'intelligence-led' policing imply approaches that target suspect populations and individuals in a highly systematic way. First established in the US with the 'war on drugs', these trends became highly evident in transnational protest policing, both in North America and in Europe.

Comparative research (della Porta, Peterson and Reiter 2006; Fernandez 2008) indicates an attempt to extend control over a population of transnational activists through a broad collection of information, shared transnationally among the different police bodies, with enforcement agencies (such as the US Department of Homeland Security Office of Domestic Preparedness) instructing and training in updated techniques of civil disobedience management (Fernandez 2008, 98).

Long-term planning included the collection of information on the protestors (who they are, how many, which groups) as well as an elaboration of the lessons learned from the policing of previous transnational events. Information collected from open source as well as infiltration (in the US, with powers increased by the Patriot Act) is then used to train officers (Fernandez 2008, 109). In fact,

> surveillance is...a policing tactic which aims to quell or weaken political activity. Technologies of surveillance include direct surveillance, such as observation and visits by officers, recording of automobile plate numbers, raids, questioning, and burglary; electronic surveillance, such as phone taps, audio eavesdropping, tracking of e-mail, and monitoring of Internet and other computer activity; use of video, photo, and car-tracking devices; undercover surveillance, including by police in disguise, and the use of informants, infiltrators, and agents provocateurs; and databasing and the sharing of databased information. (Starr, Fernandez and Scholl 2011, 73)

This information was often used in order to stop some activists reaching the protest zones. In particular in the EU, efforts have multiplied to prevent violent activists (or those presumed to be so) from reaching the city hosting the summit (Reiter and Fillieule 2006). Expanding on a 1996 Recommendation on Football Hooliganism (Official Journal 1997 C 193/1), on 26 May 1997 the European Council adopted a Joint Action with regard to cooperation on law and order and security, which stipulated that: 'Member States shall provide Member States concerned with information, upon request or unsolicited, via central bodies, if sizeable groups which may pose a threat to law and order and security are travelling to another Member State in order to participate in events.' In the preamble, the 'events' were specified as 'sporting events, rock concerts, demonstrations and road-blocking protest campaigns' (Official Journal 1997 L 147/1). The Schengen Information System (SIS), that had been introduced as a sort of compensatory measure for abolishing internal border checks, extended the possibilities for the exchange of information between police forces and intelligence services (Peers 2000, 209ff.). After the EU summit in Gothenburg, the Council for Justice and Home Affairs on 13 July 2001, adopted security measures oriented to protecting the meetings of the European Council and other comparable events, focussing on greater collaboration among the various national police forces. In order to increase information exchange, the document called for 'the use of all the legal and technical possibilities for stepping up and promoting rapid, more structured exchanges of data on violent troublemakers on the basis of national files'. Other measures included the temporary suspension of the Schengen Convention (with reintroduction of border controls) and expulsion measures and cooperation in the repatriation of expelled demonstrators. Finally, direct cooperation between judicial authorities was to be facilitated, with the aim of prosecuting and trying 'violent troublemakers...without undue delay and in conditions guaranteeing a fair trial'.

False information has also been spread in order to portray the activists as violent (della Porta, Andretta, Mosca and Reiter 2006; Fernandez 2008). In Genoa (as, before, in Washington), widespread alarmist use has been made of information later declared unreliable by the same authorities, recalling (among others) the case of the Chicago Congress of the Democratic Party in 1968 (Donner 1990, 116–17). While this alarmism did not discourage participation at the countersummits, it favoured the spreading, especially among rank-and-file police officers, of an image of demonstrators as dangerously violent, or even as terrorists (or infiltrated by terrorists). The deployment of plain-clothes police, for instance in Copenhagen, was denounced by movement activists as infiltration attempts and what was seen as *agent provocateur* behaviour.

Especially in the policing of transnational demonstrations, a massive use of data banks and exchange of information among national police forces in order to prevent individuals from participating in protest deemed dangerous for public order surfaced, particularly in the European cases, within the institutional framework of the EU. These practices, which often followed the informal rules developed for the control of football hooligans, emerged as opaque in terms of the protection of citizens' rights.

To conclude, at the turn of the millennium there was indeed a return to the massive use of police force, especially oriented towards temporary incapacitation, with protestors forced to the margins. Negotiations took place, but trust between negotiators remained low, also because of the uncompromising messages sent by the police with other interventions aimed at protection and prevention during the period leading up to the demonstrations. In fact, according to the US National Lawyers Guild, one observes a shift to a pre-emptive model focused on 'blocking access, intimidating activists, conducting broad-scale [illegal] searches, raids and mass arrests, and confiscating or incapacitating protestors' resources' (Starr, Fernandez and Scholl 2011, 68). Today, this turn is still visible in the policing of anti-austerity protests, even if not in a homogeneous fashion.

The policing of protest: some explanations

How are we to explain the policing of protest and its evolution? Social movement studies suggest some main explanations (figure 8.1) that indeed seem to have played a role in recent times.

Research on the policing of social movements has identified a tendency to use harsher styles of protest policing against social and political groups that are perceived as greater threats to political elites, or as being more ideologically driven or more radical in their aims (see della Porta and Fillieule 2004; Earl 2003; Davenport 2000, 1995). Additionally, police repression is more likely to be directed against groups that are poorer in material resources as well as in political connections (Earl, Soule and McCarthy 2003; della Porta 1998).

The police thus react to changes they perceive in the social movements. Certainly, countersummits present a specific challenge to police forces, obliged to balance respect for rights to demonstration with the maintenance of public order and the protection of domestic, and especially foreign, dignitaries (Ericson and Doyle 1999). Some characteristics of the emerging movements – not only their novelty, but also their

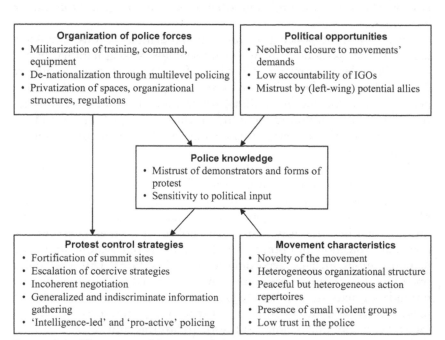

Figure 8.1   Transnational protest policing
Source: della Porta and Reiter 2011, 103

heterogeneity, loose organizational structures, and use of direct action strategies, as well as widespread distrust of the police (see della Porta and Reiter 2004; della Porta and Reiter 1998; Noakes and Gillham 2006; Peterson 2006) – have facilitated police framing of protestors as 'bad demonstrators' (or troublemakers). As Fernandez noted, 'After the 1999 WTO protests in Seattle, police developed techniques designed to deal with a decentralized, non-hierarchical, network-based movement. Such policing required thoughtful planning and careful attention to the geographical space in order to control mass movements' (2008, 137).

The resources (both material and legal) available to the police, their knowledge about protestors, as well as more general police culture, all play a role in police choices. The degree of militarization of the structure and the equipment, the legal competences and the degree of professionalization influence the strategic choices of the police. In recent years, the militarization of public order control was reflected in the augmentation of paramilitary units, used for instance in the intervention against drug dealers, as well as the growth of a military culture exemplified by police training, armament, uniforms and more (on the US, see Kraska and Kaeppler 1997; Kraska 1996). Less-lethal arms have been tested in non-political public order policing (for instance, in response to beer riots on US campuses; see McCarthy, Martin and McPhail 2004).

It has been observed that police tactics in the control of protest follow some general conceptions of the role of the police. With an original insight compared to previous research, Noakes and Gillham (2006) underline the importance of shifts in the dominant visions of the causes of crime, and in the corresponding conceptual principles underlying police intervention, for protest policing, in particular the implications of the 'new penology' with its emphasis on protection and risk management. Zero-tolerance doctrines, as well as militaristic training and equipment, are imported into the field of protest policing from other forms of public order control addressing micro-criminality or football hooliganism. The elaboration of a 'penal law of the enemy' is another case in point. The strategy of space fortification reflects the relevance of a conception of prevention as isolation from the danger (and the dangerous ones), through a reduction of rights (of demonstrations, movement, privacy) of those citizens who are considered to be potential enemies. The assumption is here that 'the implementation of the rights as well as the security of the included pass necessarily through the expulsion from those rights of the excluded, that is those who do not deserve them, who are marginals' (Pepino 2005, 262). A situation defined as an emergency is faced through the strategies experimented with in the public-order control of the different, the street enemies (migrants, petty criminals, hooligans, etc.). This intelligence-led policing is certainly facilitated by the expansion of police preventive powers (e.g. in the control of football stadiums) or the large-scale use of tapping and videocameras (originally against organized crime and terrorism). In several countries, anti-terrorism, or anti-crime policies more generally, have introduced new associational crimes (membership in or moral support of subversive or terrorist associations), or crimes against the personality of the state and heads of state, with the effect of orienting repression against categories of people rather than against specific crimes. Militarization is therefore justified by 'states of exception' that foresee, among other tactics, the use of the army.

In this situation, the new laws on terrorism that have been passed at the national level after the September 11 events, but also the enhanced international police cooperation on security issues, have provided instruments and norms that allow for a consistent restriction of demonstration rights. This is all the more the case as far as the right of protesting transnationally is concerned, with its particular sensitivity towards the possibilities for citizens to cross national borders. Stricter visa regulations, as well as police cooperation to produce proscriptive lists of potential troublemakers, risk diminishing protests about the right to demonstrate. Moreover, old and new anti-terrorism legislation is more and more used for the surveillance and intimidation of activists, who risk very high penalties for minor violations (see, e.g., Starr et al. 2008). While not used automatically, it is nevertheless available for selective implementation against the groups that are considered to be politically more dangerous.

In general, there is then a reciprocal adaptation, as in 'a dance between those who challenge authority, speak true to power, and hope for a more just world and those who wish to extend their privilege and power' (Fernandez 2008, 171). It is what Sidney Tarrow and I (della Porta and Tarrow 2012) have called 'interactive diffusion' of protestors and police tactics, with processes of learning and strategic adaptation both within protestor and police communities and across the two communities.

Social science research has also linked the style of police intervention to some characteristics of the external environment. The police have been said to be sensitive to the characteristics of the perceived threat but also to the expected demands from authorities and public opinion. Demands, especially from authorities, can be expected to be all the more relevant the more challenging a protest seems to be to their image. Research into the police has stressed that the organizational imperative is keeping control over situations, rather than enforcing the law (Rubinstein 1980; Bittner 1967; Skolnick 1966). Police officers indeed enjoy a high degree of discretion in their encounters with citizens, but they must also maintain (to different extents) the support of authorities and the public.

Political opportunities affect protest policing. The institutionalization and moderation of social movements in the 1980s and 1990s and their integration into increasingly institutionalized forms of politics contributed – also with a glorified but moderated vision of the '1968' past – to an image of the emerging global justice movement as particularly violent in its action repertoires and particularly poor in its political capacity. In the early 2000s, the isolation of protestors in the institutional sphere of politics seems to have pushed the police towards harsher strategies, adapted from those applied in preceding decades against weak (politically unprotected) groups and generally stigmatized phenomena like football hooliganism (Wahlström and Oskarsson 2006; della Porta and Reiter 2004).

A further explanation for the weak defence of rights to demonstrate observed in the policing of transnational protest events is the low formal accountability of IGOs, which, with the convergence on neoliberal policies of right-wing and left-wing political parties, has been read as closing down channels of access for political movements (della Porta, Petersen and Reiter 2006). In fact, while the targets and organization of the protest become transnational, the protest rights remain anchored at the national level (Reiter and Fillieule 2006; della Porta et al. 2006). In Genoa, but also Gothenburg and Copenhagen, the right to protest has been limited for the citizens blocked at the borders. Even though the rights to protest are recognized by the EU Convention on Human Rights and the Charter of Fundamental Rights of the European Union, there is no concrete protection of a transnational right to protest (Reiter and Fillieule 2006). Additionally, the policing of transnational events tends to involve international policing, characterized by an even lower level of democratic accountability (Sheptycki 2002, 1994; Walker 2003). The participation of multiple law enforcement agencies, as well as secret services, further reduces internal coordination and external controls on police intervention. A supranational public sphere capable of keeping a critical eye on the defence of citizens' rights is emerging (as, for instance, the wave of international protest against police brutality at the Genoa countersummit indicates), but it is still weak and surfaces only occasionally.

In the EU, the intergovernmental character of European police collaboration brought about deficient public debate, opaque decision making, and a lack of democratic accountability while increasing the difficulties for citizens to single out the institutional level which is politically and juridically responsible for limitations of their rights and which they should ask for redress (Peers 2000, 188). Integration in justice and home affairs is predominantly driven by the formalizing of informal arrangements and the structuration at the level of the EU of intergovernmental agreements.

Police matters are treated prevalently by the European Council for Justice and Internal Affairs, with a merely consultative role for the European Parliament and limited intervention by the European Court of Justice (della Porta and Reiter 2004; Reiter and Fillieule 2006). Developing through groups of experts and intelligence activities, European cooperation in the field of public order first concentrated on football hooliganism, subsequently extending to other public-order problems. In fact, a Parliament recommendation to the Council voted by the plenum on 12 December 2001 pointed at 'not a few shortcomings' in Member States' responses to the countersummits in Nice, Gothenburg and Genoa, recommending respect for European citizens' right to demonstrate. These recommendations do not seem to have been attended to by the European Council. The 'Security handbook for the use of police authorities and services at international events such as meetings of the European Council', approved in November 2002, suggested that future revisions be discussed only by the Police Chiefs Task Force and the committee of experts foreseen in Article 3 of the Joint Action of 1997 and approved by the Article 36 Committee (a coordinating committee of senior officials in the field of police cooperation and judicial cooperation in criminal matters). In 2004, a resolution on the security of Council meetings and similar events called for targeted information exchange, making possible intelligence-led checks on 'individuals or groups in respect of whom there are substantial grounds for believing that they intend to enter the Member State with the aim of disrupting public order and security at the event or committing offences relating to the event' (see Reiter and Fillieule 2006).

Conclusion

In sum, the policing of protest in the new millennium has often been characterized by police brutality and a 'show of force' attitude. Massive, highly visible police presence recalls the escalated force style, although with adaptation to new protest repertoires, police frames and technologies. Also striking in several cases of transnational protest policing is the strong presence of deterrent or even intimidating elements, among which the most visible is the fortification of summit sites and, in general, police measures aimed at its protection. Technical innovations have allowed for a broad increase in surveillance.

In general, there has been a return to massive use of force, especially oriented at temporary incapacitation, with protestors forced to the margins, in invisible places, far from the places of power. Negotiations take place, but they tend to start late and trust between negotiators of the two sides remains low, also because of the uncompromising messages sent by the police with other interventions aimed at protection and prevention during the period leading up to the demonstrations. Finally, there are clear attempts at intelligence-led policing, with much emphasis given to massive collection and frequent exchange of information, which, however, do not translate into intelligence of the differentiated protest field.

These characteristics certainly constitute a departure from the negotiated management model, with its 'demonstration-friendly' protest-policing philosophy, which had been dominant (although not exclusive) in several Western democracies in the 1980s and 1990s. In many cases, protests are made invisible if not uninfluential, by relegating them to outside the symbolic space where the powerful meet: what King and Waddington (2006) called 'exclusionary fortress-oriented policing', and Noakes and Gillham (2006) 'selective incapacitation'. The right to demonstrate seems to be recognized selectively in more than one way: weakly protected for foreigners or weak social actors, and with the exclusion of direct action protest repertoires defined as illegal and violent. Anti-terrorist legislation has further reduced protestors' rights. Some of these new trends have returned in the policing of the most recent wave of protests against the austerity crisis. The effects of these challenges to the right to demonstrate are all the more serious given the growing importance of participatory and deliberative democracy, given the crisis of representative institutions.

9

Deliberative Experiments inside Institutions

At different territorial levels, institutional experiments are called for. According to the Commission of the European Communities (2001): 'If participation in local politics is to be sustained in the twenty first century, the key challenge is to adapt the decision-making processes to meet the changing expectations of citizens. There are already many experiments and initiatives under way in several member states. In others, there are debates about wider and more sweeping reforms.... In a world where citizens are better educated and where new information and communication technologies allow the rapid spread of understanding and expertise, the case for direct involvement in the political process by citizens is more substantial than before. The key strategic issue is how to organize direct participation so that it enhances rather than diminishes the quality of local decision-making and service delivery. The facilities that are available today allow citizens to have their say on various issues, every day of the week.' Among the options available for consultation or even direct involvement of the public in decision making, the document lists classical mechanisms of referendums and citizens' initiatives; others inspired by 'New Management' that look at the public as consumers; still others that stress a politics of presence as the need to ensure the involvement of citizens who are often absent from decision making. Among them, youth parliaments, elderly people forums, neighbourhood forums, co-option procedures, community development and partnership schemes are cited. Finally, 'Another set of direct participation options attempts to create the conditions for a more deliberative democracy. Interactive websites, citizens' juries and consensus conferencing are mechanisms present in several countries' (2001). Participation is here defined as fundamental: 'The quality, relevance and effectiveness of EU policies depend on ensuring wide participation throughout the policy chain – from conception to implementation. Improved participation is likely to create more confidence in the end result and in the Institutions which deliver policies. Participation crucially depends on central governments following an inclusive approach when developing and implementing EU policies' (2001, 10).

The participatory budgeting cycle starts in January of each year with dozens of assemblies across the city designed to ensure the system operates with maximum participation and friendly interaction... Each February there is instruction from city specialists in technical and system aspects of city budgeting... In March there are plenary assemblies in each of the city's 16 districts as well as assemblies dealing with such areas as transportation, health, education, sports, and economic development. These large meetings – with participation that can reach over 1,000 – elect delegates to represent specific neighborhoods. The mayor and staff attend to respond to citizen concerns. In subsequent months these delegates meet weekly or biweekly in each district to acquaint themselves with the technical criteria involved in requesting a project be brought to a district and to deliberate about the district's needs. Representatives from the city's departments participate according to their specialties. These intermediary meetings come to a close when, at a second regional plenary, regional delegates prioritize the district's demands and elect councillors to serve on the Municipal Council of the Budget. The council is a 42-member forum of representatives of all the districts and thematic meetings. Its main function is to reconcile the demands of each district with available resources, and to propose and approve an overall municipal budget. The resulting budget is binding – the city council can suggest changes but not require them. The budget is submitted to the mayor who may veto it and remand it to the Municipal Council of the Budget, but this has never happened. (Lewit, 2002)

In the new millennium, European institutions (such as the ones cited above) recognize the need to reform existing democratic practices by introducing new instruments of citizens' participation to public deliberation. They are not the only ones: local, regional and national governments have also attempted to innovate and renew democratic procedures, reacting to the perceived decline in conventional forms of participation as well as in trust in representative institutions. A particularly innovative experiment – destined to be imitated and much discussed everywhere around the world – is the participatory budget in Porto Alegre, described above. In this chapter, I will review the main – different – logics behind these attempts, as well as assessing their capacity to improve democracy, by bridging liberal institutions with participatory and deliberative models.

Institutional experiments with deliberative democracy: an introduction

Conceptions of deliberative democracy, even when joined with participatory elements, have had effects on existing democratic institutions. As Russell Dalton (2004, 204) observed, 'the public's democratic expectations place a priority on reforms that move beyond traditional forms of representative democracy. Stronger political parties, fairer elections, more representative electoral systems will improve the democratic process, but these reforms do not address expectations that the democratic process will expand to provide new opportunities for citizen input and control.' In fact, reforms that just aim at 'turning the clock back' vis-à-vis recent transformations have been considered as either unrealistic or insufficient (Dryzek 2010, 205). Innovation implies, instead, giving citizens the possibility to participate in various ways at various levels. As Cheryl S. King, Kathryn M. Feltey and Bridget O'Neill Susel stressed, 'empowering citizens means designing processes where citizens know that their participation has the potential to have an impact, where a representative range of citizens are included, and where there are visible outcomes' (1998, 318).

In the search for complementary sources of legitimation that could allow them to face the challenge of a weak electoral accountability and the erosion of a 'legitimation by the output' (in terms of good performances), public institutions have more and more discussed various forms of involvement of citizens in decision making. At the beginning of the new millennium, the White Paper on European Governance by the Commission of the European Communities (2001) recognized the principle of participation by means of open consultation with citizens and their associations as one of the fundamental pillars of European Union governance. Building on the Charter of Fundamental Rights and within the context of the debate on 'The Future of Europe', the European Commission urged the identification of ways to constructively manage change by more actively involving European citizens in decision making: 'Failure to do so might fuel "citizenship" deficit, or even encourage protest' (2001, 10). The experience of the Convention for the Elaboration of the Charter of Fundamental Rights provided examples for a better involvement of civil society in the European Union. A conception of a government *with* the people has been put forward at EU level as a third way 'between government *by* and *of* the people at national level, and governance *for* and *with* the people at the EU level' (Schmidt 2006, 9).

At the national and, especially, at the local levels, research on co-management in public policies has noted, if not a change in paradigm, at least the experimentation with different bases of legitimacy through the incorporation of different points of view. Within the frame of governing with the people, experiments with deliberative and participatory democracy in public decision making have developed as ways of increasing the participation of citizens, in the creation of high-quality communicative arenas and, therefore, citizens' empowerment. The adopted formulas are, indeed, varied. In a study commissioned by the Organisation for Economic Co-operation and Development (OECD), David Shand and Morten Arnberg (1996) proposed a continuum of participation from minimal involvement to community control through regular referendums, with intermediate steps such as consultation, partnership and delegation (in which control over developing policy options is handed to a board of community representatives within a framework specified by the government). Similarly, Patrick Bishop and Glyn Davis (2002) distinguished among consultation, partnership and control. Consultation practices include key contracts surveys, interest group meetings, public meetings, discussion papers, public hearings; partnership includes advisory boards, citizens' advisory committees, policy community forums, public inquiries; controls include referendums, community parliaments, electronic voting. We might add the above-mentioned participatory budget as an instance of the control type of participation.

In this panoply of institutional experiments, one could distinguish, with Graham Smith (2009), two main institutional formulas: assembleary is the first, oriented to the construction of a 'mini-public'; selection by lot is the second.

As far as the *assembleary model* is concerned, institutions of participatory democracy, like neighbourhood assemblies, thematic assemblies, neighbourhood councils, consultation committees and strategic participatory plans, form part of local governance in most democratic countries. In addition, user representatives are often admitted to the institutions that govern schools or other public services, which sometimes are even handed to citizens' groups to manage. Particular interest, including at the institutional level, was attracted by the previously mentioned participatory budget in Porto Alegre. During a long-term experiment, the participatory budget acquired an articulate and complex structure, oriented to achieving two main objectives: social equality and citizen empowerment. A fundamental criterion in the distribution of public funds is, in fact, the level of privation of services and wellbeing in the different neighbourhoods. The organization of the process was oriented to controlling the limits of assemblies, in particular in terms of blocks being put on their decisions, without renouncing the advantages of direct democracy. Recognizing its success, the United Nations have defined the participatory budget as one of the forty 'best practices' at global level (Allegretti 2003, 173).

As for the *'mini-publics' model*, from the beginning of the 1960s the idea of drawing lots as a democratic method of choosing representatives was implemented in citizen juries that emerged in the United States: small groups of citizens, drawn from population registers, met to express their opinion on some decisions. Similarly, in Denmark, since the 1980s, *consensus conferences* (these too composed of citizens selected at random) are called on to discuss controversial questions, including those with high technical content, with the same happening in France in *Conférences des citoyens*, and in Germany in *Planungszellen*. Similar to this is the *deliberative poll* model, which foresees informed deliberation among citizens selected to mirror some social characteristics of the population (Sintomer 2007, 133ff.). While traditional surveys follow the logic of aggregation of individual preferences, deliberative pools – which may involve hundreds of people – aim to discover what public opinion would be if citizens had the possibility to study and discuss a certain theme.

Both types of experiments have proliferated at the national and, above all, the local level. Although participatory and/or deliberative decision-making processes continue to be the exception rather than the rule (Font 2003, 14; see also Akkerman, Hajer and Grin 2004), they are increasingly used (Lowndes, Pratchett and Stoker 2001), as well as reflected upon. 'Interactive policy-making' has thus developed, defined as the 'political practices that involve consultation, negotiation and/or deliberation between government, associations from civil society and individual citizens' (Akkerman, Hajer and Grin 2004, 83; see also Akkerman 2001).[1]

Even though the intensity of participation, its duration and influence vary greatly between the different participatory mechanisms, they do show the insufficiency of a merely representative conception of democracy. In the previously mentioned institutional experiments we find in fact, in different balances, the objectives of improving managerial capacities, through greater transparency and the circulation of information, but also of transforming social relations, reconstructing social ties and capital of solidarity and trust and, from the political point of view, of 'democratising democracy' (Bacqué, Rey and Sintomer 2005).

Research on attempts to extend policy making to citizen participation usually focuses on the capacity of such instruments to resolve problems created by local opposition to an unpopular use of the local territory (Bobbio and Zeppetella 1999). Renn, Webler and Wiedemann spoke of 'forums for exchange that are organized for the purpose of facilitating communication between government, citizens, stakeholders and interest groups, and businesses regarding a specific decision or problem' (Renn et al. 1995, 2). Several of these practices aim at reaching high deliberative quality in the sense that 'all potentially affected groups have equal opportunity to get involved in the process and equal right to propose topics, formulate solutions, or critically discuss taken-for-granted approaches, and because decision-making is by exchange of argument' (Baccaro and Papadakis 2004).

Do these institutional experiments fulfill these high expectations? If, at the end of the 1990s, James Bohman noted 'a surprising lack of empirical case studies of democratic deliberation' (1998, 419), stressing that 'empirical research is a cure for both a priori scepticism and untested idealism about deliberation' (ibid., 22), empirical research did, however, grow exponentially in the years to follow. Empirical studies have addressed the evaluation of particular deliberative programmes as well as the observation of individual behaviour in experimental groups (for surveys, Ryfe 2002; Chambers 2003). While empirical research is proliferating, its results are, however, as we are going to see, far from consistent. Aware of the difficulty of implementing normative ideals, theoreticians of deliberative democracy are becoming institutional designers, promoters and practitioners of various democratic experiments (Dryzek 2010, 8–9). The position towards these experiments by various actors, including social movements, is also ambivalent. In particular, notwithstanding their resonance with the value promoted in these institutional experiments, social movements have frequently criticized the results of 'top-down' experiments as a merely symbolic representation of citizens' participation, responding to a renewed and more sophisticated consensus strategy.

In a survey of 210 social movement organizations (active in the Social Forum process in Italy, France, Germany, Spain, Switzerland, Great Britain and at the transnational level) conducted within the comparative project on Democracy in Europe and the Mobilization of the Society, we asked our interviewees about their opinion on these experiments in participatory public decision making. We observed a significant interest among a large (although not majoritarian) part of our sample, but also some scepticism. While 42.3 per cent of the groups did not discuss this issue or have no clear stance on it, over one-third (38.5 per cent) declared that these participative experiments improve the quality of political decisions and the remaining roughly one-fifth (19.2 per cent) was sceptical. When asked to qualify their judgement on experiments in public decision making, almost one-fifth of the groups spoke of both advantages and risks. About half underlined the positive aspects and almost one-third pointed at the negative side of institution-driven experiments (della Porta 2009a and 2009b).

Critically, such experiments were considered elitist ('they involve mostly experts and not citizens'), but also useless ('no real changes occur') and even dangerous ('serve for cooptation of critical engagement', 'are used to create political consensus and legitimation of institutions'). These processes were also labelled as artificial (not true experiments with a new democratic model) or 'top-down' (promoted and implemented from the top of the political system). According to social movement activists, the 'palaces of power' were not really opened to citizens' participation, but remained accessible only to the elites (in particular the economic ones). The criticism addressed especially the missing links between the consultation, deliberation, decision and monitoring phases, but also the technocratic distortion of the political debate, the pre-selection (by institutions) of relevant social actors to be involved in consultation, and in some cases the limited significance of the stakes (as signs of a too-cautious approach by the institutions).

There were, however, also positive expectations, which concerned, first, the input side of the decision-making process. Institutional experiments are considered to be inclusive ('they stimulate active citizens' participation') and bottom-up ('they express the real needs of citizens', 'people become closer to politics'). Additionally, these experiments were positively evaluated for their potential consequences on the output of the decision-making process: to attribute more responsibility to the people, to foster transparency and publicity of the decision making, to produce a more consensual decision making and to allow for the emergence of new political styles and administrative practices.

Similar interest, but also skepticism, is confirmed also by the data from a survey of more than 1,000 participants in the fourth ESF. Notwithstanding the fact that some of the social movement organizations have actively promoted these types of experiments, only one-third of our activists (30.7 per cent) strongly believed that they were to improve the quality of decision making, while 42.5 per cent were moderately optimistic, and 14.3 per cent pessimistic (of whom, 2.6 per cent strongly). However, as much as one-third declared they had participated in such a process (della Porta and Mosca 2006; della Porta and Andretta 2006).

The performance of institutional experiments

Ambivalent research results, as well as political attitudes towards the experiments, might be linked to the 'conceptual stretching' of terms such as 'participatory' and 'deliberative democracy', as well as to the different institutional designs and political processes that have brought about their development. The above-mentioned experiments in participation are not only varied, but also still in an experimental and fluid form. In their analysis of policy making and politics in the network society, Maarten Hajer and Hendrik Wagenaar warn us that in these new spaces of politics including 'the practices of policy-making and politics coming from below', 'there are no pre-given rules that determine who is responsible, who has authority over whom, what sort of accountability is to be expected' (Hajer and Wagenaar 2003, 9). The new practices seem to 'initially exist in an *institutional void*' (2003), without clear rules. Democratic innovations vary however in terms of participation, deliberation and empowerment.

As for *participation*, major questions have addressed the real chances of participation, especially for the poorer areas and groups. Identifying the shift of attention from participation to deliberation as a significant change in the critical project of democratic theory, Emily Hauptmann has noted that 'most theorists of deliberative democracy, despite such fundamental criticisms of the participatory view, still insist that deliberation is a kind of participation or somehow essential to it' (2001, 408).

As mentioned before (see chapter 3), a good deliberation requires inclusivity. If normative theorists stress the virtues of participation, empirical research indicates, however, the difficulties these institutional experiments encounter in involving citizens. For instance, according to a survey of sixteen organizations that attempt to foster better public deliberation in local and national communities, 'participation is closely associated with educational level, which in turn is connected to indicators of socio-economic status. Given the selection techniques of these organizations (word of mouth, facilitating meetings at public institutions like libraries or town halls, advertising in local media) it is likely that their reach does not extend much beyond this highly participatory demographic base' (Ryfe 2002, 365). This, in its turn, creates problems of legitimation for institutions that risk being characterized not only by low participation, but also by reproducing (or even increasing) the social inequality observed in other forms of political participation. According to research on different forms of participation, however, with the exclusion of groups of the very poor, the social distribution of participants is broad and heterogeneous (Smith 2009, 41ff.), with even greater involvement by the popular classes in the Porto Alegre participatory budget (Gret and Sintomer 2005, 77). In terms of the level and quality of participation, the characteristics of the experiments vary according to different dimensions: 'Participation is shaped by the policy problem at hand, the techniques and resources available and, ultimately, a political judgment about the importance of the issue and the need for public involvement' (Bishop and Davis 2002, 21).

In general, maximum participation is advocated in assembly models. The participatory budget model emphasizes the participation of all citizens interested in determining decisions. As mentioned, the process of participatory budgeting in Porto Alegre involves up to 50,000 people per year, combining working groups and assemblies on various thematic policy areas and territorial sub-areas of the metropolitan city. Various rules aim at increasing active participation, among them a rigorously observed equal turn in speaking, the election of delegates in proportion to the number of participants in public assemblies, and the fixed annual agenda of the main assemblies. The participatory budget model in fact stresses participation of all citizens affected by a certain decision. Citizens are pushed to mobilize, 'because the more people that go to the meetings, the more likely they will be able to win the prioritizing vote that determines which neighborhoods will benefit first' (Abers 2003, 206). The 'extremely competitive component' of the participatory budget 'gives it its vitality', since if the participatory budget 'did not provide the prospective of providing returns to their specific needs or concerns, most people would not go to the meetings' (2003). The administration also provided incentives to participation in various ways. For instance, it hired activists and potential organizers from neighbourhood movements in order to help with the organization of the process; moreover, city administrators visited neighbourhoods where participation was low (2003, 205). In Porto Alegre, and similar experiments in West Bengal and Kerala, this brought about high rates of involvement by poorer, less-educated citizens, and women (2003, 245).

In contrast, for mechanisms such as deliberative polls, inclusiveness refers to the ideal of a broadly representative jury selection that is able to draw on a wide range of experiences and backgrounds. Numbers often remain quite low in these cases, and invited participants are selected randomly. The rationale is in fact more to see how citizens would decide in conditions that allow for an informed discussion, than to improve the democratic capacity of those specific citizens. The logic of deliberative polls is explained as follows by their inventor James Fishkin, a scholar of democracy: 'The deliberative poll is unlike any poll or survey ever conducted. Ordinary polls model what the public is thinking, even though the public might not be thinking very much or paying much attention. A deliberative poll attempts to model what the public *would* think, had it a better opportunity to consider the question at issue' (Fishkin 1997, 162).

As for *deliberation*, the discursive quality of the process is influenced by the spread of information as well as the plurality of arguments.

Political theorists have defined deliberation as a specific decision-making device likely to direct participants towards shared interests through high-quality debates. Personal involvement in the participatory process may significantly change one's attitude, perspective and value priorities. Indeed, 'rather than aggregating (exogenously generated) preferences or filtering them, deliberative democracy proceeds through a transformation of the preferences during the discussion and as a result of it' (Elster 1997, 11; also Manin and Blondiaux 2002). Participation is said to become a 'school of democracy': the more citizens participate in decision-making processes, the more they are enlightened and informed (Pateman 1970; see also chapter 4). Even participation in citizens' jury is said to promote civic engagement (Gastil et al. 2010). Notwithstanding the differences in the numbers of citizens participating, the shared assumption concerning the procedures employed for the selection of citizens is that ordinary citizens have both the will and the capacity to take important decisions and to do so in the public interest.

From the empirical point of view, while some studies conclude that citizens' participation in policy making increases efficiency and legitimacy, others express doubts about its capacity to solve free-rider problems and produce optimal decisions, or to facilitate the achievement of the public good (Renn et al. 1996; Petts 1997; Hajer and Kesselring 1999; Grant, Perl and Knoepfel 1999). Additionally, the quality of the discourse is not automatically improved through participation: research has, rather, stressed some trade-offs between participation and discursive quality.

Democratic innovations differ in terms of attention paid to the relevance of an informed arena. For the mini-publics (such as citizens' juries), the quality of discourse is related to the range of information to which citizens are exposed in the forum, their opportunity to question witnesses, their ability to reflect on the experiences and perspectives of fellow citizens with various backgrounds, and the stable expectations and relations of trust that can be fostered among participants. Deliberation is in fact here defined as 'the process by which individuals sincerely weight the merits of competing arguments in discussions together' (Fishkin 2009, 33). Mini-publics should thus show 'what people would think under good conditions' (2009, 83). So, it was noted regarding citizens' juries and the like that 'although such forums can only approximate the ideal of inclusiveness and equality of voice through sampling procedures, they do foster conditions under which informed and democratic deliberation can take place and directly involve citizens from a cross-section of society. Empirical backing is emerging for the theoretical claim made for the transformative and educative power of democratic deliberation' (Smith 2001, 82). The presence of normal citizens (rather than the self-selected ideologically committed ones that populate assemblies) should ensure open-mindedness and, therefore, better chances that arguments are sincerely weighted (Dryzek 2010, 156). Innovative democratic experiments such as deliberative opinion polls, citizens' juries and consensus conferences all share the fact that 'a cross-section of the population is brought together for three to four days to discuss an issue of public concern; citizens are exposed to a variety of information and hear a wide range of views from witnesses who they are able to cross-examine; and fairness of the proceedings is entrusted to an independent facilitating organization' (Smith 2000). In general, the environment of mini-publics is structured so as to facilitate the voice of and interaction between citizens through independent facilitators (Smith 2009, 83). Facilitators have an important role here, both in ensuring inclusiveness and in encouraging an ethos of mutual respect during deliberations.

The deliberative quality is less central for assembleary forms. About participatory budgeting, Abers expresses much doubt 'that purely deliberative processes ever occur in participatory fora', even though 'deliberation became more and more common over time as participants gained experience with public debate' and 'developed their capacity to argue and reason' (2003, 206). Only in a second move in fact does the deliberative dimension of the participatory forums come in and turn such forums into civic learning spaces. Argument and reason come to the fore – although usually not totally replacing 'strategic bargaining that is intended to give maximum advantage to one's own interests' – only because people are 'forced to confront their needs with others' (Abers 2003, 206). According to Gianpaolo Baiocchi (2001), the participatory budget in Porto Alegre also includes rules oriented to improving communication. Moreover, there is a didactic component embedded in the meetings devoted to learning procedures and rules, as well as specific competencies related to budgeting and specific skills in debating and mobilizing resources for collective goals (2003).

The quality of communication is in general expected to be negatively affected by the size of the arena. Fung observes that 'If there is a magic number for a group that is small enough so that all of its members can contribute seriously to an ongoing discussion, and yet large enough to offer diverse views and ample energies, it is probably not so far from the actual number of people that actually participate in groups constituted by the Chicago reforms' (2003, 132) – that is, between ten and twenty participants (2003, 128). In general, the larger the decisional arena, the more arduous the task of actual deliberation (and consensus): 'Beyond a very small number of participants (certainly fewer than 20), deliberation breaks down "with speech-making replacing conversation and rhetorical appeals replacing reasoned arguments"' (Parkinson 2003, 181).[2]

Nevertheless, experiments such as community dialogue aim at combining involvement of a large number of participants and discursive quality through a multi-step process: 'The dialogue proceeds through agenda setting, strategy development, and decision making. The agenda setting round asks the community to define the scope and terms of the dialogue. The strategy development round asks citizens to identify promising options and the decision making round asks citizens to select the preferred course' (Weeks 2000, 362).[3]

As far as *empowerment* is concerned, democratic experiments vary in how much decisional power is granted to the new arenas. As Graham Smith (2009, 17) sums it up, the empirical evidence suggests that 'the deep scepticism expressed by citizens about their capacity to affect the decision-making process is often justified.... The prevailing division of powers between public authorities and citizens is far from challenged.' The level of empowerment is linked to the specific place the deliberative arena occupies in policy making. Focusing attention on different empirical cases, research has highlighted a generally low level of power attribution to these institutional experiments. It is, in fact, still unclear how deliberative arrangements relate to those formal institutions that organize representation along territorial lines, and 'how deliberative procedures themselves might operate within both secondary associations and more formal political institutions' (Johnson 1998, 175–76).[4]

Dryzek distinguishes several potential impacts of mini-publics, such as making policy, influencing policy making or influencing the public opinion. Empowered policy making, however, 'almost never happens' (2010, 169). Above all, the power of the 'mini-publics', created by drawing lots to discuss relevant issues, is limited to a general *moral suasion*. As its promoter notes, 'A deliberative poll is not meant to describe or predict public opinion. Rather, it prescribes. It has recommendatory force of recommendation: these are the conclusions people come to, were they better informed on the issue, and had they the opportunity and the motivation to examine those issues seriously' (Fishkin 1997, 162). In general, the recommendations of the mini-publics are considered within complex processes, in which other actors tend to have greater influence (Smith 2009, 93). Nevertheless, some similar deliberative experiments, for example the programming cells in Germany, have had a certain influence on decisions (2009, 93).

Higher levels of empowerment can instead be found in assembleary types of experiment. In particular, the participatory budget in Porto Alegre manages up to 20 per cent of the annual budget and makes possible a positive response to about one-third of requests presented by citizens (Santos 1998, 493). As mentioned in the incipit of this chapter, decisions made through the participatory budget process are implemented by the administration.

Another central theme regards the types of citizens that are empowered. The risk of the unequal distribution of resources between the different interests in the field (wealth, social prestige, number, aggregation capacity) in these democratic experiments, resulting in political inequality, became apparent long ago. In other words, it may be that those who are further 'empowered' are those that already have power. Without the filter of parties, the lobbying pressures of the best organized can have better chances of success, and public action can move away from the pursuit of the public good. The weakening of the public function through the transfer of decision-making power to free negotiation between carriers of different interests could, in fact, reward the richest in terms of resources, individual and organized, and penalize the poorest. Direct participation tends to legitimate a recourse to collecting opinions, but the decisions that count are taken by ever more limited groups. In addition, participation is often not only limited, but also unequal, with the agenda being controlled by the most educated and well-off (Young 2000).

If it is true that one of the functions that these new arenas can fulfil is that of rendering the decision-making process more transparent (della Porta 2008a), it is, however, necessary to make sure that they do not transform into covers for decisions that are actually taken elsewhere. To avoid manipulation by the strongest groups, the need to favour above all the participation of those groups that meet with the most difficulties in organizing collectively has been underlined. In this case too, different types of existing experiments present diverse capacities for guaranteeing the empowerment of citizens that possess fewer material resources.

How to explain the different characteristics of deliberative experiments

The democratic qualities of the new models in decision making vary, then. The quality of deliberative experiments on the various dimensions is clearly linked, as we have already seen, to institutional designs, which vary, first of all, according to the *type and range of issues* addressed. Cohen and Rogers distinguished projects aimed at increasing the efficiency of specific public services by involving their users (as in policing, education and the environment) from those dealing with larger policy issues and thus involving potentially all citizens (such as town budgets). According to these authors, those of the first type 'aim to solve bounded policy challenges', and those of the second 'aim to transform fundamental balances of social power' (2003, 260). The first 'are set against a background in which imbalances of power are not of obvious relevance to decision-making' and in which the main purpose is to achieve co-ordination for mutual benefit (2003, 250). In the second, the deliberative problem-solving arrangements are 'part of much larger political projects, themselves aimed precisely at changing a more fundamental balance of power between large forces in society' (2003, 251).

Existing research indicates many possible shifts in the issues addressed. Abers, for instance, explains the participation of ordinary people in the participatory budget experiment by the fact that the programme initially focused on local issues that were important to neighbourhood residents: 'there was no need to convince poor Porto Alegre residents that basic sanitation, flood control, street pavements, bus services, schools, and health posts were important to their lives' (2003, 204). People are 'not drawn into the process because they wish to deliberate, but because they wish to get infrastructure for their own neighborhoods, to improve their lives' (2003, 206). Nevertheless, 'through the participatory process itself, people begin to perceive the needs of others, develop some solidarity, and conceptualize their own interests more broadly' (2003, 206).

Differences among the various models of deliberative democracy also depend upon the characteristics of the *policy entrepreneurs* and the political support they achieve for the democratic innovations. In terms of degree and quality of participation, the characteristics of the experiments vary according to 'the policy problem at hand, the techniques and resources available and, ultimately, a political judgment about the importance of the issue and the need for the public involvement' (Bishop and Davis 2002, 21). Administrators, citizens, stake-holders and experts may all desire participation, but for quite different reasons. Thus they may have different ideas about how the process should be conducted, and evaluate the results of specific experiments accordingly (Renn et al. 1995, 5). Relevant questions address first of all the *origin of the arena*: who took the initiative in setting it up? Who has the power to end it? In particular, we shall distinguish cases in which access to the policy-making process originates from a bottom-up initiative and those in which it originates from the top (Fung and Wright 2001).

Some democratic innovations have been promoted by social movement organizations. The model for many of these is the already-mentioned participatory budgeting, implemented since 1988 by the Municipality of Porto Alegre (Alfonsin and Allegretti 2003). Established by left-wing parties deeply rooted in civic society associations, the experiment aimed at mobilizing and activating the poor and dispossessed. There, 'the relevant participatory bodies are both effect and cause of a wider political mobilization that enabled groups to participate who had not participated before, and, importantly, those bodies have much wider powers than the more policy-specific bodies considered in the US cases' (Cohen and Rogers 2003, 251).

In Europe, this approach to local budgeting was specifically proposed by organizations of the global justice movement (i.e. Démocratiser radicalement la démocratie; Carta del nuovo municipio), discussed in the ESFs and supported by local Social Forums. European local institutions, especially those governed by the Left, began in the early 2000s to promote participatory budgeting experiments, although generally on a more limited and controlled scale than in Brazil. Moreover, environmental associations in particular promoted parts of Agenda 21, stimulating a participatory process at the local level concerning social and environmental developmental sustainability, approved at the Global Conference on the Environment in Rio de Janeiro in 1990 and characterized by a widening space of participation for citizens and their associations.[5] Most deliberative experiments have, however, been promoted top-down.

The *national administrative and political cultures* within which participatory experiments develop also play an important role (Sintomer, Herzberg and Röcke 2007). In France, where experiments with deliberative democracy have been defined mainly within a 'policy of proximity' framework, the 1992 law strengthening decentralization, and the creation in 1995 of a Commission Nationale du Débat Public (CNDP, National Commission of Public Debate), reflected an emphasis on participation (Blatrix 2003). In Spain, democratic innovations developed within a radical turn from a centralized unitary state into the semifederalism of the Comunidades Autonómicas participatory practices; in Italy they are rooted in urban planning. In Switzerland, they seem influenced by a long tradition of institutionally driven participation of citizens in decision-making processes through referendums and popular initiatives. In Germany, so-called round tables, stemming from the period after the fall of the communist regime in East Germany, continue to exist in a number of cities, focussing, for example, on problems of unemployment, integration of immigrants, and local social policies (Rocke 2009).

However, quality public deliberation requires the existence of some shared norms: a deliberative process is facilitated by the presence of common objectives, and by focussing the debate on the best way of reaching them. For this, cooperative processes are often successful in creating territorial pacts that bring together actors united by the goal of economic development. These tend, however, to exclude and be opposed by actors (such as residents', consumers', public service users' groups) that hold a different conception of development (and democracy). The definition of common norms is thus a crucial moment that cannot easily be left to negotiation between actors. The risk to be avoided is that this market self-regulates to the detriment of the weakest interests, but also of the weakest political power, snared by particularistic interests. Participation in deliberative arenas must not, therefore, lead to any removal of accountability from public institutions.

Conclusion

At the local, but also transnational, levels, social movements' criticism of representative democracy has been accompanied by proposals for alternative institutions. Deliberative and participatory forms in public decision making have been experimented with in various contexts and, especially, much discussed as possible bridging arenas between institutions and the citizens. In many cases, social movement organizations actively promoted these types of experiments, as ways of channelling the emerging demands into political institutions, but also of propagating an alternative model of politics and democracy 'from below'. The degree of inclusiveness, the quality of the discourse, and the decisional power devolved to these emerging institutions varies, in fact, significantly in the different forms (mini-public or assembleary) they take. Each of them seems to present advantages and disadvantages along these three dimensions, while it seems difficult to maximize all elements at the same time. All in all, most of these experiments do not seem to live up to the expectations they create, as standards of inclusiveness, discursive qualities and, especially, empowerment, remain low. However, they testify to the search for alternative institutions, able to combine different democratic principles and qualities. They also represent additional arenas for participation and deliberation, whose development depends on the different balance of individual and collective commitment.

10

Can Democracy Be Saved? A Conclusion

Democracies, and by far not just the new ones among them, are not functioning well. (Offe 2011, 447)

This is how a major political theorist, Claus Offe, synthesized the state of democracy today. As he observed, when reflecting around this crisis, one has to keep in mind the question, 'What is democracy good for?' (2011, 448). This question is relevant for scholars, but also for the citizens of (old and new) democracies.

The present decade started with a new wave of democratization in North Africa and the Middle East – all the more important as this geopolitical area had been long considered to be unfertile soil for democracy. They also opened, however, with a new wave of protest, especially in the Western and Northern parts of the globe, that targeted representative democracy in various ways:

- first, the financial crisis in what used to be considered 'advanced democracies' – now faced, e.g., with economic growth in authoritarian China – challenged the idea that democracy is economically more efficient and successful (an image often stressed with regard to the collapse of 'real socialism' in Eastern Europe).
- second, the policies that had produced the crisis, and were then used to address it, challenged another founding myth: that in democratic countries, equal political rights tend to spill over to social equalities. By stigmatizing economic inequalities, the mentioned protests challenged a certain understanding of democracy.

- third, 'really existing democracies' were especially criticized as politically unable to live up to their promises of equal representation: faced with evidence of corruption and collusion between economic and political power, governments (but also parliamentary oppositions) were accused of representing 'the 1%' leaving the '99%' unrepresented.

These protests developed in a context already characterized by growing dissatisfaction with a liberal conception of democracy that neoliberal trends had made all the more minimalistic in the recognition of not only social, but also political, participation rights. Research had indicated a definite decline in the quality of democracy (Diamond and Morlino 2005) as well as in citizens' satisfaction with the functioning of democratic institutions (e.g., Putnam and Pharr 2000). Political parties have lost support and trust; citizens are voting less and they are more volatile in their party preferences (e.g., Dalton 2004; della Porta 2008a). In a vicious circle, politicians tend to rely more and more on (ephemeral) personalistic appeals and less and less on the development of identifiable programmes or collective identities, thus increasing disaffection. In sum, while the number of countries recognized as meeting at least minimal democratic standards has increased steadily, the quality of existing democracy is declining. As Offe aptly synthesized:

> causal narratives on the crisis of democracy include economic globalization and the absence of effective supranational regulatory regimes; the exhaustion of the left-to-the-center political ideas and the hegemony of market-liberal public philosophies, together with their anti-statist implications; and the impact of financial and economic crises and the ensuing fiscal starvation of nation states which threatens to undermine their state capacity. (Offe 2011, 457)

In this volume, I have suggested that, in order to assess the challenges to democracy, as well as its potential 'to be saved', we have to distinguish, however, between the different and ever-changing meanings of democracy. Different conceptions of democracy are indeed discussed in theory and experimented in practice. Challenges to the liberal conception, long considered as hegemonic, bring (or bring back) our attention to participatory and/or deliberative conceptions of democracy. Formal and informal institutions develop, finding different balances between different democratic qualities. These diverse conceptions are intertwined in two recent debates: that on the potential contribution of new technologies to democratic development, and that on the perspectives for global democracy.

Throughout this volume, I have looked at challenges and opportunities for different conceptions of democracy. Indeed, I have observed that the liberal conception does not reflect in an exhaustive manner the real functioning of the democratic state in any of its different periods of existence. It is also partial insofar as it implicitly sees states as the only arena of democracy. The vision of democracy as mere electoral accountability, or a specific form of preference counting, has instead been transformed from within, as rights were extended in breadth and depth. Especially in Western Europe, the labour movement played in fact a most important role in developing ideas of collective rights and increased participation, as well as in linking (in theory and practice) political rights with social rights.

Beyond electoral accountability, research on social movements and protest, but also on other actors of civil society, has in fact focussed its attention on the many arenas in which forms of democracy are founded on diverse principles. Linked to this, research on the long processes of the first democratization has underlined the importance of non-electoral circuits for the functioning of the democratic state. The influence that protest exerted in regimes with restricted electorates did not pass through elections, even if parliaments became targets for demands. In fact, in their concrete evolution, existing democratic regimes mitigated the ideal-typical principles of liberal democracy, mixing them with others stemming from other conceptions of democracy.

These evolutions were partly produced by the claims of social movements, and partly by institutional responses oriented to overcoming perceived challenges in terms of legitimacy and efficiency. If the workers' movement has, in many diverse historical contexts, contributed to the development of liberal democracy, demanding the extension of suffrage and the right to expression and protest, it has nevertheless also contributed to transforming the liberal individualist conception, claiming collective rights and practising forms of participatory democracy. In more recent social movements, the participatory practices have become intertwined with attention to a deliberative democracy oriented to creating multiple public spheres open to the construction of collective identities.

In the past as in the present, social movements have demanded but also prefigured diverse models of democracy. As I have suggested all through this volume, in a moment of deep crisis of the liberal model, it is at these different conceptions of democracy that we have to look if we want to save democracy, transforming challenges into opportunities – or, as Rosanvallon (2006) put it, if we want to give defiance a positive outcome.

Far from being able to offer a ready-made solution, I hope, in this volume, to have contributed some knowledge on the different ways in which democracy can be conceptualized and the different democratic qualities that different democratic models emphasized. In particular, looking at normative reflections and empirical research, I have addressed the participatory and the deliberative visions of democracy, as well as looking at their convergence.

First of all, we have seen that progressive social movements have supported an expansion of the channels of political participation as well as of its forms. In normative theory, participatory democracy is conceptualized as aiming at multiplying the occasions of citizens' participation, beyond elections and also outside of political institutions. Wherever and whenever decisions are made, the participation of the citizens is not only useful as socialization to democratic values, but also a fundamental requirement for a just decisional process. In the labour movement, in various moments, related ideas of direct democracy emerged and re-emerged in criticism of the bureaucratization of mass parties and labour unions. In the late 1960s and early 1970s, a broad cycle of protest called for more social rights, but also more participation in the society. With all its imperfection and malfunctioning, the open assembly as the main decisional space for recent social movements still reflects the call for direct involvement as opposed to delegation.

If assembleary democracy had its limits, it was indeed from self-critical reflections on its pitfalls that deliberative conceptions of democracy developed. While the stress on participation challenges the representativeness of delegates, the emphasis on deliberation challenges the majoritarian principle – or at least tries to complement it. Against a minimalistic and economist conception of democracy as a market, which has spread in political science through the work of Anthony Downs (1957), deliberative theorists stress the importance not only (or not so much) of counting preferences in a democratic way (that is, that each preference counts the same), but also of opinions being *formed* in a democratic way. As preferences and/or identities are always in flux, the conditions under which they are formed are of vital importance for democracy. If Habermas' thought has been extremely influential in this enlargement of the democratic conception from preference-counting to preference-forming, critical scholars and social movements alike have promoted a vision of democracy that has bridged the creation of multiple public spheres with mobilization from below. In the wave of protest of the early 2010s, the prefiguration of public spheres, open and plural, found expression in the camps built in the occupied squares in Egypt, Spain, Greece, the United States and many other countries around the world. These represented the culminating points of visions and practices oriented to high-quality communication. Consensus building, as an alternative to majoritarian voting, has developed (once again, in theory and practice) with the evolution of the women's movement, the peace movement and, more recently, the global justice movement, and with their self-reflexive critique of the risks of merely participatory visions but also of the potential pitfalls of consensus.

We have also seen that the value of participation and deliberation is high not only for social movements in 'really existing democracies', but also for those struggling against dictatorship. Research on democratization shows in fact not only the importance of mobilizations from below, but also the tensions between the visions of democracy social movements struggle for and their achievements, when powerful 'democracy promoters' impose a liberal vision of democracy.

Can these different conceptions, combined in various forms and degrees, save democracy in our troubled times? All through the volume, I have noted how some developments provide resources for participation and deliberation. Critical citizens are not necessarily disaffected citizens. Many of them could become, as seems to have happened in 2011, committed citizens, willing to invest their time, energy and knowledge in the attempt to find solutions to complex problems. Critical citizens do not see reasons for loyalty, but often practise voice rather than exit. In fact, in the contemporary world, citizens are politically active, even if less so in conventional forms and more so in unconventional ones.

In the growth of these critical resources, social trends interact with political ones. Increasing education helps to spread the belief in one's own 'droit de parole' that, in its turn, pushes citizens to mobilize against cuts in the public education system, in investments in health and pensions, in workers' rights and the right to work. New technologies offer some instruments for these democratic innovations, even though they also present risks of increased control and growing tensions between the virtual and the real. The high density of communication also helps the development of cosmopolitan identities, at least as much as it creates localist and nationalist backlash. At the same time, however, the acknowledgement of the need to think, and act, globally raises the uneasy task of imagining institutions of global democracy, and in a moment in which even the national ones are in crisis.

At the local, national and supranational levels, institutions have reacted to challenges and claims through an incoherent mix of exclusion and adaptation. Research on protest policing indicates in fact a tendency to move away from inclusive definitions of the right to protest, with an – albeit differentiated – increase in practices of 'selective incapacitation' of protest. As said, these tendencies are much more worrying when liberal democracy appears progressively less legitimate to critical citizens and the creation of arenas of participation and deliberation as ever more urgent.

At the same time, however, participatory and deliberative conceptions and practices have also developed at the institutional level. Within the conception of 'government with the people' (Schmidt 2006, 6), experiments in participatory and deliberative democracy in public decision-making processes have indeed been carried out as a means for increasing citizen participation by creating high-quality communicative arenas and giving power to citizens. These also aim to overcome the partial solutions recently developed to confront the weaknesses of representative democracy, which appear very far from satisfactory. Technocratic models of democracy, which assume the existence of consensual objectives (such as economic development) to be reached by means of experts or bureaucracy are accused of snatching power from citizens (and alienating them) (Sanderson 1999). Media democracy, with legitimization filtered through means of mass communication, has facilitated populist appeals, while the commercialization of the media system has reduced its capacity to promote information and critical debate.

If really existing democracies suffer from a 'vast underutilization of political resources' (Offe 2011, 461), an increase in the participatory and deliberative qualities of democracy can help to overcome it. To the question, then, 'Can democracy be saved?', the answer could therefore be optimistic, but the (ever-mutable) solutions require changes in conceptions and practices of democracy as much as in our ways of looking at them. Delegation and majority voting no longer work in the face of more and more defiant citizens and complex, global problems, which require local as well as specialized knowledge. An image of democracy as a market perniciously pushes for individual egoism when collective commitment is called for instead. Conceptions and practices of democracy as participation and deliberation can help to address democracy in this 'era of defiance' (Rosanvallon 2006).

Notes

1 Models of Democracy: An Introduction

1 Unless otherwise stated, translations are by the author of this volume.

2 Liberal Democracy: Evolution and Challenges

1 Accessed 19 September 2012.

3 Participatory Democracy

1 Arnstein (1969) refers to delegated power as situations in which citizens achieve authority over a particular plan or programme through negotiations between them and public officials. 'At this level', she says, 'the ladder has been scaled to the point where citizens hold the significant cards to assure accountability of the program to them' (1969, 222). In these situations, 'power holders need to start the bargaining process rather than respond to pressure from the other end' (1969, 222). She then refers to a citizen control situation – the highest rung – as one 'which guarantees that participants or residents can govern a program or an institution, be in full charge of policy and managerial aspects, and be able to negotiate the conditions under which "outsiders" may change them' (1969, 223): a situation where 'have-not citizens obtain the majority of decision-making seats' (1969, 216).

2 In the second half of the 1700s, petitions with up to 250,000 signatures were circulated in England (Tilly 1995, 173); in the 1830s, an average of more than thirty protest events was recorded every month; hundreds of new associations were formed between 1830 and 1832 to request a reform of the parliamentary system.

3   The concept of the public sphere in fact emerged alongside the possibility – brought by the modern age – of distinguishing between the public, linked to the State, and the private, excluded from the State's sphere of intervention.

4   In Victorian Great Britain, bread riots occurred during poor harvests, when the 'Victorian poor', still without the vote, 'appeared – tumultuous, violent and not altogether ignorant of their interest – at election hustings' (Hinton 1974, 17).

5   At this time, 'More than any other, the strike confirmed itself as the major form of working-class action' (Perrot 1986, 106), increasing from around 100 in 1880 to 1,000 in 1906.

6   As Keane (2003, 82) observes, ever since the birth of the movement against slavery at the end of the eighteenth century, we can speak of *civility politics*, that is 'initiatives of organized citizens that seek to ensure that no-one appropriates or arbitrarily uses the state means of violence against civil societies, at home or elsewhere'.

7   The attitude of the Left towards movements was also influenced by internal electoral competition. The propensity to support social movements tended, in fact, to increase in situations of electoral instability, which makes the conquest of new blocs of votes particularly important, and in the presence of competition between left-wing parties. In addition, left-wing parties in opposition saw important allies against right-wing governments in social movements.

4   Deliberative Democracy: Between Representation and Participation

1   In each country and at the transnational level, we selected about thirty organizations that had been involved in the main initiatives of the global justice movement (among them the European Social Forums), ensuring variance especially on the main issues addressed. Lists of organizations that had signed calls for action at Social Forums (at the national, European and global levels) and other important movement events were used to single out the groups belonging to the 'core' of the movement networks. A common sampling strategy was agreed upon in order to collect comparable data, covering social movement organizations representing different streams within the movement (environmentalist, pacifist, women's rights, unions, gay, migrant and human rights activists, squatters and so on), organizations that stemmed from the global justice movement (local social forums, Attac), as well as Web sites of media close to it (periodical magazines, radio stations, newspapers, and networks of independent communication).

2   Though we aimed at covering the same organizations for the two types of analysis (documents and interviews with representatives), this was not always possible. We did interview the representatives of about 90 per cent of the organizations whose documents were analysed in the previous part of the research.

6 The Challenge of Global Governance

1 Traditionally, the presidency of the WB went to the USA, that of the IMF to Europe, but the international relations scholar Gilpin recognizes the influence of the United States on both institutions (2000, 48).

9 Deliberative Experiments inside Institutions

1 In the same vein, this has been labelled 'collaborative policy making' (Innes and Booher 2003) or 'cooperative democracy' (Bogumil 2002).
2 According to Parkinson, there is thus 'very little in mass public communication, including a great deal of media debate, large-scale referendum processes, or even public meetings, which merits the label "deliberative"' (2003, 181).
3 Weeks assessed the practical feasibility of the model through four large-scale implementations, each addressing controversial and politically charged issues in cities ranging in population from 100,000 to 400,000.
4 More radical critiques are presented in Sanders (1997) and Walzer (1999).
5 Research has indicated that the extent of effective implementation of Agenda 21 varies greatly cross-nationally and within countries; its local implementations also vary greatly in the extent to which they are inclusive, participatory or involved in decision making (Lafferty 2002; Lucas, Ross and Fuller 2003).

Bibliography

Abers, R. N. (2003) Reflections on What Makes Empowered Participatory Governance Happen. In: Fung, A. & Olin Wright, E. (eds.) *Deepening Democracy: Institutional Innovations in Empowered Participatory Governance.* London and New York, Verso, pp. 200–7.

Akkerman, T. (2001) Urban Debate and Deliberative Democracy. *Acta Politica* 36 (1), 71–87.

Akkerman, T., Hajer, M. & Grin, J. (2004) The Interactive State: Democratization from Above? *Political Studies* 52, 82–95.

Alfonsin, B. & Allegretti, G. (2003) Dalla gestione consensuale alla riprogettazione condivisa del territorio. In: della Porta, D. & Mosca, L. (eds.) *Globalizzazione e movimenti sociali.* Rome, Manifestolibri, pp. 121–53.

Allegretti, G. (2003) *L'insegnamento di Porto Alegre.* Florence, Alinea.

Allegretti, U. (2002) *Stato e diritti nella mondializzazione.* Troina, Oasi.

Alternativa Antimilitarista – MOC (2004) 'Declaración Ideológica', 18 July, www.antimilitaristas.org/spip.php?article476, accessed 12 November 2008.

Andretta, M., della Porta, D., Mosca, L. & Reiter, H. (2002) *Global, Noglobal, Newglobal: Le proteste di Genova contro il G8.* Rome and Bari, Laterza.

Anheier, H., Glasius, M. & Kaldor, M. (eds.) (2001) *Global Civil Society.* Oxford, Oxford University Press.

Aouraght, M. & Alexander, A. (2011) The Egyptian Experience: Sense and Nonsense of the Internet Revolution. *International Journal of Communication* 5, 1344–58.

Archibugi, D. (1998) Principles of Cosmopolitan Democracy. In: Archibugi, D., Held, D. & Kohler, M. (eds.) *Re-imagining Political Community: Studies in Cosmopolitan Democracy.* Cambridge, Polity Press, pp. 198–229.

Archibugi, D. (2003) Cosmopolitical Democracy. In: Archibugi, D. (ed.) *Debating Cosmopolitics.* London, Verso, pp. 1–15.

Archibugi, D., Held, D. & Koehler, M. (1998) Introduction. In: Archibugi, D., Held, D. & Koehler, M. (eds.) *Re-imagining Political Community: Studies in Cosmopolitan Democracy*. Cambridge, Polity Press, pp. 1–9.

Archibugi, D., Konig-Archibugi, M. & Marchetti, R. (2011) Introduction: Mapping Global Democracy. In: Archibugi, D., Konig-Archibugi, M. & Marchetti, R. (eds.), *Global Democracy: Normative and Empirical Perspectives*. Cambridge, Cambridge University Press, pp. 1–21.

Arendt, H. (1972) *La crise de la culture*. Paris, Gallimard.

Arnstein, S. R. (1969) A Ladder of Citizen Participation. *Journal of the American Institute of Planners* 35 (4), 216–24.

Ash, T. G. (2011) A Century of Civil Resistance: Some Lessons and Questions. In: Roberts, A. & Ash, T. G. (eds.) *Civil Resistance and Power Politics: The Experience of Non-violent Action from Gandhi to the Present*. Oxford, Oxford University Press, pp. 371–92.

Atkinson, J. D. (2010) *Alternative Media and Politics of Resistance*. New York, Peter Lang.

Ayers, J. M. (1999) From the Streets to the Internet: The Cyber-Diffusion of Contention. *The Annals of the American Academy of Political and Social Science*, 566, 132–43.

Attac Germany (2001) 'Zwischen Netzwerk, NGO und Bewegung, Das Selbstverständnis von ATTAC, 8 Thesen', October, www.attac.de (home page), accessed 12 November 2008.

Attac Italia (2007) 'Assemblea nazionale', 27 February, www.attac.it (home page), accessed 12 November 2008.

Baccaro, L. & Papadakis, K. (2004) The Downside of Deliberative Public Administration. Paper presented at the conference Empirical Approaches to Deliberative Politics, EUI/Swiss Chair, Florence, 21–22 May.

Bachrach, P. (1975) Interest, Participation and Democratic Theory. In: Pennock, R. & Chapman, J. (eds.) *Nomos XVI, Participation in Politics*. New York, Lieber-Atherto, pp. 39–55.

Bachrach, P. & Baratz, M. S. (1986) *Le due facce del potere*. Padua, Liviana (orig. 1970).

Bacqué, M. H., Rey, H. & Sintomer, Y. (2005) *Gestion de proximité et démocratie participative*. Paris, La découverte.

Badie, B. (1999) *Une monde sans souveraineté*. Paris, Fayard.

Baiocchi, G. (2001) Participation, Activism, and Politics: The Porto Alegre Experiment and Deliberative Democratic Theory. *Politics and Society* 29 (1), 43–72.

Baker, G. (1999) The Taming Idea of Civil Society. *Democratization*, 6 (3), 1–29.

Barber, B. (2003) *Strong Democracy*. Berkeley, University of California Press (orig. 1984).

Barisione, M. (2007) *L'immagine del leader: Quanto conta per gli elettori?* Bologna, Il Mulino.

Barnes, S. & Kaase, M. (eds.) (1979) *Political Action: Mass Participation in Five Democracies*. London, Sage.

Beck, U. (1999) *Che cos'è la globalizzazione: rischi e prospettive della società planetaria*. Rome, Carocci.

Beetham, D. (1999) *Democracy and Human Rights*. Cambridge, Polity Press.

Beissinger, M. R. (2002) *Nationalist Mobilization and the Collapse of the Soviet State*. Cambridge, Cambridge University Press.

Beissinger, M. R. (2007) Structure and Example in Modular Political Phenomena: The Diffusion of Bulldozer/Rose/Orange/Tulip Revolutions. *Perspectives on Politics* 5, 259–76.

Beissinger, M. R. (2011) The Intersection of Ethnic Nationalism and People Power Tactics in the Baltic States, 1987–91. In: Roberts, A. & Ash, T. G. (eds.) *Civil Resistance and Power Politics: The Experience of Non-violent Action from Gandhi to the Present*. Oxford, Oxford University Press, pp. 231–46.

Bendix, R. (1964) *Nation Building and Citizenship*. New York, John Wiley & Sons.

Benhabib, S. (1996) Toward a Deliberative Model of Democratic Legitimacy. In: Benhabib, S. (ed.) *Democracy and Difference: Contesting the Boundaries of the Political*. Princeton, Princeton University Press, pp. 67–94.

Bennett, L. (2003a) Communicating Global Activism: Strengths and Vulnerabilities of Networked Politics. *Information, Communication & Society* 6, 143–68.

Bennett, L. (2003b) New Media Power: The Internet and Global Activism. In: Couldry, N. & Curran, J. (eds.) *Contesting Media Power: Alternative Media in a Networked World*. Lanham, Rowman & Littlefield, pp. 17–37.

Bennett, L. (2004) Social Movements beyond Borders: Understanding Two Eras of Transnational Activism. In: della Porta, D. & Tarrow, S. (eds.), *Transnational Protest and Global Activism*. Lanham, Rowman & Littlefield, pp. 203–26.

Bentivegna, S. (1999) *La politica in rete*. Rome, Meltemi.

Bermeo, N. (1990) Rethinking Regime Change. *Comparative Politics*, 22 (3), 359–77.

Bermeo, N. (1997) Myths of Moderation: Confrontation and Conflict during Democratic Transition. *Comparative Politics*, 29 (2), 205–322.

Betsill, M. & Corell, E. (2008) *NGO Diplomacy: The Influence of Non-governmental Organizations in International Environmental Negotiations*. Cambridge, Mass., MIT Press.

Biagini, E. F. & Reid, A. J. (1991) Currents of Radicalism, 1850–1914. In: Biagini, E. F. & Reid, A. J. (eds.) *Currents of Radicalism: Popular Radicalism, Organized Labour and Party Politics in Britain, 1850–1914*. Cambridge, Cambridge University Press, pp. 1–21.

Bishop, P. & Davis, G. (2002) Mapping Public Participation in Policy Choice. *Australian Journal of Public Administration* 61 (1), 14–29.

Bittner, E. (1967) The Police Skid-Row. *American Sociological Review* 32, 699–715.

Blatrix, C. (2003) The Changing French Democracy: Patchwork Participatory Democracy and Its Impact on Political Participation. Paper presented at the ECPR Joint Sessions of Workshops, Edinburgh, 28 March to 2 April, available at: www.essex.ac.uk/ECPR/events/jointsessions/paperarchive/edinburgh/ws22/Blatrix.pdf.

Blee, K. (2011) *Democracy in the Making*. Oxford, Oxford University Press.

Bobbio, L. & Zeppetella, A. (1999) *Perchè proprio qui? Grandi opere e opposizioni locali.* Milan, FrancoAngeli.

Bobbio, N. (1983) Democrazia. In: Bobbio, N., Matteucci, N. & Pasquino, G. (eds.) *Dizionario di Politica.* Turin, UTET.

Bogumil, J. (2002) Party Competition, Constraints to Negotiate and Economisation – Changes in Municipal Decision-making, the Example of North-Rhine-Westphalia. *German Journal of Urban Studies* **41** (2), 109–26.

Bohman, J. (1997) Deliberative Democracy and Effective Social Freedom: Capabilities, Resources, and Opportunities. In: Bohman, J. & Rehg, W. (eds.) *Deliberative Democracy: Essays on Reason and Politics.* Cambridge, Mass., MIT Press, pp. 321–48.

Bohman, J. (1998) The Coming Age of Deliberative Democracy. *Journal of Political Philosophy* **6** (4), 399–423.

Boli, J. & Thomas, G. M. (1999) *Constructing the World Culture: International Nongovernmental Organizations since 1875.* Stanford, Stanford University Press.

Boudreau, C. (2004) *Resisting Dictatorship: Repression and Protest in Southeast Asia.* Cambridge, Cambridge University Press.

Branford, S. & Rocha, J. (2002) *Cutting the Wire: The Story of the Landless Movement in Brazil.* London, Latin American Bureau.

Bratton, M. & van de Walle, N. (1992) Popular Protest and Political Reform in Africa. *Comparative Politics* **24** (4), 419–42.

Bratton, M. & van de Walle, N. (1994) Neopatrimonial Regimes and Political Transitions in Africa. *World Politics,* **46** (4), 453–89.

Bratton, M. and van de Walle, N. (1997) *Democratic Experiments in Africa. Regime Transition in Comparative Perspective.* Cambridge, Cambridge University Press.

Breines, W. (1989) *Community and Organization in the New Left, 1962–1968: The Great Refusal.* New Brunswick, Rutgers University Press.

Brito, A. (1997) *Human Rights and Democratization in Latin America: Uruguay and Chile.* Oxford, Oxford University Press.

Brysk, A. (1993) From Above and Below: Social Movements, the International System, and Human Rights in Argentina. *Comparative Political Studies* **26** (3), 259–85.

Bunce, V. (1999) *Subversive Institutions: The Design and the Destruction of Socialism and the State.* Cambridge, Cambridge University Press.

Burdick, J. (1992) Rethinking the Study of Social Movements: The Case of Christian Base Communities in Urban Brazil. In: Escobar, A. & Álvarez, S. (eds.) *The Making of Social Movements in Latin America: Identity, Strategy and Democracy,* Boulder, Colo., Westview, pp. 171–84.

Burdick, J. (2004) *Legacies of Liberation: The Progressive Catholic Church in Brazil at the Start of a New Millennium.* Aldershot, Ashgate.

Calhoun, C. (1982) *The Question of Class Struggle: Social Foundation of Popular Radicalism during the Industrial Revolution.* Oxford, Blackwell.

Calise, M. (2010) I partiti e lo stato democratico. In: Pizzorno, A. (ed.) *La democrazia di fronte allo stato democratico.* Milan, Feltrinelli, pp. 299–324.

Campus, D. (2006) *L'antipolitica al governo: De Gaulle, Reagan e Berlusconi*. Bologna, Mulino.

Canel, E. (1992) Democratization and the Decline of Urban Social Movements in Uruguay: A Political-Institutional Account. In: Escobar, A. & Álvarez, S. (eds.) *The Making of Social Movements in Latin America: Identity, Strategy and Democracy*. Boulder, Colo., Westview, pp. 276–90.

Captain, S. (2011) 'The Inside Story of Occupy Wall Street', www.fastcompany.com/1785918/the-inside-story-of-occupy-wall-street, accessed 14 July 2012.

Carapico, S. (1998) *Civil Society in Yemen: The Political Economy of Activism in Modern Arabia*. Cambridge, Cambridge University Press.

Cardon, D. & Grandjou, F. (2003) Peut-on se libérer des formats mediatiques? Le mouvement alter-mondialization et l'Internet. *Mouvements* **25**, 67–73.

Casper, G. & Taylor, M. (1996) *Negotiating Democracy: Transitions from Authoritarian Rule*. Pittsburgh, University of Pittsburgh Press.

Castells, M. (2001) *The Internet Galaxy: Reflections on the Internet, Business and Society*. Oxford, Oxford University Press.

Castells, M. (2009) *Communication Power*. Oxford, Oxford University Press.

Chalmers, D. (2003) The Reconstitution of European Public Spheres. *European Law Journal* **9** (2), 27–89.

Chambers, S. (2003) Deliberative Democratic Theory. *Annual Review of Political Science* **6**, 307–26.

Chandoke, N. (2003) *The Concepts of the Civil Society*. New Delhi, Oxford University Press.

Chiodi, L. (2007) Transnational Policies of Emancipation or Colonization? Civil Society Promotion in Post-communist Albania. Ph.D. thesis, European University Institute, Florence.

Cohen, J. (1989) Deliberation and Democratic Legitimacy. In: Hamlin, A. & Pettit, P. (eds.) *The Good Polity: Normative Analysis of the State*. Oxford, Basil Blackwell, pp. 17–34.

Cohen, J. & Rogers, J. (2003) *Power and Reason*. In: Fung, A. & Wright, O. E. (eds.) *Deepening Democracy: Institutional Innovations in Empowered Participatory Governance*. London and New York, Verso, pp. 237–58.

Collier, R. B. (1999) *Paths toward Democracy: The Working Class and Elites in Western Europe and South America*. New York, Cambridge University Press.

Collier, R. B. & Mahoney, J. (1997) Adding Collective Actors to Collective Outcomes: Labor and Recent Democratization in South America and Southern Europe. *Comparative Politics* **29** (3), 285–303.

Commission of the European Communities (2001a) *European Governance: A White Paper*. Brussels, Commission of the European Communities. Available at: http://europa.eu.int/eur-lex/en/com/cnc/2001/com2001_0428en01.pdf, accessed 10 March 2012.

Conférence de citoyens (2002) *Changements climatiques et citoyenneté: Rapport officiel du panel de citoyens, avis et recommandations des citoyens à l'issue des débats des 9 et 10 février 2002*. Available at: www.ademe.fr/entreprises/polluants/themes/problematiques/contenus/rapportconfcitoyens.pdf, accessed 10 March 2012.

Corradi, J., Weiss Fagen, P. & Garretón, M.A. (eds.) (1992) *Fear at the Edge: State Terror and Resistance in Latin America.* Berkeley, University of California Press.

Costa, P. (2010) Democrazia e diritti. In: Pizzorno, A. (ed.) *La democrazia di fronte allo stato democratico.* Milan, Feltrinelli, pp. 1–48.

Cotta, M. (1990) Rappresentanza politica. In: Bobbio, N., Matteucci, N. & Pasquino, G. (eds.) *Dizionario di politica.* Turin, Utet, pp. 929–34.

Couldry, N. (2000) *The Place of Media Power: Pilgrims and Witnesses of the Media Age.* London, Routledge.

Couldry, N. (2003) Beyond the Hall of Mirrors? Some Theoretical Reflections on the Global Contestation of Media Power. In: Couldry, N. & Curran, J. (eds.) *Contesting Media Power: Alternative Media in a Networked World.* Lanham, Rowman & Littlefield, pp. 39–55.

Couldry, N. (2006) *Listening Beyond the Echoes: Media, Ethics and Agency in an Uncertain world.* New York, Paradigm.

Council of Europe (2001) *Draft Recommendation of the Committee of Ministers to Member States on 'Participation of Citizens in Local Public Life' and a Draft Explanatory Report.* Doc. 9172, 9 July. Available at: http://assembly.coe.int/Documents/WorkingDocs/doc01/EDOC9172.htm, accessed 10 March 2012.

Critcher, C. & Waddington, D. (eds.) (1996) *Policing Public Order: Theoretical and Practical Issues.* Aldershot, Avebury.

Crouch, C. (2003) *Post-Democracy.* Cambridge, Polity Press.

Crouch, C. (2010) Democracy and the Economy. In: Pizzorno, A. (ed.) *La democrazia di fronte allo stato democratico.* Milan, Feltrinelli, pp. 181–92.

Crozier, M., Huntington, S. & Watakuni, J. (1975) *The Crisis of Democracy.* New York, New York University Press.

Dahl, R.A. (1970) *After the Revolution? Authority in a Good Society.* New Haven, Yale University Press.

Dahl, R.A. (1971) *Polyarchy: Participation and Opposition.* New Haven, Yale University Press.

Dahl, R.A. (1998) *On Democracy.* New Haven, Yale University Press.

Dahlberg, L. (2001) Democracy via Cyberspace: Mapping the Rhetorics and Practices of Three Prominent Camps. *New Media and Society* 3 (2), 155–77.

Dahlgren, P. (2009) *Media and Political Engagement: Citizens, Communication and Democracy.* Cambridge, Cambridge University Press.

Dalton, R.J. (2000) Value Change and Democracy. In: Pharr, S. & Putnam, R. (eds.) *Disaffected Democracies.* Princeton, Princeton University Press, pp. 252–69.

Dalton, R.J. (2004) *Democratic Challenger, Democratic Choices: The Erosion of Political Support in Advanced Industrial Democracies.* Oxford, Oxford University Press.

Dalton, R.J. & Wattemberg, M.P. (eds.) (2000) *Parties without Partisans.* Oxford, Oxford University Press.

Davenport, C. (1995) Multi-dimensional Threat Perception and State Repression: An Inquiry into Why States Apply Negative Sanctions. *American Journal of Political Science* 39, 683–713.

Davenport, C. (ed.) (2000) *Paths to State Repression: Human Rights Violations and Contentious Politics*. Boulder, Colo., Rowman & Littlefield.

Davenport, C. (2005) Introduction: Repression and Mobilization: Insights from Political Science and Sociology. In: Davenport, C., Johnston, H. & Mueller, C. (eds) *Repression and Mobilization*. Minneapolis: The University of Minnesota Press, pp. vii–xli.

de Sousa Santos, B. (1998) Participatory Budgeting in Porto Alegre: Toward a Redistributive Politics. *Society* 26, 461–508.

Del Giorgio, E. (2002) *I figli dei Fori*. Research report. Florence, EUI.

Delany, C. (2009) *Learning from Obama: Lessons for Online Communicators in 2009 and Beyond*. Available at: www.epolitics.com/learning-from-obama/.

Delazay, Y. & Garth, B. G. (1996). *Dealing with Virtue: International Commercial Arbitration and the Construction of a Transnational Legal Order*. Chicago, The University of Chicago Press.

della Porta, D. (1995) *Social Movements, Political Violence and the State*. Cambridge and New York, Cambridge University Press.

della Porta, D. (1996) *Movimenti Collettivi e Sistema Politico in Italia, 1960–1995*. Bari, Laterza.

della Porta, D. (1998) Police Knowledge and Public Order in Italy. In: della Porta, D. & Reiter, H. (eds.) *Policing Protest: The Control of Mass Demonstrations in Western Democracies*. Minneapolis, University of Minnesota Press, pp. 228–51.

della Porta, D. (2004) Multiple Belongings, Tolerant Identities and the Construction of Another Politics: Between the European Social Forum and the Local Social Fora. In: della Porta, D. & Tarrow, S. (eds.) *Transnational Protest and Global Activism*. Lanham, Rowman & Littlefield, pp. 175–202.

della Porta, D. (2005a) Making the Polis: Social Forums and Democracy in the Global Justice Movements. *Mobilization* 10 (1), 73–94.

della Porta, D. (2005b) Deliberation in Movement: Why and How to Study Deliberative Democracy and Social Movements. *Acta Politica* 40 (3), 336–50.

della Porta, D. (2007) *The Global Justice Movement in Cross-National and Transnational Perspective*. Boulder, Colo., Paradigm.

della Porta, D. (ed.) (2009a) *Another Europe*. London, Routledge.

della Porta, D. (ed.) (2009b) *Democracy in Social Movements*. London, Palgrave.

della Porta, D. (2010) Social Movements and Civil Society: How Emerging Social Conflicts Challenge Social Science Approaches. In: Baert, P., Koniordos, S. M., Procacci, G. & Ruzza, C. (eds.), *Conflict, Citizenship and Civil Society*. London, Routledge, pp. 51–68.

della Porta, D. & Andretta, M. (2006) *Global Activists. Conceptions and Practices of Democracy in the European Social Forums*, WP5 Report, Democracy in Movement and the Mobilization of the Society – DEMOS, European Commission, 2006.

della Porta, D., Andretta, M., Mosca, L. & Reiter, H. (2006) *Globalization from Below: Transnational Activists and Protest Networks*. Minneapolis, The University of Minnesota Press.

della Porta, D. & Caiani, M. (2009) *Social Movements and Europeanization*. Oxford, Oxford University Press.

della Porta, D. & Diani, M. (2004) *Movimenti senza protesta? L'ambientalismo in Italia*. Bologna, Il Mulino.

della Porta, D. & Diani, M. (2006) *Social Movements. An Introduction*. Oxford, Blackwell.

della Porta, D. & Fillieule, O. (2004) Policing Social Movements. In: Snow, D. A., Soule, S. A. & Kriesi, H. (eds.) *The Blackwell Companion to Social Movements*. Oxford, Blackwell, pp. 217–41.

della Porta, D. & Gbikpi, B. (2008) La partecipazione nelle istituzioni: concettualizzare gli esperimenti di democrazia deliberative e partecipativa. *Partecipazione e conflitto* 0, 15–42.

della Porta, D. & Mattina, L. (1986) Ciclos políticos y movilización étnica: el caso Vasco. *Revista Española de Investigaciones Sociológicas* 35, 123–48.

della Porta, D. & Mosca, L. (2005) Global-net for Global Movements? A Network of Networks for a Movement of Movements. *Journal of Public Policy* 25 (1), 165–90.

della Porta, D. & Mosca, L. (2006) *Organizational Structures and Practices of Democracy in the Global Justice Movement*, WP4 Report, Democracy in Movement and the Mobilization of the Society – DEMOS, European Commission.

della Porta, D., Peterson, A. & Reiter, H. (2006) *The Policing of Transnational Protest: In the Aftermath of the 'Battle of Seattle'*. Aldershot, Ashgate.

della Porta, D. and Piazza, G. (2008) *Voices of the Valley, Voices of the Straits: How Protest Creates Communities*. Berghahn Books.

della Porta, D. & Reiter, H. (eds.) (1998) *Policing Protest: The Control of Mass Demonstrations in Western Democracies*. Minneapolis, The University of Minnesota Press.

della Porta, D. & Reiter, H. (2003) *Polizia e ordine pubblico*. Bologna, Il Mulino.

della Porta, D. & Reiter, H. (2004) *La protesta e il controllo: Movimenti e forze dell'ordine nell'era della globalizzazione*. Milan, Altraeconomia & Piacenza, Berti.

della Porta, D. & Reiter H. (2006) *Organizational Ideology and Vision of Democracy in the Global Justice Movement*. WP3 Report, Democracy in Movement and the Mobilization of the Society – DEMOS, European Commission.

della Porta, D. & Reiter, H. (2006) *Organizational Structures and Practices of Democracy in the Global Justice Movement*. WP4 Report, Democracy in Movement and the Mobilization of the Society – DEMOS, European Commission.

della Porta, D. & Reiter, H. (2011) State Power and the Control of Transnational Protests. In: Oleson, T. (ed.) *Power and Transnational Activism*. London and New York, Routledge.

della Porta, D. & Reiter, H. (2012) Desperately Seeking Politics. *Mobilization: An International Quarterly* 17 (3), 349–61.

della Porta, D. & Rucht, D. (1995) Left-Libertarian Movements in Context: Comparing Italy and West Germany, 1965–1990. In: Jenkins, C.L. &

Klandermans, B. (eds.) *The Politics of Social Protest*. Minneapolis and London, University of Minnesota Press, pp. 299–372.

della Porta, D. and Rucht, D. (eds.) (forthcoming) *Meeting Democracy*. Cambridge, Cambridge University Press.

della Porta, D. & Tarrow, S. (eds.) (2005) *Transnational Protest and Global Activism*. Lanham, Rowman & Littlefield.

della Porta, D. & Tarrow, S. (2012) Interactive Diffusion: The Coevolution of Police and Protest Behavior with an Application to Transnational Contention. *Comparative Political Studies* 20, 1–34.

della Porta, D., Valiente, C. & Kousis, M. (forthcoming) Sisters of the South: The Women's Movement and Democratization. In: Gunther, R., Diamandouros, P. & Puhle, H. (eds.) *Democratic Consolidation in Southern Europe: The Cultural Dimension*. Baltimore, Johns Hopkins University Press.

della Porta, D. & Zamponi, L. (forthcoming) Protest and Policing on October 15th, Global Day of Action. The Italian Case. *Policing and Society*.

Derechos para Tod@s (n.d.) Who we are.

Deutsch, Karl W. 1964, *The Nerves of Government. Models of Political Communication*, New York, Free Press.

Deutscher Bundestag (2002) *Schlussbericht der Enquete-Kommission Globalisierung der Weltwirtschaft – Herausforderungen und Antworten*. Drucksache 14/9200. Berlin, Deutscher Bundestag.

di Palma, G. (1991) Legitimation from the Top to Civil Society: Politico-Cultural Change in Eastern Europe. *World Politics* 44 (1), 49–80.

Diamanti, I. (2007) La democrazia degli interstizi: Società e partiti in Europa dopo la caduta del Muro. *Rassegna italiana di sociologia* 48, 387–412.

Diamond, L.J. & Gunther, R. (eds.) (2001) *Political Parties and Democracy*. Baltimore and London, Johns Hopkins University Press.

Diamond, L.J. & Morlino, L. (eds.) (2005) *Assessing the Quality of Democracy*. Baltimore, Johns Hopkins University Press.

Dissent! A Network of Resistance against the G8 (2008) *Introduction to the Dissent! Network*, www.dissent.org.uk (home page), accessed 12 November 2008.

Donker, T. (2012) *Mobilizing for Democracy: The Tunisian Case*. Report for the ERC Project on Mobilizing for Democracy. Florence, EUI.

Donner, F. (1990) *Protectors of Privilege*. Berkeley, University of California Press.

Dore, R. (1998) A chi giova la convergenza? In: Berger, S. & Dore, R. (eds.) *Differenze nazionali e capitalismo globale*. Bologna, Il Mulino, pp. 241–51.

Dore, R. (2010) The Dynamics of Economic Change and What it Means for the Democratic State. In: Pizzorno A. (ed.) *La democrazia di fronte allo stato democratico*. Milan, Feltrinelli, pp. 165–80.

Downing, J. (1984) *Radical Media: The Political Experience of Alternative Communication*. Boston, South End Press.

Downs, A. (1957) *An Economic Theory of Democracy*. New York, Harper and Row.

Dryzek, J.S. (2000a) Discursive Democracy vs. Liberal Constitutionalism. In: Saward, M. (ed.) *Democratic Innovation: Deliberation, Representation and Association*. London and New York, Routledge and ECPR, pp. 78–89.

Dryzek, J. S. (2000b) *Deliberative Democracy and Beyond*. New York, Oxford University Press.

Dryzek, J. S. (2010) *Foundations and Frontiers of Deliberative Governance*. Oxford, Oxford University Press.

Dzur, A. W. (2002) Public Journalism and Deliberative Democracy. *Policy* 34 (3), 313–36.

Earl, J. (2003) Tanks, Tear Gas and Taxes. *Sociological Theory* 21, 44–68.

Earl, J., Soule, S. A. & McCarthy, A. (2003) Protest Under Fire? Explaining Protest Policing. *American Sociological Review* 69, 581–606.

Eckstein, S. (ed.) (2001) *Power and Popular Protest: Latin American Social Movements*, 2nd edition. Berkeley, University of California Press.

Eder, K. (2003) Identity Mobilization and Democracy: An Ambivalent Relation. In: Ibarra, P. (ed.) *Social Movements and Democracy*. New York, Palgrave, pp. 61–80.

Eder, K. (2010) The Transformations of the Public Sphere and their Impact on Democratization. In: Pizzorno, A. (ed.) *La democrazia di fronte allo stato democratico*. Milan, Feltrinelli, pp. 247–83.

Eisinger, P. K. (1973) The Conditions of Protest Behavior in American Cities. *American Political Science Review* 67, 11–28.

Eliasoph, N. (1998) *Avoiding Politics: How Americans Produce Apathy in Everyday Life*. Cambridge, Cambridge University Press.

Elster, J. (1997) The Market and the Forum: Three Varieties of Political Theory. In: Bohman, J. & Rehg, W. (eds.) *Deliberative Democracy: Essays on Reason and Politics*. Cambridge, Mass., MIT Press, pp. 3–33.

Elster, J. (1998) Deliberation and Constitution Making. In: Elster, J. (ed.) *Deliberative Democracy*. Cambridge, Cambridge University Press, pp. 97–122.

Eltantawy, N. & Wiest, J. B. (2011) Social Media in the Egyptian Revolution: Reconsidering Resource Mobilization Theory. *International Journal of Communication* 5, 1207–24.

Epstein, J. A. (1994) *Radical Expression: Political Language, Ritual, and Symbol in England, 1790–1850*. Oxford, Oxford University Press.

Ericson, R. & Doyle, A. (1999) Globalization and the Policing of Protest: The Case of APEC 1997. *British Journal of Sociology* 50, 589–608.

Escobar, A. & Álvarez, S. (eds.) (1992) *The Making of Social Movements in Latin America: Identity, Strategy and Democracy*. Boulder, Colo., Westview.

EuroMayDay (2004) *Middlesex Declaration of Europe's Precariat 2004*, www.euromayday.org (home page), accessed 12 November 2008.

Evans, R. J. (ed.) (1989) *Kneipengespräche im Keiserreich. Stimmungsberichte der Hamburger Politische Polizei 1892–1914*. Hamburg, RoRoRo.

Evans, S. & Boyte, H. (1986) *Free Spaces: The Sources of Democratic Changes in America*. New York, Harper and Row.

Ferejohn, J. (2000) Instituting Deliberative Democracy. In: Shapiro, I. & Macedo, S. (eds.) *Designing Democratic Institutions*. New York and London, New York University Press, pp. 75–104.

Fernandez, L. A. (2008) *Policing Dissent: Social Control and the Anti-Globalization Movement*. New Brunswick, NJ, Rutgers.

Ferrarese, M. R. (2000) *Le istituzioni della globalizzazione: Diritto e diritti nella società transnazionale*. Bologna, Il Mulino.

Fillieule, O. & Jobard, F. (1998) The Policing of Protest in France: Towards a Model of Protest Policing. In: della Porta, D. & Reiter, H. (eds.) *Policing Protest: The Control of Mass Demonstrations in Western Democracies*. Minneapolis, The University of Minnesota Press, pp. 70–90.

Fischer, F. (2003) Citizens and Experts: Democratizing Policy Deliberation. In: Fischer, F. (ed.) *Reframing Public Policy: Discursive Politics and Deliberative Practices*. New York, Oxford University Press, pp. 205–20.

Fishkin, J. (1997) *The Voice of the People*. Durham, Duke University Press.

Fishkin, J. (2003) Consulting the Public through Deliberative Polling. *Journal of Policy Analysis and Management* 22 (1), 128–33.

Fishkin, J. (2009) *When the People Speak: Deliberative Democracy and Public Consultation*. Oxford, Oxford University Press.

Fitzpatrick, T. (2002) The Two Paradoxes of Welfare Democracy. *International Journal of Social Welfare* 11, 159–69.

Flam, H. (2001) *Pink, Purple, Green: Women's, Religious, Environmental and Gay/Lesbian Movements in Central Europe Today*. New York, Columbia University Press.

Flybjerg, B. (1998) Habermas and Foucault: Thinkers for Civil Society? *The British Journal of Sociology* 49, 211–33.

Font, J. (ed.) (2003) *Public Participation and Local Governance*. Barcelona, ICPS.

Foweraker, J. & Landman, T. (1997) *Citizenship Rights and Social Movements: A Comparative and Statistical Analysis*. Oxford, Oxford University Press.

Francisco, R. A. (1996) Coercion and Protest: An Empirical Test in Two Democratic States. *American Journal of Political Science* 40, 1179–204.

Francisco, R. A. (2005) The Dictator's Dilemma. In: Davenport, C., Johnston, H. & Mueller, C. (eds.) *Repression and Mobilization*. Minneapolis, The University of Minnesota Press, pp. 58–83.

Franklin, M. N. & van der Eijk, E. (2004) *Voter Turnout and the Dynamics of Electoral Competition in Established Democracies since 1945*. Cambridge and New York, Cambridge University Press.

Fraser, N. 1997. *Justice Interruptus*. London, Routledge.

Freedom House (2012) *Freedom in the World 2012*. New York, Freedom House.

Freeman, J. (1970) *The Tyranny of the Structurelessness*, http://flag.blackened.net/revolt/hist_texts/structurelessness.html, accessed 28 October 2008.

Freschi, A. C. (2002) *La società dei saperi: Reti virtuali e partecipazione sociale*. Rome, Carocci.

Fruci, G. L. (2003) *La nuova agorà: i social forum tra spazio pubblico e dinamiche organizzative*. In: Ceri, P. (ed.) *La democrazia dei movimenti*. Rubettino, Soveria Mannelli, pp. 169–200.

Fung, A. (2003) Deliberative Democracy, Chicago Style: Grassroots Governance in Policing and Public Education. In: Fung, A. & Olin Wright, E. (eds.) *Deepening Democracy: Institutional Innovations in Empowered Participatory Governance*. London and New York, Verso, pp. 111–43.

Fung, A. & Olin Wright, E. (2001) Deepening Democracy, Innovations in Empowered Participatory Governance. *Politics and Society* 29 (1), 5–41.

Fuster, M. (2010) Governance of Online Creation Communities: Provision of Infrastructure for the Building of Digital Commons. Ph.D. thesis, European University Institute, Florence.

Gamson, W. A. (1992) The Social Psychology of Collective Action. In: Morris, A. D. & McClung Muller, C. (eds.) *Frontiers in Social Movement Theory*. New Haven, Yale University Press, pp. 53–76.

Gamson, W. A. (2004) Bystanders, Public Opinion and the Media. In: Snow, D. A., Soule, S. A. & Kriesi, H. (eds.) *The Blackwell Companion to Social Movements*. Oxford, Blackwell, pp. 242–61.

Gamson, W. A., Croteau, D., Hoynes, W. & Sasson, T. (1992) Media Images and the Social Construction of Reality. *Annual Review of Sociology* 18, 373–93.

Gamson, W. A. & Modigliani, A. (1989) Media Discourse and Public Opinion on Nuclear Power. *American Journal of Sociology* 95, 1–37.

Gastil, J., Dees, E. P., Weiser, P. J. & Simmons, C. (2010) *The Jury and Democracy*. Oxford, Oxford University Press.

Geddes, B. (1999) What Do We Know about Democratization after Twenty Years? *Annual Review of Political Science* 2, 115–44.

Gerhard, J. & Neidhardt, F. (1990) *Strukturen und Funktionen moderner Öffentlichkeit: Fragestellung und Ansätze*. Discussion Paper FS III: 90–101. Berlin, Wissenschaftszentrum Berlin.

Gilpin, R. (2000) *The Challenge of Global Capitalism*. Princeton, NJ, Princeton University Press.

Gimmler, A. (2001) Deliberative Democracy, the Public Sphere and the Internet. *Philosophy and Social Criticism* 27 (4), 21–39.

Gitlin, T. (1980) *The Whole World is Watching: Mass Media in the Making and Unmaking of the New Left*. Berkeley and Los Angeles, University of California Press.

Glenn, J. (2003) Contentious Politics and Democratization: Comparing the Impact of Social Movements on the Fall of Communism in Eastern Europe. *Political Studies* 55, 103–20.

Goodin, R. E. (2003) *Reflective Democracy*. Oxford, Oxford University Press.

Grant, W., Perl, A. & Knoepfel, P. (eds.) (1999) *The Politics of Improving Urban Air Quality*. Aldershot, Edward Elgar.

Gret, M. & Sintomer, Y. (2005) *The Porto Alegre Experiment: Learning Lessons for Better Democracy*. London, Zed Books.

Gunning, J. (2007) *Hamas in Politics: Democracy, Religion, Violence*. New York, Columbia University Press.

Gunther, R. & Mughan, A. (eds.) (2000) *Democracy and the Media: A Comparative Perspective*. Cambridge, Cambridge University Press.

Gupta, D. K., Singh, H. & Spargue, T. (1993) Government Coercion of Dissidents: Deterrence or Provocation? *Journal of Conflict Resolution* 37, 301–39.

Gutmann, A. (1996) Democracy, Philosophy, and Justification. In: Benhabib, S. (ed.) *Democracy and Difference: Contesting the Boundaries of the Political*. Princeton, Princeton University Press, pp. 340–7.

Gutmann, A. & Thompson, D. (1996) *Democracy and Disagreement*. Cambridge, Mass., Harvard University Press.

Habermas, J. (1981) *Theorie des kommunikativen Handelns*. Frankfurt am Main, Suhrkamp.

Habermas, J. (1988) *Storia e critica dell'opinione pubblica*. Rome and Bari, Laterza (orig. 1966).

Habermas, J. (1996) *Between Facts and Norms: Contribution to a Discursive Theory of Law and Democracy*. Cambridge, Mass., MIT Press.

Habermas, J. (2001) *The Postnational Constellation*. Cambridge, Polity Press.

Hafez, M. (2003) *Why Muslims Rebel*. Boulder, Colo., Lynne Rienner.

Hajer, M. & Kesselring, S. (1999) Democracy in the Risk Society? *Environmental Politics* 8 (3), 1–23.

Hajer, M. & Wagenaar, H. (eds.) (2003) *Deliberative Policy Analysis: Understanding Governance in the Network Society*. Cambridge, Cambridge University Press.

Haug, C. (2010) Discursive Decision-making in Meetings of the Global Justice Movements: Culture and Practices. Ph.D. thesis, Freie Universität Berlin, Berlin.

Hauptmann, E. (2001) Can Less Be More? Leftist Deliberative Democrats' Critique of Participatory Democracy. *Polity* 33 (3), 397–421.

Held, D. (1997) *Modelli di democrazia*. Bologna, Il Mulino.

Held, D. (1998) *Democracy and Globalization*. In: Archibugi, D., Held, D. & Kohler, M. (eds.) *Re-imagining Political Community: Studies in Cosmopolitan Democracy*. Cambridge, Polity Press, pp. 11–27.

Held, D. (2006) *Models of Democracy*, 3rd edition. Cambridge, Polity Press.

Held, D. & McGrew, A. (2007) *Globalization and Antiglobalization*, 2nd edition. Cambridge, Polity Press.

Hick, S. & McNutt, J. (2002) Communities and Advocacy on the Internet: A Conceptual Framework. In: Hick, S. & McNutt, J. (eds.) *Advocacy, Activism and the Internet*. Chicago, Lyceum Books, pp. 3–18.

Higley, J. & Gunther, R. (1992) *Elites and Democratic Consolidation in Latin America and Southern Europe*. New York, Cambridge University Press.

Hinton, J. (1974) *Labour and Socialism: A History of the British Labour Movement 1867–1974*. Brighton, Wheatsheaf.

Hipsher, P. (1998a) Democratic Transitions as Protest Cycles: Social Movements Dynamics in Democratizing Latin America. In: Meyer, D. & Tarrow, S. (eds.) *The Social Movement Society: Contentious Politics for a New Century*. Lanham, Rowman & Littlefield, pp. 153–72.

Hipsher, P. (1998b) Democratic Transitions and Social Movements Outcomes: The Chilean Shantytown Dwellers' Movement in Comparative Perspective. In: Giugni, M., McAdam, D. & Tilly, C. (eds.) *From Contention to Democracy*. Lanham, Rowman & Littlefield, pp. 149–67.

Hirst, P. (1994) *Associative Democracy: New Forms of Economic and Social Governance*. Cambridge, Polity Press.

Howard, P.N. (2010) *The Digital Origins of Dictatorship and Democracy: Information Technology and Political Islam*. Oxford, Oxford University Press.

Huntington, S. (1965) *Political Order in Changing Societies*. New Haven, Yale University Press.

Huntington, S. (1975) The United States. In: Crozier, M., Huntington, S. & Watakuni, J. (eds.) *The Crisis of Democracy*. New York, New York University Press.

Huntington, S. (1991) *The Third Wave: Democratization in the Late Twentieth Century*. Norman, University of Oklahoma Press.

Idle, N. & Nunns, A. (eds.) (2011) *Tweets from Tahrir: Egypt's Revolution as it Unfolded, in the Words of the People Who Made It*. New York, OR Books.

Indymedia (2002) *Principles of Unity*, http://italy.indymedia.org (home page), accessed 12 November 2008.

Innes, J.E. and Booher, D.E. (2003) Collaborative Policy Making: Governance through Dialogue. In: Hajer, M.A. & Wagenaar, H. (eds.), *Deliberative Policy Analysis: Understanding Governance in the Network Society*. Cambridge, Cambridge University Press, pp. 33–59.

Jamal, M.A. (2012) Democracy Promotion, Civil Society Building, and the Primacy of Politics. *Comparative Political Studies* 45 (1), 3–31.

Jasper, J. (1997) *The Art of Moral Protest: Culture, Biography, and Creativity in Social Movements*. Chicago, University of Chicago Press.

Jelin, E. (ed.) (1987) *Movimientos Sociales y Democracia Emergente*, 2 vols. Buenos Aires: Centro Editor de América Latina.

Jiménez, M. & Calle, A. (2006) Organizational Ideology and Visions of Democracy in Spanish GJMOs. In: della Porta, D. & Reiter, H. (eds.) *Organizational Ideology and Vision of Democracy in the Global Justice Movement*, WP3 Report, Democracy in Movement and the Mobilization of the Society – DEMOS, European Commission, pp. 265–89.

Joerges, C. and Neyer, J. (1997) From Intergovernmental Bargaining to Deliberative Political Processes: The Constitutionalisation of Comitology. *European Law Journal* 3 (3), 273–99.

Johnston, H. (2011) *States and Social Movements*. Cambridge, Polity Press.

Johnson, J. (1998) Arguing for Deliberation: Some Skeptical Considerations. In: Elster, J. (ed.) *Deliberative Democracy*. Cambridge, Cambridge University Press, pp. 161–84.

Juris, J.F. (2012) Reflections on #Occupy Everywhere: Social Media, Public Spaces, and Emerging Logics of Aggregation. *American Ethnologist* 39 (2), 259–79.

Kaldor, M. (2003) *Global Civil Society: An Answer to War*. Cambridge, Polity Press.

Karatnycky, A. & Ackerman, P. (2005) *How Freedom is Won: From Civic Resistance to Durable Democracy*. New York, Freedom House.

Karl, T.L. (1990) Dilemmas of Democratization in Latin America. *Comparative Politics* 23 (1), 1–21.

Keane, J. (2003) *Global Civil Society?* Cambridge, Cambridge University Press.

Keck, M. & Sikkink, K. (1998) *Activists beyond Borders: Advocacy Networks in International Politics*. Ithaca, Cornell University Press.

Kelsen, H. (1995) *La democrazia*. Bologna, Il Mulino (orig. 1929).

Khamis, S. & Vaughn, K. (2011) Cyberactivism in the Egyptian Revolution: How Civic Engagement and Citizen Journalism Tilted the Balance. *Arab Media and*

Society 14, www.arabmediasociety.com/index.php?article=769&printarticle (accessed 5 May 2012).

King, C.S., Feltey, K.M. & O'Neill Susel, B. (1998) The Question of Participation: Toward Authentic Public Participation in Public Administration. *Public Administration Review* 58 (4), 317–26.

King, M. & Waddington, D. (2006) The Policing of Transnational Protest in Canada. In: della Porta, D., Peterson, A. & Reiter, H. (eds.) *Policing Transnational Protest: In the Aftermath of the 'Battle of Seattle'*. Aldershot, Ashgate.

Kitschelt, H. (1986) Political Opportunity Structures and Political Protest: Anti-Nuclear Movements in Four Democracies. *British Journal of Political Science* 16, 57–85.

Kitschelt, H. (1993) Social Movements, Political Parties, and Democratic Theory. *The Annals of the AAPSS* 528, 13–29.

Klandermans, B. (1989) Introduction: Social Movement Organizations and the Study of Social Movements. In: Klandermans, B. (ed.) *Organizing for Change*. Greenwich, JAI Press, pp. 1–17.

Klein, N. (2002) *Fences and Windows: Dispatches from the Front of the Globalization Debate*. London, Flamingo.

Klimke, M. & Scharlot, J. (2008) *1968 in Europe: A History of Protest and Activism*. London, Palgrave Macmillan.

Kocka, J. (1986) Problems of Working Class Formation in Germany: The Early Years, 1800–1875. In: Katnelson, I. & Zolberg, A.R. (eds.) *Working-Class Formation: Nineteenth-Century Patterns in Western Europe and the United States*. Princeton, Princeton University Press, pp. 279–351.

Koelbe, T. (2009) Democracy. *APSA-CP Newsletter* 20 (2), 9.

Kraska, P.B. (1996) Enjoying Militarism: Political/Personal Dilemmas in Studying U.S. Paramilitary Units. *Justice Quarterly* 13, 405–29.

Kraska, P.B. & Kaeppler, V.E. (1997) Militarizing American Police: The Rise and Normalization of Paramilitary Units. *Social Problems* 44 (1), 1–18.

Kriesi, H. (1991) *The Political Opportunity Structure of New Social Movements*. Discussion Paper FS III: 91–103. Berlin, Wissenschaftszentrum Berlin.

Kriesi, H. (1996) The Organizational Structure of New Social Movements in a Political Context. In: McAdam, D., McCarthy, J. & Zald, M.N. (eds.) *Comparative Perspective on Social Movements: Political Opportunities, Mobilizing Structures, and Cultural Framing*. Cambridge and New York, Cambridge University Press, pp. 152–84.

Kriesi, H., Koopmans, R., Duyvendak, J.W. & Giugni, M. (1995) *New Social Movements in Western Europe*. Minneapolis, The University of Minnesota Press and London, UCL Press.

Kuran, T. (1991) Now Out of Never: The Element of Surprise in the East European Revolution of 1989. *World Politics* 44 (1), 7–48.

Laclau, E. & Mouffe, C. (2001) *Hegemony and Socialist Strategy*. London, Verso.

Lafferty, W.M. (ed.) (2002) *Sustainable Communities in Europe*. London, Earthscan.

Lane, J.E. & Ersson, S. (1999) *Politics and Society in Western Europe*. London, Sage.

Lawrence, J. (1991) Popular Politics and the Limitations of Party: Wolverhampton, 1867–1900. In: Biagini, E. F. & Reid, A. J. (eds.) *Currents of Radicalism. Popular Radicalism, Organized Labour and Party Politics in Britain, 1850–1914*. Cambridge, Cambridge University Press, pp. 65–85.

Le Bon, G. (1895) *La psychologie des foules*. Paris, PUF.

Lello, E. (2007) La rappresentanza politica nella 'vecchia' Europa: crisi o mutamento? *Rassegna italiana di sociologia* 48, 413–61.

Levine, D. & Mainwaring, S. (2001) Religion and Popular Protest in Latin America: Contrasting Experiences. In: Eckstein, S. (ed.) *Power and Popular Protest: Latin American Social Movements*, 2nd edition. Berkeley, University of California Press.

Lewit, D. (2002) Porto Alegre's Budget Of, By, and For the People, 31 December, www.yesmagazine.org/issues/what-would-democracy-look-like/562, accessed 7 August 2012.

Lichbach, M. I. (1987) Deterrence or Escalation? The Puzzle of Aggregate Studies of Repression and Dissent. *Journal of Conflict Resolution* 31, 266–97.

Linz, J. & Stepan, A. (1996) *Problems of Democratic Transition and Consolidation: Southern Europe, South America, and Post-Communist Europe*. Baltimore, Johns Hopkins University Press.

Lipset, S. M. (1959) Some Social Requisites to Democracy: Economic Development and Political Legitimacy. *American Political Science Review* 55, 69–105.

London Social Forum (2003) *Why a London Social Forum now*, www.londonsocialforum.org (home page), accessed 12 November 2008.

Lotan, G., Graeff, E., Ananny, M., Gaffney, D., Pearce, I. & Boyd, D. (2011) Information Flows During the 2011 Tunisian and Egyptian Revolutions. *International Journal of Communication* 5, 1375–405.

Lowden, P. (1996) *Moral Opposition to Authoritarian Rule in Chile, 1973–1990*. London, Macmillan.

Lowndes, V., Pratchett, L. & Stoker, G. (2001) Trends in Public Participation: Local Government Perspectives. *Public Administration* 79 (1), 202–22.

Lucas, K., Ross, A. & Fuller, S. (2003) *What's in a Name? Local Agenda 21, Community Planning and Neighbourhood Renewal*. York, Joseph Rowntree.

Macdonald, T. (2008) *Global Stakeholder Democracy: Power and Representation beyond the Liberal State*. New York, Oxford University Press.

Mainwaring, S. (1987) Urban Popular Movements, Identity, and Democratization in Brazil. *Comparative Political Studies* 20 (2), 131–59.

Manin, B. (1987) On Legitimacy and Political Deliberation. *Political Theory* 15 (3), 338–68.

Manin, B. (1995) *Principes du gouvernement représentatif*. Paris, Flammarion.

Manin, B. & Blondiaux, L. (2002) L'idée de démocratie déliberative dans la science politique contemporaine: Introduction, généalogie et éléments critiques. *Politix* 15 (57), 37–55.

Mansbridge, J. (1996) Using Power / Fighting Power: The Polity. In: Benhabib, S. (ed.) *Democracy and Difference: Contesting the Boundaries of the Political*. Princeton, Princeton University Press, pp. 46–66.

Maravall, J. M. (1982) *The Transition to Democracy in Spain*. London, Croom Helm.

Marchetti, R. (2008) *Global Democracy: For and Against. Ethical Theory, Institutional Design and Social Struggles.* London, Routledge.

Marchetti, R. (2011) Models of Global Democracy: In Defence of Cosmo-Federalism. In: Archibugi, D., Konig-Archibugi, M. & Marchetti, R. (eds.) *Global Democracy: Normative and Empirical Perspectives.* Cambridge, Cambridge University Press, pp. 22–46.

Margolis, M. & Resnick, D. (2000) *Politics as Usual: the Cyberspace 'Revolution'.* Thousand Oaks, Sage.

Markoff, J. (1999) Globalization and the Future of Democracy. *Journal of World-System Research* 2, 277–309.

Marks, G., Mbaye, H.D. & Kim, H.M. (2009) Radicalism or Reformism? Socialist Parties before World War I. *American Sociological Review* 74, 615–35.

Marshall, T.H., (1992) Citizenship and Social Class. In: Marshall, T.H. & Bottomore, H.D. (eds.) *Citizenship and Social Class.* London, Pluto Press, pp. 3–51.

Mattoni, A. (2012) *Media Practices and Protest Politics.* Aldershot, Ashgate.

Mayer, N. & Perrineau, P. (1992) *Les comportements politiques.* Paris, Armand Colin.

McAdam, D. & Rucht, D. (1993) The Cross-National Diffusion of Movement Ideas. *The Annals of the American Academy of the Political and Social Sciences* 52, 56–74.

McAdam, D., Tarrow, S. & Tilly, C. (2001) *The Politics of Contention.* Cambridge, Cambridge University Press.

McCarthy, J., Martin, A. & McPhail, C. (2004) The Policing of U.S. University Campus Community Disturbances, 1985–2001. Paper presented at the conference Policing Political Protest after Seattle, Fiskebackekil, Sweden, 1–5 May.

McPhail, C., Schweingruber, D. & McCarthy, J. (1998) Policing Protest in the United States. In: della Porta, D. and Reiter, H. (eds.) *Policing Protest: The Control of Mass Demonstrations in Western Democracies.* Minneapolis, The University of Minnesota Press, pp. 49–69.

McWilliam, R. (1991) Radicalism and the Popular Culture: The Tichborne Case and the Politics of 'Fair Play'. In: Biagini, E.F. & Reid, A.J. (eds.) *Currents of Radicalism: Popular Radicalism, Organized Labour and Party Politics in Britain, 1850–1914.* Cambridge, Cambridge University Press, pp. 44–64.

Milan, S. (2009) Stealing the Fire. Ph.D. thesis, European University Institute, Florence.

Mill, J.S. (1947) *On Liberty.* New York, Appleton-Century-Crofts (orig. 1859).

Miller, D. (1993) Deliberative Democracy and Social Choice. In: Held, D. (ed.) *Prospects for Democracy.* Cambridge, Polity Press, pp. 74–92.

Moore, B., Jr (1973) *Social Origins of Dictatorship and Democracy: Lord and Peasant in the Making of the Modern World.* Harmondsworth, Penguin (orig. 1966).

Moore, W.H. (1998) Repression and Dissent: Substitution, Context and Timing. *American Journal of Political Science* 42, 851–73.

Morlino, L. (1996) Crisis of Parties and Change of Party System in Italy. *Party Politics* 2, 5–30.

Morlino, L. (2011) *Changes for Democracy.* Oxford, Oxford University Press.

Mosca, L. & della Porta, D. (2009) Unconventional Politics Online. In: della Porta, D. (ed.) *Democracy in Social Movements.* London, Palgrave, pp. 194–216.

Mosca, L. & della Porta, D. (2009) Searching the Net: Websites' Qualities in the Global Justice Movement. *Information, Communication and Society* 12, 771–92.

Mouffe, C. (2000) *The Democratic Paradox.* London, Verso.

Mouffe, C. (2005) *On the Political.* London, Routledge.

Mouffe, C. (2009) The Book Interview. *New Statesman*, 19 November.

Myers, D.J. (2001) Social Activism through Computer Networks. In: Burton, O.V. (ed.) *Computing in the Social Sciences and Humanities.* Urbana, University of Illinois Press, pp. 124–39.

Neumann, F. (1968) Entstehung und Entwicklung der politischen Parteien. In: Abendrot, W. & Lenk, K. (eds.) *Einführung in die politische Wissenschaft.* Munich, Francke Verlag.

Neumann, S. (1956) *Towards a Comparative Study of Political Parties.* In: Neumann, S. (ed.) *Modern Political Parties.* Chicago, University of Chicago Press.

Neveu, E. (1999) Media, mouvements sociaux, espace public. *Reseaux* 98, 17–85.

Noakes, J. & Gillham, P.F. (2006) Aspects of the 'New Penology' in the Police Response to Major Political Protests in the United States, 1999–2000. In: della Porta, D., Peterson, A. & Reiter, H. (eds.) *Policing Transnational Protest: In the Aftermath of the 'Battle of Seattle'.* Aldershot, Ashgate, pp. 97–116.

Nolan, M. (1986) Economic Crisis, State Policy, and Working Class Formation. In: Katnelson, I. & Zolberg, A.R. (eds) *Working-Class Formation: Nineteenth-Century Patterns in Western Europe and the United States.* Princeton, Princeton University Press.

Norris, P. (2001) *Digital Divide? Civic Engagement, Information Poverty and the Internet Worldwide.* New York, Cambridge University Press.

O'Brian, R., Goetz, A.M., Scholte, J.A. & Williams, M. (2000) *Contesting Global Governance.* New York, Cambridge University Press.

O'Donnell, G. (1978) Reflections on Patterns of Change in the Bureaucratic-Authoritarian State. *Latin American Research Review* 13 (1), 3–38.

O'Donnell, G. (1979) Tensions in the Bureaucratic-Authoritarian State and the Question of Democracy. In Collier, D. (ed.) *The New Authoritarianism in Latin America.* Princeton, Princeton University Press, pp. 285–318.

O'Donnell, G. (1993) *On the State, Democratization and some Conceptual Problems (A Latin American View with Glances at some Post-Communist Countries)*, Working Paper Series No. 92. Notre Dame, The Helen Kellogg Institute for International Studies, University of Notre Dame.

O'Donnell, G. (1994) Delegative Democracy? *Journal of Democracy* 5, 56–69.

O'Donnell, G. & Schmitter, P. (1986) *Transitions from Authoritarian Rule: Tentative Conclusions about Uncertain Democracies.* Baltimore, Johns Hopkins University Press.

Oberschall, A. (2000) Social Movements and the Transitions to Democracy. *Democratization* 7 (3), 25–45.

Offe, C. (1985) New Social Movements: Changing Boundaries of the Political. *Social Research* 52, 817–68.

Offe, C. (1997) Microaspects of Democratic Theory: What Makes for the Deliberative Competence of Citizens? In: Hadenius, A. (ed.) *Democracy's Victory and Crisis.* New York, Cambridge University Press, pp. 81–104.

Offe, C. (2011) Crisis and Innovation of Liberal Democracy: Can Deliberation Be Institutionalized? *Czech Sociological Review* 47, 447–72.

Olesen, T. (2005) *International Zapatismo: The Construction of Solidarity in the Age of Globalization.* London, Zed Books.

Olivo, C. (2001) *Creating a Democratic Civil Society in Eastern Germany: The Case of the Citizen Movements and Alliance 90.* London, Palgrave.

Opp, K.-D. & Roehl, D. (1990) Repression, Micromobilization, and Political Protest. *Social Forces* 69, 521–47.

Osa, M. (2003) Networks in Opposition: Linking Organizations through Activists in the Polish People's Republic. In: Diani, M. and McAdam, D. (eds.) *Social Movements and Networks: Relational Approaches to Collective Action.* Oxford, Oxford University Press, pp. 77–104.

Osa, M. and Cordunenanu-Huci, C. (2003) Running Uphill: Political Opportunity in Non-Democracies. *Comparative Sociology* 2, 606–29.

Pagnucco, R. (1995) The Comparative Study of Social Movements and Democratization: Political Interaction and Political Process Approaches. In: Dobkowski, M., Wallimann, I. & Stojanov, C. (eds.) *Research in Social Movements: Conflict and Change.* London, JAI Press, pp. 145–83.

Parkinson, J. (2003) Legitimacy Problems in Deliberative Democracy. *Political Studies* 51 (1), 180–96.

Parsa, M. (2000) *States, Ideologies and Social Revolutions.* Cambridge, Cambridge University Press.

Pateman, C. (1970) *Participation and Democratic Theory.* Cambridge, Cambridge University Press.

Peers, S. (2000) *EU Justice and Home Affairs Law.* London, Longman.

Pepino, L. (2005) La giustizia, i giudici e il paradigma del nemico. *Questione giustizia* 3, 844–71.

Perczynski, P. (2000) Active Citizenship and Associative Democracy. In: Saward, M. (ed.) *Democratic Innovation: Deliberation, Representation and Association.* London and New York, Routledge, pp. 161–71.

Perrot, M. (1974) *Les ouvriers en grève: France 1871–1890.* Paris, Mouton.

Perrot, M. (1986) On the Formation of the French Working Class. In: Katnelson, I. & Zolberg, A.R. (eds.) *Working-Class Formation: Nineteenth-Century Patterns in Western Europe and the United States.* Princeton, Princeton University Press, pp. 71–110.

Peterson, A. (2006) Policing Contentious Politics in Transnational Summits: Darth Vader or the Keystone Cops? In: della Porta, D., Peterson, A. & Reiter,

H. (eds.) *Policing Transnational Protest: In the Aftermath of the 'Battle of Seattle'*. Aldershot, Ashgate, pp. 43–74.

Petts, J. (1997) The Public–Expert Interface in Local Waste Management Decisions: Expertise, Credibility and Process. *Public Understanding of Science* 6, 359–81.

Pharr, S. J. & Putnam, R. D. (eds.) (2000) *Disaffected Democracies: What's Troubling the Trilateral Countries*. Princeton, Princeton University Press.

Pianta, M. (2001) *Globalizzazione dal basso: Economia mondiale e movimenti sociali*. Rome, ManifestoLibri.

Pianta, M. (2012) *Nove su dieci*. Rome, Laterza.

Pickerill, J. (2003) *Cyberprotest: Environmental Activism Online*. Manchester, Manchester University Press.

Pieper, U. & Taylor, L. (1998) The Revival of the Liberal Creed: the IBM, the World Bank and Inequalities in a Globalized Economy. In: Baker, D., Epstein, G. & Podin, R. (eds.) *Globalization and Progressive Economic Policy*. Cambridge, Cambridge University Press.

Pizzorno, A. (1981) Interests and Parties in Pluralism. In: Berger, S. (ed.) *Organizing Interests in Western Europe*. Cambridge, Cambridge University Press (now in: Pizzorno, A. (1993) *Le radici della politica assoluta*. Milan, Feltrinelli, pp. 232–82).

Pizzorno, A. (1996) Mutamenti nelle istituzioni rappresentative e sviluppo dei partiti politici. In: Bairoch, P. & Hobsbawm, E. J. (eds.) *La storia dell'Europa Contemporanea*. Turin, Einaudi, pp. 961–1031.

Pizzorno, A. (2010) Introduzione. In: Pizzorno, A. (ed.) *La democrazia di fronte allo stato democratico*. Milan, Feltrinelli, pp. xi–xxvii.

Pizzorno, A. (2012) In nome del popolo sovrano? *Il mulino* 2, 261–70.

Poe, S. C. & Neal Tate, C. (1994) Repression of Human Rights to Personal Integrity in the 1980s: A Global Analysis. *American Political Science Review* 88, 853–72.

Poe, S. C., Neal Tate, C. & Camp Keith, L. (1999) Repression of Human Rights to Personal Integrity Revised: A Global Cross-national Study Covering the Years 1976–1993. *International Study Quarterly* 43, 291–313.

Polletta, F. (2002) *Freedom is an Endless Meeting: Democracy in American Social Movements*. Chicago, University of Chicago Press.

Polletta, F. (2006) *It Was Like a Fever*. Chicago, University of Chicago Press.

Postill, J. (2012) New Protest Movements and Viral Media. *Media/Anthropology*, 26 March.

Preuss, U. (1995) *Constitutional Revolution*. Atlantic Highlands, Humanities Press.

Princen, T. & Finger, M. (1994) Introduction. In: Princen, T. & Finger, M. (eds.) *Environmental NGOs in World Politics: Linking the Local and the Global*. London, Routledge, pp. 1–25.

Przeworski, A. (1991) *Democracy and Market: Political and Economic Reforms in Eastern Europe and Latin America*. Cambridge, Cambridge University Press.

Putnam, R. (2000) *Bowling Alone*. Princeton, Princeton University Press.

Raniolo, F. (2007) *La partecipazione politica*, 2nd edition. Bologna, Il Mulino.

Ratza, M. & Kurnik, A. (2012) The Occupy Movement in Žižek's Hometown: Direct Democracy and a Politics of Becoming. *American Ethnologist* 39 (2), 238–58.

Rauch, J. (2010) Group Think: Inside the Tea Party's Collective Brain. *National Journal* 11 September 2010.

RCADE (2001) *Final Draft about the Organization, 5th General Meeting*, www.rcade.org (home page), accessed 12 November 2008.

Reiter, H. & Fillieule, O. (2006) Formalizing the Informal: The E.U. Approach to Transnational Protest Policing. In: della Porta, D. & Reiter, H. (eds.) *Policing Protest: The Control of Mass Demonstrations in Western Democracies.* Minneapolis, The University of Minnesota Press, pp. 145–74.

Renn, O., Webler, T. & Wiedemann, P. (1995) A Need for Discourse on Citizen Participation: Objectives and Structure of the Book, in Renn, O., Webler, T. & Wiedemann, P. (eds.) *Fairness and Competence in Citizen Participation. Evaluating Models for Environmental Discourse.* Dordrecht, Kluwer Academic Publishers, pp. 1–15.

Rete Lilliput (2001) Criteri di fondo condivisi, www.retelilliput.org/index.php?module=ContentExpress&func=display&ceid=34&meid=, accessed 12 November 2008.

Risse, T., Ropp, S. & Sikkink, K. (1999) *The Power of Human Rights: International Norms and Domestic Change.* Cambridge, Cambridge University Press.

Rocke, A. (2009) Frames of Citizen Participation and Participatory Budget Institutions in France, Germany, and Great Britain. Ph.D. thesis, European University Institute, Florence.

Rokkan, S. (1982) *Cittadini, elezioni, partiti.* Bologna, Il Mulino (orig. 1970).

Rosanvallon, P. (2006) *La contre-démocratie: la politique à l'âge de la défiance.* Paris, Seuil.

Rose, R. (2005) A Global Diffusion Model of E-Governance. *Journal of Public Policies* 25 (1), 5–7.

Rosenau, J. (1998) Governance and Democracy in a Globalizing World. In: Archibugi, D., Held, D. & Kohler, M. (eds.) *Re-imagining Political Community: Studies in Cosmopolitan Democracy.* Cambridge, Polity Press, pp. 28–57.

Rossi, F. & della Porta, D. (2009) Social Movement, Trade Unions and Advocacy Networks. In: Haerpfer, C., Bernhagen, P., Inglehart, R. & Welzel, R. (eds.) *Democratization.* Oxford, Oxford University Press, pp. 172–85.

Rubinstein, J. (1980) Cops' Rules. In: Landman, R. J. (ed.) *Police Behavior.* New York, Oxford University Press.

Rueschemeyer, D., Stephens, E. H. & Stephens, J. (1992) *Capitalist Development and Democracy.* Chicago, University of Chicago Press.

Russett, B. & Starr, H. (1996) *World Politics: The Menu for Choice.* New York, W. H. Freeman and Company.

Ryan, C. (1991) *Prime Time Activism: Media Strategies for Grassroots Organizing.* Boston, South End.

Ryfe, D.-M. (2002) The Practice of Deliberative Democracy: A Study of 16 Deliberative Organizations. *Political Communication* 19 (3), 359–417.

Sampedro, V. B. (2005) *15-M: Multitudes Online.* Madrid, Los Libros de la Catarata.

Sanders, L.M. (1997) Against Deliberation. *Political Theory* **25** (3), 347–76.

Sanderson, I. (1999) Participation and Democratic Renewal: From 'Instrumental' to 'Communicative Rationality'? *Policy & Politics* **27** (3), 325–41.

Santos, B.S. (ed.) (2005) *Democratizing Democracy: Beyond the Liberal Democratic Canon*. London, Verso.

Sartori, G. (1969) *Democrazia e definizioni*. Bologna, Il Mulino.

Sartori, G. (1976). *Parties and Party Systems: A Framework of Political Analysis*. Cambridge, Cambridge University Press.

Sartori, G. (1987) *Theory of Democracy Revisited*. New York, Chatham House Publishers.

Sartori, G. (1990) *Elementi di teoria politica*. Bologna, Il Mulino.

Sassen, S. (2001) Fuori controllo? Lo Stato e la nuova geografia del potere. In: D'Andrea, D. & Pulcini, E. (eds.) *Filosofie della globalizzazione*. Pisa, Edizioni ETS, pp. 111–40.

Schmidt, M.G. (2010) *Demokratietheorien: Eine Einfürhung*. Bonn, Bundeszentrale für politische Bildung.

Schmidt, V.A. (2006) *Democracy in Europe: The EU and National Politics*. Oxford, Oxford University Press.

Schmitter, P.C. (1974) Still the Century of Corporatism? *Review of Politics* **1**, 85–131.

Schmitter, P.C. (1981) Interest Intermediation and Regime Governabilità in Contemporary Western Europe and North America. In: Berger, S. (ed.) *Organizing Interest in Western Europe*. Cambridge, Cambridge University Press, pp. 287–327.

Schmitter, P.C. (2001) Parties Are Not What They Once Were. In: Diamond, L. & Gunther, R. (eds.), *Political Parties and Democracy*. Baltimore, Johns Hopkins University Press, pp. 67–89.

Schneider, C. (1992) Radical Opposition Parties and Squatter Movements in Pinochet's Chile. In: Escobar, A. & Álvarez, S. (eds.) *The Making of Social Movements in Latin America: Identity, Strategy and Democracy*. Boulder, Colo., Westview, pp. 60–75.

Schneider, C. (1995) *Shantytown Protests in Pinochet's Chile*. Philadelphia, Temple University Press.

Schock, K. (2005) *Unarmed Insurrections: People Power Movements in Nondemocracies*. Minneapolis, The University of Minnesota Press.

Scholte, J.A. (ed.) (2011) *Building Global Democracy? Civil Society and Accountable Governance*. Cambridge, Cambridge University Press.

Schosberg, D., Zavestoski, S. & Shulman, S. (2005) 'To Submit a Form or Not to Submit a Form, that is the (Real) Question': Deliberation and Mass Participation in U.S. Regulatory Rule-Making. Paper presented at the Western Political Science Association annual meeting.

Schumpeter, J.A. (1967) *Capitalismo, socialismo, democrazia*. Milan, Etas Kompass (orig. 1954).

Sewell, W.H., Jr (1980) *Work and Revolution in France: The Language of Labour from the Old Regime to 1848*. Cambridge, Cambridge University Press.

Sewell, W.H., Jr (1986) Artisans, Factory Workers, and the Formation of the French Working Class, 1789–1848. In: Katnelson, I. and Zolberg, A.R. (eds.)

Working-Class Formation: Nineteenth-Century Patterns in Western Europe and the United States. Princeton, Princeton University Press, pp. 45–70.

Shand, D. & Arnberg, M. (1996) Background Paper. In: OECD (ed.) *Responsive Government: Service Quality Initiatives.* Paris, OECD, pp. 17–32.

Shapiro, I. (2003) *The State of Democratic Theory.* Princeton, Princeton University Press.

Shaw, M. (1994) Civil Society and Global Politics: Beyond a Social Movement Approach. *Millennium* 23 (3), 647–67.

Sheptycki, J. W. E. (1994) Law Enforcement, Justice and Democracy in the Transnational Arena: Reflections on the War on Drugs. *International Journal of the Sociology of Law* 24 (1), 61–75.

Sheptycki, J. W. E. (2002) *In Search of Transnational Policing: Towards a Sociology of Global Policing.* Aldershot, Ashgate.

Sheptycki, J. W. E. (2005) Policing Protest When Politics Go Global: Comparing Public Order Policing in Canada and Bolivia. *Policing and Society* 15 (3), 327–52.

Sikkink, K. (1996) The Emergence, Evolution, and Effectiveness of the Latin American Human Rights Network. In: Jelin, E. & Hershberg, E. (eds.) *Constructing Democracy: Human Rights, Citizenship, and Society in Latin America.* Boulder, Colo., Westview, pp. 59–84.

Sikkink, K. & Smith, J. (2002) Infrastructures for Change: Transnational Organizations 1953–1993. In: Khagram, S., Riker, J. V. & Sikkink, K. (eds.) *Reconstructing World Politics: Transnational Social Movements, Networks and Norms.* Minneapolis, The University of Minnesota Press, pp. 22–44.

Sil, R. & Katzenstein, P. J. (2010) Analytic Eclecticism in the Study of World Politics: Reconfiguring Problems and Mechanisms across Research Traditions. *Perspective on Politics* 8, 411–31.

Silver, B. (2003) *Forces of Labor.* New York, Cambridge University Press.

Sintomer, Y. (2001) Participatory Democracy and Governance: Local Participation in France. Paper prepared for the ECPR Joint Session of Workshops, Grenoble, 6–11 April.

Sintomer, Y. (2007) *Le pouvoir du peuple.* Paris, La découverte.

Sintomer, Y., Herzberg, C. & Röcke, A. (2007) *Démocratie participative et modernization des services publics: des affinités electives? Les budget participatifs en Europe.* Paris, La Découverte.

Skolnick, J. H. (1966) *Justice Without Trial: Law Enforcement in Democratic Society.* New York, John Wiley and Sons.

Slater, D. (1985) *New Social Movements and the State in Latin America.* Amsterdam, CEDLA.

Slater, D. (2010) *Ordering Power: Contentious Politics and Authoritarian Leviathan in Southeast Asia.* Cambridge, Cambridge University Press.

Smith, G. (2000) Toward Deliberative Institutions. In: Saward, M. (ed.) *Democratic Innovation: Deliberation, Representation and Association.* London and New York, Routledge, pp. 29–39.

Smith, G. (2001) Taking Deliberation Seriously: Institutional Design and Green Politics. *Environmental Politics* 10 (3), 72–93.

Smith, G. (2009) *Democratic Innovations: Designing Institutions for Citizen Participation.* Cambridge, Cambridge University Press.

Smith, G. & Wales, C. (2000) Citizens' Juries and Deliberative Democracy. *Political Studies* **48** (1), 51–65.

Smith, J. (1995) Transnational Political Processes and the Human Rights Movement. *Research in Social Movements: Conflict and Change* 18, 187–221.

Smith, J. (1997) Characteristics of the Modern Transnational Social Movement Sector. In: Smith, J., Chatfield, C. & Pagnucco, R. (eds.) *Transnational Social Movements and Global Politics.* Syracuse, Syracuse University Press, pp. 42–58.

Smith, J. (2001) Globalizing Resistance: The Battle of Seattle and the Future of Social Movements. *Mobilization* 6, 1–20.

Snow, D. A., Rochford, E. B., Worden, S. K. & Benford, R. D. (1986) Frame Alignment Processes, Micromobilization, and Movement Participation. *American Sociological Review* 51, 464–81.

Somers, M. R. (2008) *Genealogies of Citizenship: Markets, Statelessness, and the Right to Have Rights.* New York, Cambridge University Press.

Spain, J. (1991) Trade Unionists, Gladstonian Liberals, and the Labour Law Reforms of 1875. In: Biagini, E. F. & Reid, A. J. (eds.) *Currents of Radicalism. Popular Radicalism, Organized Labour and Party Politics in Britain, 1850–1914,* Cambridge, Cambridge University Press.

Stark, D. & Bruszt, L. (1998) *Postsocialist Pathways: Transforming Politics and Property in East Central Europe.* Cambridge, Cambridge University Press.

Starr, A., Fernandez, L., Amster, R. & Wood, L. (2008) The Impacts of State Surveillance on Political Assembly and Association: a Socio-Legal Analysis. *Qualitative Sociology* 31 (3), 251–70.

Starr, A., Fernandez, L. & Scholl, C. (2011) *Shutting Down the Streets. Political Violence and Social Control in the Global Era.* New York, New York University Press.

Steffek, J., Kissling, C. & Nanz, P. (2008) *Civil Society Participation in European and Global Governance: A Cure for the Democratic Deficit?* London, Palgrave Macmillan.

Steiner, J., Bächtiger, A., Spörndli, M. & Steenbergen, M. R. (2004) *Deliberative Politics in Action: A Cross-National Study of Parliamentary Debates.* Cambridge, Cambridge University Press.

Sunstein, C. (2001) *Republic.com.* Princeton and Oxford, Princeton University Press.

Szas, A. (1995) Progress Through Mischief: The Social Movement Alternative to Secondary Associations. In: Wright, E. O. (ed.) *Associations and Democracy.* New York, Verso, pp. 148–55.

Tallberg, J. & Uhlin, A. (2011) Civil Society and Global Democracy: An Assessment. In: Archibugi, D., Konig-Archibugi, M. & Marchetti, R. (eds.) *Global Democracy: Normative and Empirical Perspectives.* Cambridge, Cambridge University Press, pp. 210–32.

Talpin, J. (2011) *Schools of Democracy: How Ordinary Citizens become Competent in Participatory Budgeting Institutions.* Colchester, ECPR Press.

Tarrow, S. (1989) *Democracy and Disorder: Protest and Politics in Italy, 1965–1975*. Oxford and New York, Oxford University Press.

Tarrow, S. (1995) Mass Mobilization and Regime Change: Pacts, Reform and Popular Power in Italy (1918–1922) and Spain (1975–1978). In: Gunther, R., Diamandouros, P. & Puhle, H. (eds.) *Democratic Consolidation in Southern Europe: The Cultural Dimension*. Baltimore, Johns Hopkins University Press, pp. 204–30.

Tarrow, S. (1998) *Power in Movement*. Cambridge, Cambridge University Press.

Tarrow, S. (2005) *The New Transnational Contention*. Cambridge and New York, Cambridge University Press.

Tarrow, S. & McAdam, D. (2004) Scale Shift in Transnational Contention. In: della Porta, D. & Tarrow, S. (eds.) *Transnational Protest and Global Activism*. Lanham, Rowman and Littlefield, pp. 121–49.

Teorell, J. A. (1999) Deliberative Defence of Intra-party Democracy. *Party Politics* 5 (3), 363–82.

Thacker, S. C. (1998) The High Politics of IMF Lending. *World Politics* 51, 39–75.

Thompson, E. P. (1978) *The Poverty of Theory and Other Essays*. London, Merlin Press.

Thompson, E. P. (1991) *The Making of the English Working Class*. London, Penguin Books (orig. 1963).

Tilly, C. (1986) *The Contentious French*. Cambridge, Mass., Harvard University Press.

Tilly, C. (1995) *Popular Contention in Great Britain: 1758–1834*. Cambridge, Mass., Harvard University Press.

Tilly, C. (2004) *Social Movements: 1768–2004*. Boulder, Colo., Paradigm.

Tilly, C. (2007) *Democracy*. New York, Cambridge University Press.

Tocqueville, A. de (1986) *De la démocratie en Amérique*. Paris, Gallimard (orig. 1835).

Tolomelli, M. (2008) *Il sessantotto: Una breve storia*. Rome, Carocci.

Topf, R. (1995) Beyond Electoral Participation. In: Klingemann, A.-D. & Fuchs, D. (eds.) *Citizens and the State*. New York, Oxford University Press, pp. 52–91.

Torcal, M. & Montero, J. S. (eds.) (2006) *Political Disaffection in Contemporary Democracies*. London, Routledge.

Torino Social Forum (2008) *Proposta di struttura organizzativa*, www.lacaverna. it (home page), accessed 12 November 2008.

Uhr, J. (2000) Testing Deliberative Democracy: The 1999 Australian Republic Referendum. *Government and Opposition* 35 (2), 189–210.

Ulfelder, J. (2005) Contentious Collective Action and the Breakdown of Authoritarian Regimes. *International Political Science Review* 26 (3), 311–34.

Uysal, A. (2005) Organisation du maintien de l'ordre et répression policière en Turquie. In: della Porta, D. & Fillieule, O. (eds.) *Maintien de l'ordre et police des foules*. Paris, Presses de Science Po.

Vedres, B., Bruszt, L. & Stark, D. (2005) Shaping the Web of Civic Participation: Civil Society Websites in Eastern Europe. *The Journal of Public Policy* 25 (1), 149–63.

Veltri, F. (2003) Non si chiama delega, si chiama fiducia: La sfida organizzativa della Rete Lilliput. In: Ceri, P. (ed.) *La democrazia dei movimenti: Come decidono i no global*. Rubbettino, Soveria Mannelli.

Vitale, A. (2005) From Negotiated Management to Command and Control: How the New York City Police Department Polices Protest. *Policing and Society* 15 (3), 283–304.

Waalgrave, S. & Rucht, D. (eds.) (2010) *The World Says No to War*. Minneapolis, The University of Minnesota Press.

Waddington, D. (1992) *Contemporary Issues in Public Disorder: A Comparative and Historical Approach*. London, Routledge.

Waddington, D. & Critcher, C. (2000) Policing Pit Closures, 1984–1992. In: Bessel, R. & Emsley, C. (eds.) *Patterns of Provocation: Police and Public Disorder*. Oxford, Berghahn Books.

Waddington, D., Jones, K. & Critcher, C. (1989) *Flashpoints: Studies in Public Disorder*. London, Routledge.

Waddington, P. A. J. (1994) *Liberty and Order: Public Order Policing in a Capital City*. London, UCL Press.

Wahlström, M. & Oskarsson, M. (2006) Negotiating Political Protest in Gothenburg and Copenhagen. In: della Porta, D., Peterson, A. & Reiter, H. (eds.) *Policing Transnational Protest: In the Aftermath of the 'Battle of Seattle'*. Aldershot, Ashgate, pp. 117–44.

Walker, N. (2003) The Pattern of Transnational Policing. In: Newburn, T. (ed.) *Handbook of Policing*. Willan, Uffculme, pp. 111–35.

Wall, M. & El Zahed, S. (2011) 'I'll Be Waiting for You Guys': A YouTube Call to Action in the Egyptian Revolution. *International Journal of Communication* 5, 1333–43.

Walzer, M. (1999) Deliberation and What Else? In: Macedo, S. (ed.) *Deliberative Politics: Essays on Democracy and Disagreement*. Oxford, Oxford University Press, pp. 58–69.

Wapner, P. (1995) Politics Beyond the State: Environmental Activism and the World Civic Politics. *World Politics* 47, 311–40.

Warkentin, C. (2001) *Reshaping World Politics: NGOs, the Internet and Global Civil Society*. Lanham, Rowman & Littlefield.

Warkotsch, J. (2012) *Mobilizing for Democracy: The Egyptian Case*. Report for the ERC project on Mobilizing for democracy, Florence, European University Institute.

Weber, M. (1974) *Economia e società*. Milan, Edizioni di comunità (orig. 1922).

Weeks, E. C. (2000) The Practice of Deliberative Democracy: Results from Four Large-scale Trials. *Public Administration Review* 60 (4), 360–72.

Wiktorowicz, Q. (ed.) (2004) *Islamic Activism: A Social Movement Perspective*. Bloomington, Indiana University Press.

Wilhelm, A. G. (2000) *Democracy in the Digital Age: Challenges to Political Life in Cyberspace*. New York, Routledge.

Winter, M. (1998) Police Philosophy and Protest Policing in the Federal Republic of Germany, 1960–1990. In: della Porta, D. & Reiter, H. (eds.) *Policing Protest: The Control of Mass Demonstrations in Western Democracies*. Minneapolis, The University of Minnesota Press, pp. 188–212.

Wisler, D. & Kriesi, H. (1998) Public Order, Protest Cycles, and Political Process: Two Swiss Cities Compared. In: della Porta, D. & Reiter, H. (eds.) *Policing Protest: The Control of Mass Demonstrations in Western Democracies.* Minneapolis, The University of Minnesota Press, pp. 91–116.

Wombles (2008) 'Background to the Wombles', www.wombles.org.uk/article20060318.php, accessed 3 November 2008.

Wood, E.J. (2000) *Forging Democracy from Below: Insurgent Transitions in South Africa and El Salvador.* New York, Cambridge University Press.

Yashar, D. (2005) *Contesting Citizenship in Latin America: The Rise of Indigenous Movements and the Postliberal Challenge.* New York, Cambridge University Press.

Young, I.M. (1990) *Justice and the Politics of Difference.* Princeton, Princeton University Press.

Young, I.M. (1996) Communication and the Other: Beyond Deliberative Democracy. In: Benhabib, S. (ed.) *Democracy and Difference: Contesting the Boundaries of the Political.* Princeton, Princeton University Press, pp. 120–35.

Young, I.M. (2000) *Inclusion and Democracy.* Oxford, Oxford University Press.

Young, I.M. (2003) Activist Challenges to Deliberative Democracy. In: Fishkin, J.S. & Laslett, P. (eds.) *Debating Deliberative Democracy.* Malden, Blackwell, pp. 102–20.

Zittel, T. (2003). Political Representation in the Networked Society: The Americanization of European Systems of Responsible Party Government? *The Journal of Legislative Studies* 9 (3), 1–22.

Zittrain, J. (2008) *The Future of the Internet and How to Stop It.* New York, Yale University Press

Zola, D. and R. Marchetti, The Organizational Ideology and Visions of Democracy of Global Justice Movement Organisations: The Transnational Movement Organizations. In: della Porta, D. & Reiter, H. (eds.) *Organizational Ideology and Vision of Democracy in the Global Justice Movement,* WP3 Report, Democracy in Movement and the Mobilization of the Society – DEMOS, European Commission.

Zolo, D. (2004) *Globalizzazione: Una mappa dei problemi.* Rome and Bari, Laterza.

Zürn, M., Binder, M. & Ecker-Ehrhardt, M. (2010) *International Political Authority and Its Politicization.* BERLIN, Social Science Research Center Berlin, Transnational Conflicts and International Institutions (TKI)

Zürn, M. & Ecker-Ehrhardt, M. (2011) *Gesellschaftliche Politisierung und internationale Institutionen.* Frankfurt am Main, Suhrkamp.

Index